Artificial Intelligence and Actuarial Science

This book aims to explore how to automate, innovate, design, and deploy emerging technologies in actuarial work transformations for the insurance and finance sector. It examines the role of artificial intelligence with process automation in daily monitoring of solvency, governance, compliance, data processes, etc. It also explores the usage of machine learning, telematics system, AI-enabled claim processing software, Big Data and Algorithms, Explainable AI, and AI-enabled risk management tools in various actuarial processes.

This book:

- Presents case studies and best practices with real-world examples of successful and unsuccessful actuarial work transformation initiatives and transformation with emerging technologies.
- Offers deployment solutions for different applications of AI in actuarial work.
- Discusses how organizations can effectively incorporate AI into their current practices of actuarial work.
- Covers diverse emerging technologies, practices, and processes of actuaries from around the globe.
- Elaborate upon a framework for comprehending how big data and AI developments may affect insurance offers and their supervision.
- Explains how insurance companies may review and modify their current Risk Management Framework (RMF) to take into account some of the significant differences while implementing AI use cases.

This reference book is for scholars, researchers, and professionals interested in Artificial Intelligence and Actuarial Science.

Artificial Intelligence and Actuarial Science

Applications and Case Studies from Finance and Insurance

Edited by
Sonal Trivedi, M.K. Nallakaruppan,
Balamurugan Balusamy,
and Nithya Rekha Sivakumar

CRC Press
Taylor & Francis Group
Boca Raton London New York

CRC Press is an imprint of the
Taylor & Francis Group, an **informa** business
A CHAPMAN & HALL BOOK

Designed cover image: ShutterStock

First edition published 2025
by CRC Press
2385 NW Executive Center Drive, Suite 320, Boca Raton FL 33431

and by CRC Press
4 Park Square, Milton Park, Abingdon, Oxon, OX14 4RN

CRC Press is an imprint of Taylor & Francis Group, LLC

ISBN: 9781032751337 (hbk)
ISBN: 9781032751344 (pbk)
ISBN: 9781003472551 (ebk)

DOI: 10.1201/9781003472551

Typeset in Times
by codeMantra

Contents

Preface

The actuarial teams of insurers are involved in a variety of activities, such as product development, pricing, compliance, and research and development. In recent years, they have also taken on new and challenging duties both inside and outside of the traditional insurance industry. Actuarial work is being transformed by the integration of artificial intelligence (AI) and process automation. This book examines the role of AI with process automation in daily monitoring of solvency, governance, compliance, data processes, etc. It also explores the usage of machine learning (ML), telematics system, AI-enabled claim processing software, Big Data and Algorithms, Explainable AI, and AI-enabled risk management tools in various actuarial processes.

This book covers a huge application of emerging technologies in the transformation of actuarial work in insurance, as well as almost all the areas where the various emerging cutting-edge technologies can be applied in the actuarial process. This book also talks about how organizations can effectively incorporate them into their current practices of actuarial work.

This book is divided into four sections – Introduction, Application of AI, Technological advancement, and Conclusion.

SECTION A: INTRODUCTION

This section presents an introduction to actuarial systems, which play a significant role in the insurance industry. The actuarial system ensures the profitability and stability of insurance companies by setting premiums and assessing risks. This section presents an overview of the evolution of actuarial system and its challenges. This section consists of one chapter.

The first chapter titled 'Evolutions of Actuarial Systems in the Insurance Industry and Challenges in the Existing System' aims to present the profession of actuary with specific reference to the financial business and, more specifically, the insurance industry. This study examines the evolution and development trends of the insurance actuarial system.

SECTION B: APPLICATION OF AI

The application of AI in the actuarial process is vast from improving the quality of service, bringing transparency in decision-making to enhancing the quality of service. This section explores the role of AI in various actuarial processes. This section consists of ten chapters.

The first chapter titled 'Generative AI: Adoption and Challenges in Actuarial Science,' which is the second chapter of this book, aims to introduce the different categories of ML algorithms, types of ML algorithms, and current related work done using these algorithms. It will also throw light on the opportunities for actuaries and AI experts to create new business Generative AI models, as well as applications of Generative AI, its benefits, and challenges in the field of actuarial science.

The second chapter titled 'AI: A revolutionary tool for actuarial work in insurance,' which is the third chapter of this book, aims to study the application of AI in actuarial science. The study deals with the in-depth analysis of different segments where AI is helping in actuarial work in the insurance industry.

The third chapter titled 'AI Explainability: A Key Driver for Enhanced Quality of Service in Actuarial Practices,' which is the fourth chapter of this book, aims at the significance of explainability as a core driver for augmenting service quality in actuarial practices.

The fourth chapter titled 'Explainability of AI in Improving the Quality of Service in the Actuarial Industry,' which is the fifth chapter of this book, aims to provide a comprehensive analysis of the XAI. It provides valuable insights for professionals, legislators, and researchers who aim to improve service quality while embracing the transformational potential of AI.

The fifth chapter titled 'AI Transformation of the Insurance Industry: A Systematic Review of Progress and Possibilities,' which is the sixth chapter of this book, aims to provide a comprehensive and systematic review of the progress and possibilities surrounding the application of AI in the insurance sector.

The sixth chapter titled 'Examining the Factors Influencing AI Adoption in the Insurance Industry Specifically in Actuarial Process,' which is the seventh chapter of this book, discusses the various fields available in actuarial science that can hugely benefit from the application of artificial intelligence to it. This chapter also looks at some court judgments to consider as case studies. This chapter also refers to the secondary survey data in order to look at the relevance of the field along with the opportunity of the application of AI to it.

The seventh chapter titled 'Role of Artificial Intelligence (AI) in Insurance Industry: Scope, Benefits, and Adoption Roadmap,' which is the eighth chapter of this book, aims to explore the integration possibilities of AI in the insurance sector. To that end, it delves deeply into the benefits of AI and how these can be tapped by the insurance industry to optimize its operations, enhance efficiency, and expand adoption beyond its traditional strongholds.

The eighth chapter titled 'AI's role in improving the quality of Insurance services,' which is the ninth chapter of this book, deals with a new perspective of AI as a tool for improving the quality of services from the customer point of view. This chapter will provide insights into the varied benefits of AI.

The ninth chapter titled 'Fuzzy Artificial Intelligence as a Technique to Find Relative Desirability for Automated Insurance Premium Assignment,' which is the tenth chapter of this book, presents FAI as a powerful tool to transform premium allocation and highlights its potential to improve decision-making processes in the insurance industry.

The tenth chapter titled 'Opportunities and Challenges of Combining Artificial Intelligence Power with the Richness of Healthcare Claims Data,' which is the eleventh chapter of this book, explores key issues on this evolving panorama, emphasizing the importance of transparency, accountability, and accountable innovation.

SECTION C: TECHNOLOGICAL ADVANCEMENT

Technological advancement has revolutionized the actuarial process in the insurance industry, specifically artificial intelligence, machine learning, and blockchain. This section provides insight into the implementation of advanced techniques in the actuarial process and explores the practical application of technological advancement in the actuarial process. This section consists of three chapters.

The first chapter titled 'Implementing Machine Learning in Actuarial Practice: Real-World Applications and Insight,' which is the twelfth chapter of this book, explores the use of machine learning in actuarial practice. In order to improve risk assessment, pricing, underwriting, and claims handling, actuaries are using advanced data analytics more often.

The second chapter titled 'Telematics System in Usage-Based Motor Insurance,' which is the thirteenth chapter of this book, aims to investigate the use of telematics in auto insurance and consumers' attitudes about it. It also discusses the technology's future directions. The advantages and disadvantages of telematics have been examined for this study.

The third chapter titled 'Secured and Scalable: Integrating Blockchain Solutions for Health Insurance Claim Using Client Support Chatbot Automation,' which is the fourteenth chapter of this book, aims to explore real-world blockchain deployments inside healthcare insurance organizations, assessing the difficulties encountered during adoption and the subsequent advantages gained. The insights learned from these deployments are useful for professionals and legislators looking to integrate blockchain technology into their health insurance operations. Furthermore, the research tackles privacy issues by adopting modern encryption techniques, ensuring the confidentiality of customer-sensitive information throughout the claims process.

SECTION D: CONCLUSION

To understand the future of actuarial work and the role of advanced technologies in reshaping the process of actuarial work, it is important to understand the challenges and opportunities in actuarial work. This section presents the role of AI in reshaping the future of actuarial work. This section consists of two chapters.

The first chapter titled 'Law and AI-Powered Actuarial Revolution: Navigating the Future of Insurance Risk Assessment,' which is the fifteenth chapter of this book, aims to investigate the evolving role of AI in risk assessment within insurance, scrutinizing legal frameworks, regulations, and ethical guidelines governing AI's integration into actuarial processes.

The second chapter titled 'Charting the Future: Artificial Intelligence's Role in Revolutionizing Actuarial Work in Insurance Sector', which is the last and sixteenth chapter of this book, aims to critically examine the role of AI in revolutionizing actuarial work in the insurance sector.

Editors

Dr. Sonal Trivedi is an assistant professor at VIT Bhopal University, India. She has more than 12 years of teaching experience. She has published two books in national publications and has two edited books with international publishers in the process of publishing. She has 27 documents in Scopus indexed journal. She has six patents granted. She has 22 research papers in UGC-approved journals and presented 15 papers at international and national conferences. She has acted as conference chair for five international conferences. She is a reviewer for four reputed journals. She did her Ph.D. in Management (Finance) with a thesis titled 'A Study on Risk Management Tools and Techniques in Life Insurance Industry in India' from the University of Kota (Rajasthan) in 2017. She has also worked as a teaching assistant at S.V. National Institute of Technology (NIT), Surat (Institute of National Importance under Ministry of Human Resource Development (MHRD), Government of India). Her areas of interest are blockchain, finance, banking, and insurance.

Dr. M.K. Nallakaruppan is an assistant professor in Balaji Institute of Modern Management Sri Balaji University Pune India. He completed his bachelor's degree (B.E.) Electronics and Communication Engineering at J.J. College of Engineering and Technology. He completed his master's degree (M.E.) in Software Engineering at Anna University. He completed his Ph.D. in "Decision Support Systems for IoT based Infrastructures" at VIT University, Vellore. His areas of expertise are IoT and smart networks, machine learning, soft computing, decision science, and deep learning. He has 32 international publications in various international journals under his area of interest. This includes 20 research papers, 9 conferences, and 3 book chapters, all with various reputed publishers.

Dr. Balamurugan Balusamy is Associate Dean of Students at Shiv Nadar University, Delhi-NCR. Prior to this assignment, he was a professor at the School of Computing Sciences & Engineering and Director of International Relations at Galgotias University, Greater Noida, India. His contributions focus on engineering education, blockchain, and data sciences. His academic degrees and 12 years of experience working as a faculty in a global university like VIT University, Vellore, have made him more receptive and prominent in his domain. He has over 200 papers with high impact factor published in multiple reputed journals. He has edited and authored more than 80 books, as well as collaborated with eminent professors across the world from top QS-ranked universities. He has served up to the position of associate professor in his stint of 12 years of experience with VIT University, Vellore. He had completed his bachelor's, master's, and Ph.D. degrees from India's top premier institutions. His passion is teaching, and he adapts different design thinking principles while delivering his lectures. He has published over 80 books on various technologies and has visited over 15 countries for his technical course. He has attended several top-notch conferences and has published over 200 high-quality journal, conference, and book chapters combined. He serves on the advisory committee for several start-ups and forums, as well as does consultancy work for industry on industrial IOT. He has given over 195 talks at various events and symposiums.

Dr. Nithya Rekha Sivakumar received a grant from UGC and completed her Ph.D. as a full-time research scholar at Periyar University awarded with "UGC BSR Research Fellowship in Science for Meritorious Students" by the University Grants Commission, New Delhi, Govt. of India, from 2010 to 2013. She received a travel grant from the Department of Science and Technology (DST), Govt. of India, to go to United States for her Ph.D. research. She received the "Best Distinguished Researcher Award" for the year 2015–2016 from the College of Computer, Qassim Private Colleges, Buraydah, Kingdom of Saudi Arabia. She has received a research grant for the Research Identity Fast-track Funding Program from the Deputyship for Research & Innovation, as well as the Ministry of Education and Researchers Supporting Project Award from Princess Nourah Bint Abdulrahman University in Saudi Arabia four times. She is on a Panel of External Examiners for Ph.D. for more than 25 candidates who have been awarded Ph.D. She is the author of over 50 peer-reviewed articles. She also has three patents. She is a reviewer for reputed journals. She is supervising several graduates (B.S. and M.S.). Her research interests include mobile computing, artificial intelligence, Internet of Things, deep learning, machine learning, wireless networks, network/cyber security, blockchain, VANET, cognitive radio networks, and cloud computing. She is currently an associate professor in the Department of Computer Sciences, College of Computer and Information Sciences, Princess Nourah Bint Abdulrahman University, Riyadh, Saudi Arabia. She has 17 years of teaching experience in the field of computer science and 15 years of research experience.

Contributors

Firos A
Dept. of Computer Science and Engineering
Rajiv Gandhi University
Papum Pare, India

Revathi A
Department of Computer Science
Rathinam College of Arts and Science
Coimbatore, India

Vanitha A
Department of Computer Science
Rathinam College of Arts and Science
Coimbatore, India

Rashmi Aggarwal
Chitkara Business School
Chitkara University
Chandigarh, India

Anshull Bhalla
School of Management and Commerce
Manav Rachna University
Faridabad, India

Pravin Chavan
Department of Management
Dr. D.Y. Patil Vidyapeeth
Pimpri-Chinchwad, India

Vinita Choudhary
School of leadership and Management
Manav Rachna International Institute of Research and Studies
Faridabad, India

Subrata Chowdhury
Department of Computer Science and Engineering
Sreenivasa Institute of Technology and Management Studies
Chittoor, India

Arwin Sandesh D'Souza
Department of Business Administration
Nitte University
Mangalore, India

Rukudzo Dzapasi
Department of Business Management
Midlands State University
Midlands, Zimbabwe

Mufaro Dzingirai
Department of Business Management
Midlands State University
Midlands, Zimbabwe

Thippa Reddy Gadekallu
The College of Mathematics and Computer Science
Lebanese American University
Beirut, Lebanon

Rama Moorthy Hejamdi
Department of Computer Applications
Nitte University
Mangalore, India

Dhanashri Sanadkumar Havale
Department of Agribusiness Management
MIMA Institute of Management
Pune, India

Madhwaraj Kango Gopal
Dept of Master of Computer Applications
Mangalore Institute of Technology & Engineering
Mangalore, India

Neha Kamboj
IILM School of Management
IILM University
Greater Noida, India

Arvinder Kaur
School of Management and Commerce
University School of Business
Chitkara University
Chandigarh, India

Gurpreet Kaur
School of Management and Commerce
Manav Rachna University
Faridabad, India

Seema Khanum
Indian Computer Emergency Response Team (ICERT)
MeitY Electronics Niketan
New Delhi, India

Hrishikesh Gajananrao Kokate
Department of Management
Dr. D.Y. Patil Vidyapeeth
Pimpri-Chinchwad, India

Shalender Kumar
Chitkara Business School
Chitkara University
Chandigarh, India

Praveen Kumar Reddy Maddikunta
School of Computer Science Engineering and Information
Vellore Institute of Technology
Vellore, India

Daksha Malagatti
Department of Business Administration
Nitte University
Mangalore, India

Mamta
CUIET
Chitkara University
Chandigarh, India

Ramalingam Murugan
School of Computer Science Engineering and Information
Vellore Institute of Technology
Vellore, India

Dinesh N
Jain Deemed to be University
Bengaluru, India

Manawati Panwar
Jaipur School of Business
JECRC University
Vidhani, India

Neha Parveen
Crescent School of Law
B.S. Abdur Rahman Crescent Institute of Science and Technology
Peerakankaranai, India

R S M Lakshmi Patibandla
Department of Computer Science and Engineering
Koneru Lakshmaiah Education Foundation
Vijayawada, India

Danilo Pelusi
Department of Communication Science
University of Teramo
Teramo, Italy

Ravi Prakash Bylappa
Department of Computer Applications
Nitte University
Mangalore, India

Sachin Rawat
School of Management and Commerce
Manav Rachna University
Faridabad, India

Janarthanan S
Department of Computer Science
Rathinam College of Arts and Science
Coimbatore, India

Jayashri Shetty
Department of Master of Business Administration
Mangalore Institute of Technology Engineering
Mangalore, India

Gurpreet Singh
CUIET
Chitkara University
Chandigarh, India

Puneet Singh
EXL Services
Noida, India

Sridevi Jayavelu
School of Management
Vel Tech Rangarajan Dr. Sagunthala R&D Institute of Science and Technology
Chennai, India

Anita Tanwar
Chitkara Business School
Chitkara University
Chandigarh, India

Sonal Trivedi
VIT Business School
VIT Bhopal University
Bhopal, India

Chandrasekar Vijai
School of Commerce
Vel Tech Rangarajan Dr. Sagunthala R&D Institute of Science and Technology
Chennai, India

Vijayakumar T
School of Computer Science
Rathinam College of Arts and Science
Coimbatore, India

Wing-Keung Wong
Department of Finance, Fintech & Blockchain Research Center, and Big Data Research Center
The Hang Seng University
Hong Kong

Rajesh Kumar Yadav
Amity School of Business
Amity University
Noida, India

Gokul Yenduri
VIT-AP University
Amaravati, India

Section A

Introduction

1 Evolutions of Actuarial Systems in the Insurance Industry and Challenges in the Existing System

Manawati Panwar and Danilo Pelusi

1.1 INTRODUCTION

1.1.1 Who Is an Actuary?

An "actuary" is a person who is trained to assess subsequent events to increase financial and commercial implications, as well as the uncertainty and risk associated with them. They do this by applying sophisticated models and procedures based on future scenarios in circumstances encompassing finance, economics, social science, technology, demographics, and probability, as shown in Figure 1.1.

Frees and Huang (2023) believed that founded on mathematical modelling, the field of actuarial science has always addressed real-world insurance issues. Applied arithmetic lectures were more well-known afterwards. The following is how the International Actuarial Association (IAA) defines the actuarial profession: In the areas of risk management, social protection, and finance, the actuarial profession is regarded as essential to making the right decisions, all of which benefit society as a whole. Actuaries, who are experts in mathematics, statistics, and financial theory, evaluate and estimate the risks associated with certain events such as natural disasters, accidents, and the deaths of large numbers of people. The Insurance Information Institute (2010) defines an actuary as a qualified insurance professional who studies, evaluates, and manages statistical data. They evaluate insurance companies' reserves, resolve rate and rating difficulties, and identify commercial and financial risks. Actuarial science is a developing vocation and one of the most popular careers in the United States because of good working conditions.

1.1.2 Statutory Bodies of Actuaries

To oversee the actuarial profession in India, the Actuaries Act 2006 (35 of 2006) established the Institute of Actuaries of India (IAI), a governmental body. The Act became effective on November 10, 2006, following a notification issued by the Ministry of Finance, Department of Economic Affairs on November 8, 2006.

DOI: 10.1201/9781003472551-2

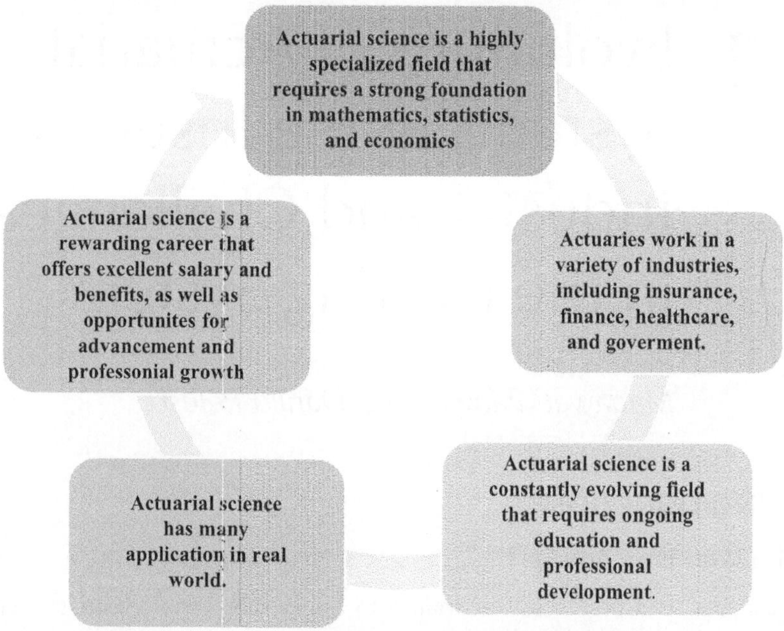

FIGURE 1.1 Introduction of actuarial system. (Developed by Author.)

The Actuarial Society of India (ASI) was established in September 1944. The ASI has been a Full Member of the International Actuarial Association (an umbrella body for all actuarial bodies worldwide) since 1979, and it actively participates in its operations. The ASI was created in 1982 under the Registration of Literary, Scientific, and Charitable Societies Act XXI of 1860 and the Bombay Public Charitable Trust Act of 1950. The ASI began administering tests up to the Associate level in 1989, followed by fellowship-level examinations leading to professional certification as an actuary in 1991.

1.2 EVOLUTION OF ACTUARIAL SYSTEMS

Over time, actuarial systems in the insurance sector have undergone a number of significant advances, as shown in Figure 1.2. These changes have been prompted by technological breakthroughs, legislative upheavals, and the increasing complexity of threats. This is a timeline that summarizes the development:

1.2.1 Manual Calculation Era (Pre-20th Century)

Watson et al. (2015) studied that actuaries had less access to information than they do now. Actuaries used basic mathematical methods to determine premiums, reserves, and annuity values. Pen and paper or basic mechanical calculators were frequently used for manual actuarial computations. Trivedi, Mehta, and Sharma (2021) studied that during this time, basic life insurance and annuities were the main insurance

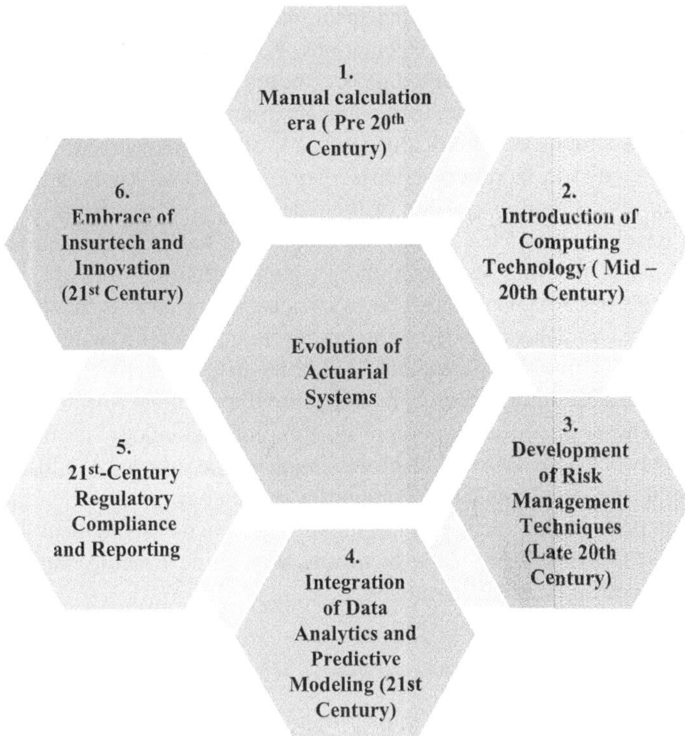

FIGURE 1.2 Evolution of actuarial systems. (Developed by Author.)

products available. Actuaries were essential to the insurance sector because of their knowledge of risk assessment, financial management, and pricing. Actuaries employ actuarial tables and models to approximate the likelihood of different events, such as disability or death, by utilizing past data (Barigou, Chen, and Dhaene 2019). By today's standards, the regulatory framework that governed insurance companies was laxer.

All things considered, the Manual Calculations Era established basic concepts and methods that still influence the insurance sector today, laying the foundation for contemporary actuarial science. Despite data and technology restrictions, actuaries of this era played a critical role in enabling the insurance sector's expansion and sustainability through their skills in risk management and financial analytics.

1.2.2 Introduction of Computing Technology (Mid-20th Century)

The introduction of computing technological advances in the mid-20th century marked a significant milestone in the evolution of actuarial systems, transforming the way actuaries conducted calculations, analysed data, and managed risks as per Harris, Rawson, and Hanson (2010).

Electronic computers were developed and widely used in the middle of the 20th century. These machines could execute complex computations far faster than manual techniques, changing several industries, including insurance. Actuaries started using computers' power to automate actuarial calculations. Feng, Runhuan, and Garrido (2011) explained that jobs that once needed days or hours of physical effort might now be finished in a fraction of the time, increasing accuracy and efficiency. As technological advances in computers, specifically actuarial software developed. These software tools were designed to facilitate actuaries work out various kinds of computations such as pricing of premiums, value of their deposits, and modelling of risks. The continued development of technology for computing has helped actuaries to work in the field aside from life insurance and payouts. Actuaries were able to examine more quantities of data and perform more intricate examinations thanks to computers. Computing technology has led to major developments for managing risks in the insurance field. Computers have made it simpler to put together regulatory documents including accounting records, making sure that insurers fulfilled the laws and regulations. The widespread adoption of information technology has facilitated collaboration between actuaries and IT professionals in the insurance industry.

In general, the development of computing technology in the mid-20th century reshaped the profession of actuarial through enabling actuaries to meet the evolving requirements of the insurance sector by means of machine learning, statistical analysis, and advanced simulation techniques.

1.2.3 Development of Risk Management Techniques (Late 20th Century)

In the second half of the 20th century, there was an important development in risk management practices within the field of insurance. An increasing amount of sophisticated approaches for determining, assessing, and controlling risk occurred throughout this time frame. There are various remarkable elements of this time frame.

Risk management techniques are implemented into the procedures for making strategic choices by the use of enterprise risk management (ERM), and they incorporate multiple kinds of risks such as operational, financial, reputational, and strategic. Nonlinear modelling has been used by actuaries to determine the implications of unexpected happening on insurance portfolios. During this time frame, analysing scenario was essential for the management of risks. Stress testing has become an important risk management technique in the midst of numerous financial meltdowns and economic changes. The management of capital was considered the greatest attention in the insurance sector in the latter part of the 20th century. Actuaries served as a vital part in establishing capital models and figuring out the amount of funding needs to fulfil the demand of regulations and risk tolerance constraints. To encourage rational risk-handling processes and assure the monetary sustainability of insurance companies, regulatory bodies developed risk-based capital (RBC) systems. According to RBC requirements, insurance companies must maintain levels of capital that correspond to the risks they deal with, encompassing insurance underwriting, capital, and operational uncertainty. Insurance firms have incorporated management of risk into their long-term planning, development of products, underwriting, and financial planning. Malik and Trivedi (2022) in his study mentioned that actuaries worked collectively with insurance underwriting, finance, legal compliance, and other departments to implement risk management thoughts into workflows and frameworks for making decisions.

In summary, the second half of 20th century witnessed a significant change in risk management techniques in the insurance sector owing to progress in modelling techniques, compliance with regulations, and an understanding of the significance of great risk governance. Actuaries were primarily responsible for formulating and implementing these strategies, which enabled insurers manage a growing, complex, and volatile operating environment.

1.2.4 Integration of Data Analytics and Predictive Modelling (21st Century)

The combination of data analytics and statistical modelling has reshaped the insurance sector in the 21st century, helping insurers to use immense quantities of data to make decisions with greater certainty, enhance risk assessment capabilities, and improve their operational effectiveness (Balbas et al., 2023).

As a consequence of the widespread adoption of technological advances, huge quantities of both organized and unorganized data are produced from an assortment of resources, which includes social networking sites, IoT technology, and interactions with clients and other outside databases. Artificial intelligence, predictive modelling, and data mining serve as essential instruments used by insurers to evaluate risk and forecast results. Data analytics and statistical modelling have transformed insurance underwriting and pricing procedures. Data analytics support insurers in identifying fraudulent claims, simplifying processing, and boosting prediction accuracy. Predictive models assess past claims data to identify trends that could point to fraud or inconsistencies, helping insurers in minimizing losses and enhancing claims management efficiency. Data analytics helps insurers to more effectively segment their clients' base and customize product and services to personal needs and preferences. Dhaene et al. (2017) pointed out that insurers examine customer data to determine categories of individuals that have identical characteristics and behaviour. Insurers apply predictive modelling to evaluate data gathered from gauges, IoT equipment, and other resources in order to recognize risk factors such as car crashes, collisions with vehicles, damage to property, or health-related issues. Data analytics and statistical modelling promote operational efficiency and effectiveness, decision-making throughout every facet of the insurance business. Data analytics and predictive modelling are used by insurers to ensure compliance with regulatory standards or requirements like soundness examinations and financial reporting risk management statements. Predictive models enable insurers to review financial adequateness, verify compliance with regulatory requirements, and prepare regulatory submissions with greater efficiency.

In general, the combination of data analytics and statistical modelling has shifted the insurance industry by enabling insurers to derive pertinent information from statistics, strengthen risk management capabilities, and offer more customized goods and services to customers. According to Choudhary, Kamboj and Trivedi (2023) highlighted that actuaries play a significant role in the development and implications of these leading-edge analytical approaches, ensuring that insurers utilize data effectively and efficiently to achieve their objectives while managing risks.

1.2.5 21st-Century Regulatory Compliance and Reporting

In the 21st century, there is a greater focus on legal compliance, as well as disclosure and transparency in the insurance sector. According to Byrne and Pattavina (2008), regulatory obligations have become ever more stringent, and insurers are anticipated to comply with a more complicated framework of rules and regulations intended to protect policyholder's interest, ensure financial stability, and safeguard the integrity of the marketplace. Choudhary and Trivedi (2023) studied that in order to protect clients' information and adhere to regulations regarding data privacy, insurers have to implement security precautions for data, which include the use of encryptions, access control, and data violation alert notifications such as the General Data Protection Regulations (GDPR) in Europe and the Health Insurance Portability and Accountability Act (HIPAA) in the United States.

Overall, the implementation of regulations and reporting obligations in the 21st century indicates regulatory bodies' efforts to foster transparency, responsibility, and protection for consumers in the insurance industry. To successfully navigate the rapidly changing regulatory or statutory environment, insurance firms must prioritize conformance activities, invest in an effective conformity infrastructure, and sustain a culture of compliance with regulatory requirements.

1.2.6 Embrace of Insurtech and Innovation (21st Century)

The insurance industry has enthusiastically welcomed Insurtech (Insurance Technology) and its development in the 21st century, which has brought in significant modifications to top business models, operations, and client engagement.

Insurers have adopted AI, machine learning, IoT, blockchain, and cloud computing to enhance operations, risk evaluations, and clients' experience. These technologies allow insurers to streamline processes, evaluate data more effectively and efficiently, and develop new goods and services. Insurtech firms use digital platforms and online markets to directly communicate with clients, bypassing conventional channels of distribution. New insurance products and coverage alternatives that are suited for changing client demands and preferences are being introduced by Insurtech entrepreneurs who are spearheading product innovation. Insurers invest in digital platforms, smartphone apps, chatbots, and virtual assistants to engage customers across the insurance lifecycle, from quotation generation to claims processing. Insurtech enterprises use data analytics and predictive modelling to improve risk assessment, pricing accuracy, and underwriting efficiency. Insurers are partnering with Insurtech startups, technology partners, and industry stakeholders to drive innovation and co-create solutions for industry challenges and opportunities. Insurtech enterprises must navigate regulatory compliance and manage risks related to innovative technology and business strategies.

Overall, the use of Insurtech and innovation is altering the insurance business, accelerating digital transformation, increasing competitiveness, and improving the entire customer experience. Insurance companies that embrace technology and innovation are better positioned to react to changing market dynamics, capitalize on emerging possibilities, and remain relevant in a quickly developing industry.

1.3 CHALLENGES

1.3.1 Data Quality and Management

Inaccurate risk assessments, underwriting choices, and claims handling can result from poor data quality, which compromises the efficacy of actuarial systems, as shown in Figure 1.3.

Maintaining trustworthy information is a significant issue for insurance companies. Inaccurate and inadequate information can lead to inaccurate actuarial models, leading to inaccurate risk forecasts, pricing challenges, and financial losses. Insurance companies consistently collect data and information from numerous databases and resources, which leads to variations in discretions, formats, and quality prerequisites. Establishing effective data governance mechanisms has become essential for safeguarding the integrity of data and compliance with regulatory requirements. Integrating numerous data resources and technologies is an important challenge for the insurance industry. Two of the most significant challenges for insurance companies are protecting confidential customer data and guaranteeing that security guidelines are complied.

1.3.2 The Complexity of Regulatory Compliance

The regulatory framework that controls the insurance industry is multifaceted and constant. Insurers have to deal with plenty number of legal requirements, particularly

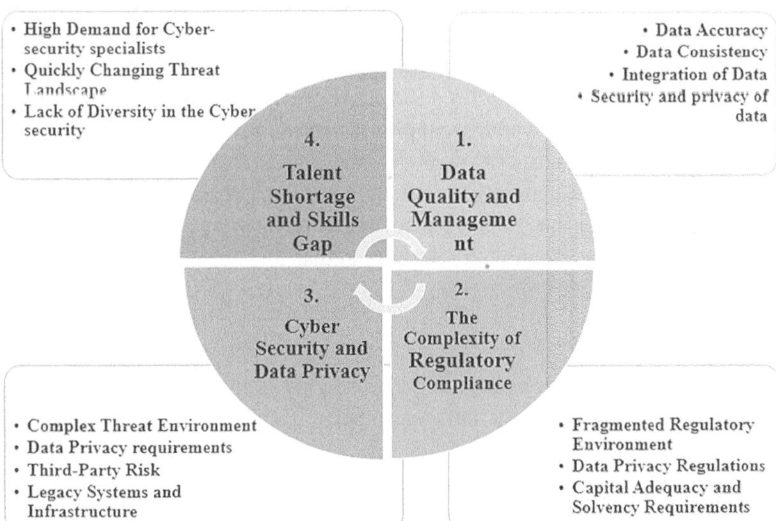

FIGURE 1.3 Challenges faced. (Developed by Author.)

financial standards, accounting responsibilities, and laws pertaining to customer protection. Compliance with regulations such as GDPR, CCPA and IFRS 17 poses major challenges for insurers, demanding strong data management, transparency, accountability, and responsibility.

The insurance industry functions in a decentralized administrative environment that has various standards and regulations across jurisdictions. Regulatory requirements in the insurance industry are frequently changing to suit market realities, potential risks, and geopolitical considerations. The General Data Protection Regulation (GDPR) in Europe and California Consumer Privacy Act (CCPA) in the United States include stringent guidelines for collecting, keeping, and processing personally identifiable data. In order to prevent government fines and negative publicity or harm to image, insurers need to establish effective data security steps and surveillance adherence to these rules and regulations. The solvency regulations, such as Solvency II, which have recently been in effect in Europe, allow insurance companies to preserve adequate funds to cover risks. In order to guarantee impartial treatment of policyholders and compliance with consumer protection legislations, regulatory authorities closely monitor insurance industry market conduct and practices.

1.3.3 Cybersecurity and Data Privacy

Because they deal with highly confidential data, insurers have become especially susceptible to cybersecurity attacks and data privacy issues. Given the highly confidential nature of the information they control, insurers encounter increasing cybersecurity attacks and data privacy concerns. Insurance companies have to conform with strict data privacy rules and regulations including General Data Protection Regulation (GDPR) in the European Union and the California Consumer Privacy Act (CCPA) in the United States. Insurance companies gather and store immense volume of highly confidential data like personally identifiable information (PII), financial statements, and health data. Insurance companies generally depend on third-party supplier, partners, and service providers to manage data processing, settlement of claims, and IT infrastructure administrations. Several insurance companies depend on outmoded infrastructure and technologies that could be missing fundamental safety and security measures, as well as safeguards from growing cyberattacks. Legacy technologies are generally more vulnerable to security concerns, malware assaults, and cyber hacking, making it difficult for insurers to maintain safety and reliability of their information technology systems.

1.3.4 Talent Shortage and Skills Gap

The insurance industry has encountered a growing demand for competent professionals with past experience in data engineering, projections, and advanced statistical analysis. As cyber risks are becoming more prevalent and complex, there is an increasing need for cyberspace security professionals in several businesses including the insurance industry. Cyberspace security responsibilities in the insurance sector generally require specialized skills and knowledge like management of risk, compliance with rules and regulations, intelligence regarding threats, handling security incidents, and digital forensics. Insurance companies may struggle to identify personnel who possess the ideal balance of technical competence and industry-specific expertise.

Insurance companies encounter strong competition from other industries like information technology, banking and healthcare, each of which demands cybersecurity professionals to safeguard digital assets while constraining cyberattacks. Due to the increased competition, insurance firms may find it challenging to find and keep skilled cybersecurity professionals.

1.3.5 Legacy and Integration Issues

Several insurance companies have old systems that are outdated structures, disorganized, and unreliable. The widespread use of old systems restricts responsiveness, adaptability, and creative thinking, making it challenging for insurers to cater to shifting marketplace circumstances and client's needs. Integrating past systems with modern actuarial platforms as well as developing technologies offers significant technological and operational barriers for insurers.

The traditional systems adopted by insurance companies are generally antiquated, developed on outdated technology, and may not have the adaptability and capacity essential to accommodate modern business processes. Insurance companies typically employ multiple systems and software programs between departments including insurance policy administration, managing of claims, underwriting, and customer relationship management. Older technologies might have inherent security challenges, rendering them subject to cyber threats, data theft, and illegal access. Legacy systems are often incompatible with modern technologies and external channels, restricting insurer's ability to make investments on advancing technologies, engage with partners, and connect with third-party systems. Transforming outdated systems into modern platforms needs an immense amount of effort and resources. Insurance companies have to analyse traditional systems dependency issues, transfer data needs, and continuity of operational requirements while limiting disruption to current operations.

1.4 EMERGING TRENDS

1.4.1 AI and Machine Learning

Figure 1.4 explains how insurers are increasingly employing AI and machine learning algorithms to enhance actuarial modelling, risk evaluation, and decision-making. Hacariz et al (2022) explained that AI-powered statistical analysis enables insurers to evaluate huge datasets, determine trends, and develop relevant insights, which leads to better improved pricing, underwriting, and settlement of claims.

Machine learning algorithms and AI have the potential to streamline the underwriting procedures, enhance accuracy, and boost risk selection, leading to improved efficiency in operations and risk management. Artificial Intelligence platforms may streamline activities such as claim intake, verification, and settlements. Machine learning algorithms may examine claim statistics, determine trends in fraud or inconsistencies, and

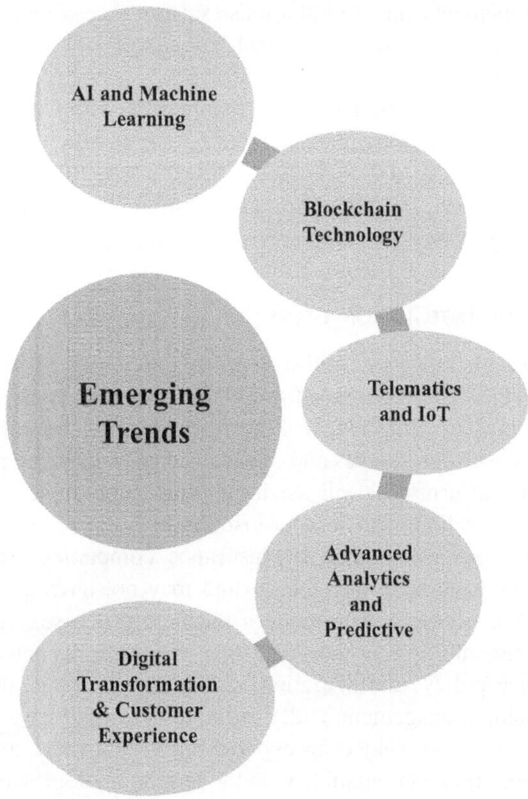

FIGURE 1.4 Emerging trends in the insurance industry. (Developed by Author.)

accelerate the process of claim settlement while minimizing the risk of omissions and fraudulent claims. Using predictive analytics, insurance business may identify high-risk people, predict the likelihood of claims, and customize pricing techniques in order to accurately represent the underlying risk factors. AI-driven chatbots and digital assistants can respond to customer enquiries, propose items, and manage policies. Machine learning algorithms can detect trends of fraudulent behaviour in insurance claims including incorrect information, fabricated situations, and exaggerated losses. By examining previous claims data and identifying discrepancies, artificial intelligence platforms can enable insurers to detect fraud, minimize financial losses, and secure their reputation. AI and machine learning may assist insurers in preemptively finding and mitigating risks through statistical modelling as well as real-time surveillance. IoT equipment, including telematics sensors or smart home appliances, can gather data on driving patterns or property conditions permitting insurers to supply risk minimizing services and benefits to policyholders. AI and Machine learning can be utilized for tailored pricing and suggested products, portfolio optimization and management of risk, and natural language processing for policy analysis.

Insurer can utilize AI and machine learning in order to monitor policyholders health and well-being data such as fitness trackers, smartwatches, and connected devices. Insurance firms will get a competitive advantage and be able to adapt to the emerging demands of the digital era if they manage to implement these advances in technologies.

1.4.2 Blockchain Technology

Blockchain technology has the capability to change various aspects of the insurance industry such as management of contract, processing of claims, and identifying fraudulent activities. Turnbull and Turnbull (2017) suggest that insurers are investigating towards solutions that utilize blockchain technology for enhancing data security, accountability, and operational effectiveness while reducing administrative expenditures and minimizing the risk of fraud. For example, automated agreements for policy management, fraud detection and mitigation, Simplified Reinsurance Processes, Better Data safety, security and Privacy, Catastrophe bonds and customizable insurance, advances in claim settlement and processing, logistics and insurance, Peer-to-peer (P2P) and small-scale insurance services monitoring and regulatory compliance, and cooperation and data sharing.

1.4.3 Telematics and IoT

Telematics gadgets and Internet of Things (IoT) sensors offer insurer to gather real-time data on policyholder behaviour, consumption habits, and risk exposures. Blacklow (2007) observed that integrating telematics data with actuarial algorithms enables insurers to develop usage-based insurance products and services, customized pricing, and preemptive risk management strategies tailored towards particular clients' requirements. Telematics information from IoT gadgets can assist insurers in accurately assessing specific risk profiles. Telematics data can be analysed by insurers to validate a claim's conditions, evaluate liability, and accelerate claims settlement, leading to quicker resolution, minimal fraud, and improved client satisfaction. Telematics information may disclose risky behaviours such as reckless driving, abrupt stops, drinking and driving, or driving while distracted.

IoT-enabled telematics services are usually utilized in corporate fleet administration to monitor vehicle locations, analyse behaviour of drivers, and streamline route planning and logistics. Smart watches, smart sensors, cameras, and alarms are examples of IoT gadgets that keep track of property conditions and identify potential risk or reasons of damages like fire, theft, and water damage. Home insurer may offer premium discounts to clients who adopt IoT-enabled surveillance and safety systems, stimulating risk management and damage mitigation practices. Telematics information from IoT devices enables insurance companies significant insights for statistical or mathematical modelling and data analytics. IoT technology and Telematics are implemented by insurance companies to communicate with clients and encourage safe driving habits through gamification, incentive schemes, and individual feedback.

When gathering and utilizing telematics data from IoT devices, insurers need to make sure they are in line with privacy laws and data protection rules.

1.4.4 Advanced Analytics and Predictive Modelling

Insurers are investing in sophisticated analytics and predictive modelling to better risk prediction, portfolio optimization, and client segmentation. Buck and Huber (2014) believed that through the use of predictive analytics, insurers can better predict future trends, spot new hazards, and create proactive plans for mitigating those risks – all of which improve overall business performance and resilience. Advanced analytics and predictive modelling improve Risk Assessment and Underwriting, Fraud Detection and Prevention, Consumer Segmentation and Targeted Marketing, Retention and Churn Prediction Strategies, Claim Severity and Loss Reserving, Disaster Modelling and Risk Mitigation, Analysis of Customer Lifetime Value (CLV), Adaptive Pricing and Customized Products, Innovation and Product Development, and Optimizing processes and operational efficiency. Trivedi and Malik (2022a) explained that Insurance companies can improve overall productivity and performance by analysing data on claims processing times, customer service indicators, and resource utilization.

1.4.5 Digital Transformation and Customer Experience

Insurers are implementing digital transformation strategies to improve consumer interaction, streamline operations, and provide personalized experiences. Meyers and Hoyweghen (2018) studied that customers may easily manage their insurance plans, obtain real-time information, and connect with insurers across many channels thanks to digital platforms, smartphone apps, and self-service portals. Insurance firms make use of digital equipment's to facilitate clients' onboarding. Insurance businesses are applying multi-channel techniques to connect with customers across several channels including social media, mobile application, websites, and customer care lines. These internet-based platforms allow customers to manage their insurance schemes, update individual details, and access important documents online. Delong (2013) observed that insurance firms can minimize expenses by implementing Ser-service Kiosks, enhancing efficiency and productivity, and offering policyholders a wide range of options and flexibility. Using advanced analytics and machine learning algorithms, insurers may analyse customer information and preferences to offer customized product recommendations. Smartphone application enables policyholders to conveniently file claims, upload documentation, and track their coverage status.

According to Trivedi (2023a), introducing mobile claim management enables insurers to speed up the processing of claims, improve transparency, and proactively assist customers during critical times. To deliver faster services to customers, insurance companies use chatbots and automated assistants. Insurance companies can use data analytics to offer personalized recommendations to their customers on risk prevention measures, loss evasion, and insurance coverage augmentation. Virtual platforms enable insurer to promptly collect and review clients' feedback and sentiments data. Trivedi and Malik (2022a) highlighted that insurance businesses are digitizing their claim request processing workflow to improve productivity and speed up claim handling. Computerized procedures, online paperwork, and digital signatures simplify claims settlement, minimize processing times, and offer a better customer experience whenever processing claims. Insurer can maintain continuing interaction and communication with customers at every stage of their respective lives because of the digital revolution.

Trivedi (2023b) discovered that insurance companies may build long-term relationship, develop credibility, and improve clients' confidence by offering targeted interaction, meaningful updates, and assertive alarms. Due to the digital revolution, insurance companies can keep perpetual communication and connection with their customers at every stage of life.

1.4.6 Regulatory Technology (RegTech)

The proliferation of regulatory technology (Reg Tech) systems has been helping insurance companies to simplify regulatory techniques, automate regulatory reporting, and control risk related to regulation with greater efficiency. Reg Tech platforms integrate artificial intelligence, data analytics, and blockchain to monitor regulatory compliance, comply with legislative developments, and minimize compliance-related expenses and risk. Reg Tech solutions automate compliance processes such as legislative disclosure, monitoring and auditing procedures, assuring insurance companies satisfy rigorous regulatory obligations. Reg Tech systems streamline reporting for regulatory purposes by standardizing formats of information automating collections and verification, and facilitating submission to regulatory authorities. Trivedi et al. (2024) observed that by concentrating on automating the reporting process, insurance companies can ensure that regulatory submissions are true, timely, and identical, minimizing the risk of oversights, fines, and penalties for noncompliance. Reg Tech tools enable insurance firms to execute stringent KYC and AML verification on clients and counterparties, eliminating frauds, money laundering, and terrorist financing. Reg Tech technologies allow insurance companies to handle data safety and security concerns by effective management, two-way encryption, and access management processes. Reg Tech solutions allow insurance firms to effectively handle functional, financial, and regulatory risks by offering modern risk evaluation and monitoring tools. Reg Tech systems help insurance companies in navigating regulatory shifting by monitoring patterns, analysing rules and regulation, and swapping relevant data with counterparties. According to Brindopke (2021), Reg Tech solutions help insurance companies to make sure that staff understand and grasp their regulatory responsibilities, conform to compliance specifications, and effectively and efficiently handle compliance risk through offering interactive virtual training programs, tests, and certification. Reg Tech systems strengthen audits and ensure productivity by automating disclosure, paperwork, and verification processes.

Thanks to Reg Tech systems, insurance businesses are able to participate in regulatory sandbox environment, development centers, or regulatory testing space developed by regulatory authorities. Reg Tech products serve insurance companies to confront the issues of international compliance and developments in globalization by offering their businesses with resources and instruments they require to handle regulatory obligations across multiple jurisdictions.

1.5 CONCLUSION

The changes from slide rules to AI demonstrate the actuarial profession's persistence and agility. Every advancement in technology has opened up new opportunities that are transforming the actuarial profession and helping actuaries to overcome ever more complex issues. To remain an influential player in the risk management and resilience sector, the actuarial community needs to keep focusing on innovative thinking, collaborations, and ethical conduct as we confront new technological breakthroughs.

Finally, the expansion of actuarial systems in the insurance industry has been distinguished by major developments that were caused by technological advancements, regulatory reforms, and changing expectations. From manual calculations in the 19th century to the implementations of advanced analytics and digital technologies in the 21st century, actuarial systems have transformed remarkably, allowing insurers to enhance the assessment of risks, increase operational efficiency while offering more customized goods and services to clients. Several minds of challenges with the insurance sector's present structure make it challenging to manage risk, function effectively and efficiently, and delight clients.

REFERENCES

Balbas, Alejandro, Beatriz Balbas, Raquel Balbas, and Antonio Heras. "Actuarial pricing with financial methods." *Scandinavian Actuarial Journal* 5 (2023): 450–476.

Barigou, Karim, Ze Chen, and Jan Dhaene. "Fair dynamic valuation of insurance liabilities: Merging actuarial judgement with market-and time-consistency." *Insurance: Mathematics and Economics* 88 (2019): 19–29.

Blacklow, Robert S. "Actuarially speaking: An overview of life expectancy. What can we anticipate?" *The American Journal of Clinical Nutrition* 86, no. 5 (2007): 1560S–1562S.

Brindopke, Susanne. "Actuarial Data Science." In Volker Liermann, Claus Stegmann (Eds.), *The Digital Journey of Banking and Insurance, Volume I: Disruption and DNA*, 119–136. Cham, Switzerland: Palgrave Macmillan, 2021.

Buck, Robert E., and Michael R. Huber. "Introduction to the special issue on actuarial education." *PRIMUS* 24, no. 9–10 (2014): 775–779.

Byrne, James M., and April Pattavina. "The Emerging Role of Clinical and Actuarial Risk Assessment in an Evidence-Based Community Corrections System Issues to Consider." In *Correctional Counseling and Treatment: Evidence-Based Perspectives*, 15. NJ: Pearson/Prentice Hall, 2008

Choudhary, Vinita, Neha Kamboj, and Sonal Trivedi. "Scoping Review of Literature on the Application of Blockchain in Finance." In Sonal Trivedi, Rashmi Aggarwal, and Gurmeet Singh (Eds.), *Perspectives on Blockchain Technology and Responsible Investing*, 1–28. USA: IGI Global, 2023.

Choudhary, Vinita, and Sonal Trivedi. "The Role of Internal Audit in Risk Management with a Perspective of Sustainability Development." In Kiran Sood, Simon Grima, Peter Young, Ercan Ozen, and Balamurugan Balusamy (Eds.), *The Impact of Climate Change and Sustainability Standards on the Insurance Market*, 287–315. Beverly, MA: Scrivener Publishing, 2023.

Delong, Łukasz. *Backward Stochastic Differential Equations with Jumps and Their Actuarial and Financial Applications*. London: Springer, 2013.

Dhaene, Jan, Ben Stassen, Karim Barigou, Daniël Linders, and Ze Chen. "Fair valuation of insurance liabilities: Merging actuarial judgement and market-consistency." *Insurance: Mathematics and Economics* 76 (2017): 14–27.

Feng, Runhuan, and Jose Garrido. "Actuarial applications of epidemiological models." *North American Actuarial Journal* 15, no. 1 (2011): 112–136.

Frees, Edward W., and Fei Huang. "The discriminating (pricing) actuary." *North American Actuarial Journal* 27, no. 1 (2023): 2–24.

Hacarız, Oytun, Torsten Kleinow, and Angus S. Macdonald. "An actuarial model of arrhythmogenic right ventricular cardiomyopathy and life insurance." *Scandinavian Actuarial Journal* 2022, no. 2 (2022): 94–114.

Harris, Andrew John Rawson, and R. Karl Hanson. "Clinical, actuarial and dynamic risk assessment of sexual offenders: Why do things keep changing?" *Journal of Sexual Aggression* 16, no. 3 (2010): 296–310.

Insurance Information Institute (2010). https://www.iii.org/sites/default/files/docs/pdf/Insurance_Handbook_20103.pdf

Malik, Reena, and Sonal Trivedi. "Blockchain Technology and Healthcare: Towards Combating COVID-19." In Kiran Sood, Rajesh Kumar Dhanaraj, Balamurugan Balusamy, and Seifedine Kadry (Eds.), *Blockchain Technology in Corporate Governance: Transforming Business and Industries*, 57–74. Wiley, 2022.

Meyers, Gert, and Ine Van Hoyweghen. "Enacting actuarial fairness in insurance: From fair discrimination to behaviour-based fairness." *Science as Culture* 27, no. 4 (2018): 413–438.

Trivedi, Sonal. "Blockchain framework for insurance industry." *International Journal of Innovation and Technology Management* 20, no. 6 (2023a): 2350034.

Trivedi, Sonal. "Blockchain Technology and Structural Change in Financial Services." In Kiran Sood, Simon Grima, Ganga Sharma, Balamurugan Balamurugan (Eds.), *The Application of Emerging Technology and Blockchain in the Insurance Industry*, 249–263. Denmark: River Publishers, 2023b.

Trivedi, Sonal. "Convention of Blockchain in Financial Services: A State-of-the-Art Literature Review." In Kiran Mehta, Renuka Sharma, Poshan Yu (Eds.,) *Revolutionizing Financial Services and Markets through FinTech and Blockchain* (2023c). USA: IGI Global 237–250.

Trivedi, Sonal, Vinita Choudhary, Neha Kamboj, and Nirmaljeet Kaur Virk. "New Avenues of Opportunities and Challenges for Start-Ups, MSMEs, the Indian Financial Sector, and the Indian Insurance Sector." In Simon Grima, Shilpa Chaudhary, Kiran Sood, and Sanjeev Kumar (Eds.), *Business Drivers in Promoting Digital Detoxification*, 226–250. USA: IGI Global, 2024.

Trivedi, Sonal, and Reena Malik. "Blockchain Technology as an Emerging Technology in the Insurance Market." In Kiran Sood, Rajesh Kumar Dhanaraj, Balamurugan Balusamy, Simon Grima, and R. Uma Maheshwari (Eds.), *Big Data: A Game Changer for Insurance Industry*, 81–100. England: Emerald Publishing, 2022a.

Trivedi, Sonal, and Reena Malik. "Role and Significance of Data Protection in Risk Management Practices in the Insurance Market." In Kiran Sood, Balamurugan Balusamy, Simon Grima, Pierpaolo Marano (Eds.), *Big Data Analytics in the Insurance Market*, 263–273. Emerald Publishing, 2022b.

Trivedi, Sonal, Kiran Mehta, and Renuka Sharma. "Systematic literature review on application of blockchain technology in E-finance and financial services." *Journal of Technology Management & Innovation* 16, no. 3 (2021): 89–102.

Turnbull, Craig, and Craig Turnbull. "A Brief History of Financial Economics for Actuaries." In Craig Turnbull (Ed.), *A History of British Actuarial Thought*, 145–185. UK: Palgrave Macmillan 2017.

Watson, Hannah, A. A. Cohen, and Caroline Isaksson. "A theoretical model of the evolution of actuarial senescence under environmental stress." *Experimental Gerontology* 71 (2015): 80–88.

Section B

Application of AI

2 Experts Opinion on Generative AI

Adoption and Challenges in Actuarial Science

Madhwaraj Kango Gopal, Jayashri Shetty, Gokul Yenduri, Praveen Kumar Reddy Maddikunta, Ramalingam Murugan, and Thippa Reddy Gadekallu

2.1 INTRODUCTION

Artificial intelligence (AI) is one such concept that tries to bring human knowledge onto machines. It was being used initially in specific disciplines, but nowadays it is being used in multidisciplinary environments. Laporta et al. (2024) described that a lot of benefits have been achieved with the use of AI and its associated technologies. Lozano-Murcia et al. (2024) described that sustainable AI helps in creating systems that are socially acceptable while minimizing computing resources on the whole. Finally, we have the generative AI that has evolved in recent times and focuses on generating content based on the input supplied to a system. Many generative AI tools have been developed such as Ada, Genni, ChatBot, RAD AI, Yooz, ChatGPT, GPT-4, and DeepDream. All these types of AI have been used extensively across several disciplines like Insurance, Healthcare, Education, Tourism, Marketing, Agriculture, Banking, Entertainment, Accounting, and E-commerce applications. In this chapter, we will discuss generative AI and its adoption in actuarial science.

Ridzuan et al. (2024) describe that technological advancements have led to new opportunities in actuarial science. Amerirad et al. (2023) describe that the use of AI across several fields has become a reality today, actuarial science is no exception. Actuarial science can adapt and incorporate new techniques to find solutions to problems amicably.

Perla et al. (2024) described that the need was felt mainly in the life insurance sector, where the volume of future liability was known but the timing was unknown. Therefore, there was a major challenge of discounting backward to know what the present value of the future liability would be. This led to the growth of actuarial science. Edmond Halley, an astronomer, laid the foundation for modern actuarial science.

DOI: 10.1201/9781003472551-4

Das et al. (2024) explained that using past events, experiences, and learning, a linear model was devised to answer the question of when in the future the liability would become due. du Preez et al. (2024) studied that once the future date is known and the future value is already available, all one needs to do is to discount the future value using a prudent discount rate to obtain how much the company should set aside today to pay for the liability in the future.

Etzler et al (2024) described that Actuaries analyze the financial impact of risk, particularly looking ahead into the future. So, Boucher and Valdez (2021) explained that recently the scope of actuarial science has widened to include investment advice, healthcare, finance, asset management, risk management, and even population forecasting.

Adeoye et al. (2024) explained that Machine learning (ML) algorithms can identify patterns and correlations within data that may be challenging for traditional actuarial methods to uncover. Ngwenduna and Mbuvha (2021) suggested that this allows actuaries to make more informed decisions while setting insurance premiums or estimating pension liabilities. The use of technology has become imperative because of the benefits it offers while studying systems, actuarial science is no exception.

2.2 PROGRAMMING LANGUAGES THAT SUPPORT ACTUARIES

Large amounts of datasets are available in different domains, which require the support of programming languages to process the data to acquire task-oriented results. Python helps to perform several tasks as follows:

- Using specific ML and DL algorithms depending on the business context.
- Advancing scientific research in actuarial data will aid in arriving at decisions due to its large volume.
- Data analysis can be performed with several tools, libraries, and functions.
- Predictive modeling is the essence of any domain, and this will hold good to the actuarial context.
- It helps to connect with traditional and non-traditional databases like SQL, NOSQL, and MongoDB.

2.3 APPLICATIONS IN THE ACTUARIAL CONTEXT

2.3.1 Effective Automation of Actuarial Content

Excel sheets were used in the olden days and even today. Richman and Wüthrich (2023) described that entering data manually in Excel spreadsheets has become a very tedious task, and therefore, all manual tasks on a day-to-day basis that are being done by actuaries can be automated depending on the inputs supplied to the application.

2.3.2 Availability of Several Python Libraries

Several Python libraries would help in analyzing the actuarial content. Data visualization can be done using Matplotlib. Data Analysis can be done using the Pandas library. Scipy can be used for solving scientific problems and calculations and the Numpy library can be used for scientific and numerical computations.

2.3.3 Reusing Use Cases

du Preez et al. (2024) described that some common techniques that are used are Data Cleaning and Web Scraping, which can be effectively used to make business decisions quicker on any pricing or selling strategy, predictive modeling of business use cases, performing regression and other statistical techniques, detection of frauds during claim settlement, etc.

2.4 ML ALGORITHMS – CATEGORIES

Four different categories of algorithms exist in ML. They are supervised algorithms, semi-supervised algorithms, unsupervised algorithms, and reinforcement learning algorithms.

2.5 TYPES OF ML ALGORITHMS AND RELATED WORK

Now that we have understood all of the different categories of ML algorithms, we will dwell on different types of algorithms that exist in one of these categories. These algorithms have been used in many disciplines including actuarial science.

2.6 A LOOK AT THE MACHINE LEARNING ALGORITHMS TODAY

Amerirad et al. (2023) described that any model that gets generated using ML or DL consists of the following datasets, i.e., a training dataset, a testing dataset, and the activation function. Parodi (2012) studied that several activation functions are used to understand the behavior of the dataset over some time.

2.6.1 Artificial Neural Networks

A modified version of the ANN algorithm was created by Laporta et al. (2024) to estimate conditional quantiles of aggregate claim amounts using the neural network approach. Zhu and Huang have observed the development of advanced models in better forecasting and performance in actuarial applications.

2.6.2 Decision Tree Algorithm

Ridzuan et al. (2024) performed a comparative study between the logistic regression model, decision tree, and neural networks using SAS Enterprise Miner, and found that the decision tree was the best model for health insurance premium pricing.

2.6.3 Convolutional Neural Networks

Perla et al. (2024) adapted the LocalGLMnet model proposed by Richman and Withrich (2023), used auto-encoders, and observed that mortality rates can be forecasted more efficiently.

2.6.4 K-Nearest Neighbors (KNN)

Power, Cote, and Duchesne (2024) described that there has not been much work with the use of this algorithm in the actuarial context. There is an opportunity for researchers to work on the use of this algorithm in making actuarial decisions.

2.6.5 Support Vector Machine (SVM)

This is a supervised ML algorithm that is used to solve classification and regression problems effectively. Data gets separated with a boundary or hyperplane concept. This helps in identifying data within a particular boundary and even distinguishing them accordingly.

2.6.6 Random Forest

Etzler et al. (2024) compared logistic regression with the Random Forest algorithm and found no superior performance of the Random Forest than the conventional logistic regression model. He, Jin, and Li (2024) reviewed cyber risk research across several disciplines with an important objective to help researchers in the fields of insurance and actuarial science by identifying potential gaps in the literature.

2.6.7 Stochastic Gradient Descent

Sun, Wang, and Wang (2024) studied the concept of prediction intervals of prices in variable annuities. They found the gradient boosting model with the bootstrap method to evaluate the prediction interval in large variable annuity policies. Power et al. (2024) proposed a hierarchical model that refined the traditional ways of predicting future claims using the XGBoost, a scalable gradient-boosting algorithm.

2.6.8 Ensemble Learning

Das et al. (2024) designed a new ensemble approach using the DeepAR and XGBoost regression models. They found that this ensemble approach performed better than benchmarked statistical models by 50%.

2.6.9 Generative Models

These algorithms are a class of statistical model that generates new instances based on an input dataset. Several algorithms have a generative nature like Adversarial ML, Diffusion Model, Autoregressive models, and Bayesian Networks.

2.6.10 Time Series Forecasting

These algorithms are used to forecast trends, understand different patterns of data, and make conclusions. Using time series algorithms helps in predicting business decisions and would help in the context of actuarial science.

2.6.11 Supervised Dimensionality Reduction Techniques

These algorithms have an objective of representing the data in low-dimensional space, which helps in making the data classifications easier.

2.7 GENERATIVE AI MODELS

Generative AI is an artificial intelligence technology that is designed to generate new content, such as images, text, audio, or video, which is supported by existing data. He, Jin and Li (2024) described that these models learn the underlying patterns and structures of the data they are trained on and can then generate new samples that resemble the original data.

2.7.1 Predictive Modeling

AI-powered predictive models can improve the reliability of forecasting future events, such as mortality rates, accident frequencies, or financial market trends. This allows actuaries to make more informed decisions while fixing insurance premiums or estimating pension liabilities.

2.7.2 Data Visualization

Actuaries use data visualization tools for general reporting and analysis. This enables the actuaries to do quicker summarization of data and get detailed results. It helps with pricing and underwriting.

2.7.3 Better Risk Assessment

Traditionally, insurers depended on historical data and actuarial models for risk assessment and calculation of premiums. On the other hand, generative AI enables actuaries to incorporate extensive factors into their risk assessment models, including non-traditional data sources such as social media, network of physical devices, and satellite images.

2.7.4 Cost Savings

Generative AI helps insurers reduce operational costs by automating manual processes and improving operational efficiency.

2.7.5 Cloud Computing

The technology foundation of actuarial modeling is redefined by cloud computing. AI technologies demand considerable computational power and data storage, which is efficiently addressed by cloud computing.

2.7.6 Customized Products

Generative AI enables insurers to create personalized insurance products and services tailored to the unique needs and preferences of individual policyholders based on the insights from prospective customer's queries.

2.7.7 Quick Decision-Making

Generative AI automates repetitive and time-consuming tasks, such as data processing and model development, which allows actuaries to engage in more strategic activities.

2.7.8 Competitive Advantage

Adeoye et al. (2024) have found that AI-driven analytics will certainly help insurers with instant solutions for satisfying individual customers, attaining higher levels of satisfaction, and thereby improving overall business growth.

2.8 ADOPTION OF GENERATIVE AI

There is no day without news on new AI applications. There is a shift in the usage of AI. It was assumed that some fields are not open to AI. But today domains like insurance, marketing, education, banking, and tourism are open to AI. Now, let us explore the adoption of generative AI in different areas:

2.8.1 Generative AI and Risk Management

du Preez et al. (2024) have studied the risks related to AI from an actuarial angle and laid down the challenges while using modeling languages in actuarial science. Technologies' ability to handle and analyze large volumes of data at a faster speed with lower human intervention has made the work of actuaries simpler. Clemente et al. (2023) studied that by training AI models on historical data, one can generate data that accurately represents real-world scenarios.

2.8.2 Generative AI and Fraud Detection

Using generative AI for fraud detection helps to identify potential risk factors. For example, in banking, AI algorithms are assigned the task of continuous monitoring of accounts; they analyze transaction patterns to detect signs of fraud, such as unexpected overseas transactions or unexpected huge amounts of withdrawals.

2.8.3 Generative AI and Underwriting

Generative AI can assist underwriters in evaluating potential risks by analyzing large volumes of data, including medical records, lifestyle habits, historical claims, customer information, and external factors, to generate risk profiles and recommend appropriate coverage levels, helping underwriters to make more informed decisions with better efficiency and accuracy.

2.8.4 Generative AI and Claim Processing

Claim processing involves certain steps, which are time-consuming and prone to errors. Each step involves careful attention to detail and often requires the claim managers to review lengthy and narrative documents.

2.8.5 Generative AI and Customer Service

As the technology continues to unfold, AI opens up new ways of doing things, which enhances customer service. With access to the right data and customer context, bots can make personalized recommendations to customers.

2.9 CHALLENGES IN USING GENERATIVE AI

Actuarial models rely heavily on historical data such as financial, demographic, and insurance-specific information. The data must be accurate and sufficient to adapt to the situation. Actuarial data often contains sensitive personal details. The important challenges of the application of generative AI are:

2.9.1 Data Quality

The major challenge of using AI in actuarial science is to safeguard the quality and reliability of data that feeds the algorithms. The fruitfulness of AI models relies heavily on the quality and representativeness of the data used for training.

2.9.2 Regulatory Compliance

The major challenge of using AI in actuarial science is going along with the upcoming and existing regulations that govern the actuarial field and the restrictions on the use of data and technology. Amerirad et al. (2023) prescribed a taxonomy for adversarial networks consistent with the current regulatory framework concerning claims falsification in health insurance.

2.9.3 Cyber Threats

Cyber threat is a challenge for actuaries like many other professionals. Actuaries may face such threats in different ways, such as loss or theft of client's personal data, loss or theft of confidential and commercially sensitive information, domain name disputes, physical damage caused by the use of the internet, and denial of hardware or software malfunction. In addition, it may harm the reputation of actuaries.

2.9.4 Ethical Issues

The ethical implications of the decisions and actions that the algorithms generate are another challenge of using AI in actuarial science. If the algorithms are based on protected and sensitive attributes, such as race, gender, and health status, AI models may produce outcomes harmful to certain individuals or groups.

2.9.5 Human Oversight

Maintaining the appropriate level of human intervention in AI models and their outputs is another challenge in actuarial science.

Sun, Wang, and Wang (2024) explained that, while many actuaries have a high level of understanding of AI concepts, there is a lack of practical experience in applying these concepts.

2.9.6 Views of Experts

To get valuable insights into generative AI in the present actuarial science context, an effort was made to contact some practicing actuaries and people who are working in the insurance sector.

2.9.6.1 Expert 1: Mr. Vamsidhar Ambatipudi, MBA (IIM – Indore), FRM, FIAI, CERA, Associate Professor, Head-Management Group (Off-Campus), BITS Pilani.

1. **What do you think actuarial science is all about?**

   At its core, actuarial science is a discipline that applies mathematical and statistical methods to assess risk in insurance, finance, and other sectors. It's the backbone of decision-making in the insurance industry, balancing financial theory with human behavior to predict future events. This precise field is pivotal in designing policies that safeguard against uncertain future losses.
2. **How actuarial science was used in business/insurance?**

   Historically, actuarial science has played a pivotal role in the insurance sector, determining premiums, setting reserves for future claims, and ensuring that companies remain solvent and can meet their future obligations. Actuaries analyze past data, identify trends, and use complex mathematical models to predict risk and financial outcomes, making informed decisions about policy pricing and the terms of insurance contracts.

3. **What are the issues actuaries face today?**

   Actuaries today face several challenges, including dealing with the uncertainty of new risks such as cyber threats, the impact of climate change on insurance models, and navigating the complex landscape of regulatory changes. Additionally, the increasing volume and velocity of data demand more sophisticated tools and approaches for analysis and prediction.
4. **Are there any pertinent traditional models that are used by actuaries?**

   Traditional actuarial models have largely been deterministic, relying on historical data and established statistical methods to estimate future outcomes. Techniques such as the life table for mortality, annuity calculations for pensions, and loss models for property and casualty insurance are foundational. However, these models often assume static conditions and may not fully capture the complexities of real-world scenarios.
5. **Is AI used? If used, how is it used by actuaries today?**

   AI has begun to revolutionize actuarial science, offering tools that can handle vast datasets more efficiently and uncover insights that were previously inaccessible. AI techniques, including ML algorithms, are used to enhance predictive modeling, risk assessment, and customer segmentation. This has led to more accurate premium calculations, better risk management strategies, and personalized insurance products.
6. **What changes over some time has the actuarial science undergone?**

   Over the years, actuarial science has undergone significant transformations, evolving from manual calculations and simple deterministic models to sophisticated statistical and computational techniques. The integration of AI and ML represents the latest phase in this evolution, driving greater efficiency, accuracy, and innovation in the field.
7. **Was technology used in solving problems with actuaries?**

   Technology, particularly software and computational models, has been instrumental in solving complex actuarial problems. High-speed computing allows for the simulation of millions of scenarios, providing actuaries with a broader perspective on potential outcomes and enabling more informed decision-making.
8. **What are the pressing issues actuaries face today?**

   Dealing with the unpredictable effects of global phenomena like pandemics and climate change and navigating the complexities of cyber risk are the most pressing problems facing actuaries today. Moreover, ensuring data privacy and meeting the ever-tightening regulatory requirements present ongoing challenges.
9. **Can generative AI help or not help actuaries?**

   Generative AI, with its ability to create new data instances and simulate various scenarios, holds significant potential in actuarial science. It can help in stress testing insurance models under various conditions, generating synthetic data to improve model robustness, and exploring innovative insurance products and services. However, the use of generative AI also requires careful consideration of ethical standards, data integrity, and regulatory compliance.

2.9.6.2 Expert 2: Mrs. Supreetha P. Pakkala, Associate Regional Head, Bajaj Allianz Life Insurance Co. Ltd., Mangalore

1. **What do you think actuarial science is all about?**
   Actuarial science assesses financial risks in the insurance and finance fields using precise and statistical methods. Actuarial science applies probability analysis and statistics to define, analyze, and solve the financial impact of uncertain future events. Actuarial science helps insurance companies forecast the probability of an event occurring to determine the funds needed to pay claims. Actuarial science tries to measure the risk of an event occurring using probability analysis so that its financial impact can be determined.
2. **How actuarial science was used in business/insurance?**
   Suppose an insurance broker is calculating what is the price to be charged for term insurance to a 25-year-old client and a 40-year-old client, in this situation, the current health of the client, expected lifespan, and lifestyle choices will be considered. It's not possible to do a quick calculation to come up with a price. This is where the genius of the actuary becomes useful. The actuary can access historical data across genders and age groups using an accurate model; the actuary can estimate the possibilities of survival for each of the sections, thereby obtaining how risky the client is to insure.
3. **What are the issues actuaries face today?**
   The need to maintain public trust and confidence. To keep up with changing technology and data analytics. To have a top talent for accurate results. There is a need to manage risk in an increasingly complex world.
4. **Are there any pertinent traditional models that are used by actuaries?**
   The models that actuaries typically use in their work are deterministic or stochastic, which represent possible outcomes relative to future contingent events. A contingent event is an event whose occurrence, timing, or severity is uncertain.
5. **Is AI used? If used, how is it used by actuaries today?**
   Actuaries play a crucial role in assessing and managing financial risk, and with the start of AI, their profession has evolved significantly. Here are some ways that actuaries can directly use AI:

   Rating, reserving, and forecasting: Actuaries employ AI techniques to enhance their pricing models, especially in areas like long-term care (LTC) experience studies and ML, which helps update pricing assumptions based on real-world data.

   Telematics for vehicle insurance: AI-driven telematics systems analyze driving behavior to determine personalized insurance premiums for vehicle owners.

   Underwriting: AI assists in automating risk assessment during underwriting processes.

   Marketing: Actuaries leverage AI to identify target markets and optimize marketing strategies.

Population health interventions: AI aids in predicting health outcomes and designing effective interventions.

Claims processing: Automation streamlines claim handling and fraud detection.

AI enables actuaries to analyze large datasets efficiently while automating routine tasks.

6. **What changes over some time has the actuarial science undergone?**

Some of the key developments:

Emerging technologies: The field of actuarial science has been impacted by emerging technologies. These technologies include data analytics, ML, and AI. Actuaries now use advance tools to analyze large datasets, model risks, and make informed decisions.

Climate change: Actuaries are increasingly involved in assessing the impact of climate-related risks. As climate change accelerates, actuaries play a crucial role in evaluating risks to health, livelihoods, food security, water supply, and economic growth.

Collaboration with other professions: Actuaries now collaborate more closely with professionals from other fields, such as data scientists, economists, and engineers. This interdisciplinary approach enhances their ability to address complex challenges.

Regulatory changes: Actuarial work is influenced by evolving regulations and standards. Actuaries must stay updated on changes in accounting rules, solvency requirements, and risk management guidelines.

Risk modeling: Actuaries now employ sophisticated risk models to assess various risks, including cybersecurity, pandemics, and longevity. These models help insurers and organizations make informed decisions.

7. **Was technology used in solving problems with actuaries?**

Technology plays a crucial role in the field of actuarial science. Actuaries use various tools and technologies to analyze data, model risk, and make informed decisions. Here are some ways technology is utilized by actuaries:

Statistical modeling software: Actuaries frequently employ statistical models and tablets to evaluate large amounts of data.

Basic computer skills and proficiency with tools like Microsoft Office are important. Actuaries benefit from programming knowledge in statistical languages such as SQL, Python, and R.

Data visualization: Actuaries use data visualization tools to present complex information in a clear and concise manner.

Cloud computing and storage: Cloud platforms enable actuaries to store and access data securely. They can analyze data remotely and collaborate with colleagues across different locations.

Predictive models: Actuaries leverage predictive modeling techniques to forecast future events. These models help assess risks and guide decision-making.

Artificial intelligence (AI): ML algorithms can enhance risk assessment and automate processes.

8. **What are the pressing issues actuaries face today?**

   Actuaries face many pressing challenges, including actuarial modernization.

   The insurance landscape is growing fast, and actuarial departments are at the lead of this change. Efficiency, regulatory compliance, process quality, and management insights are key drivers for modernization efforts.

   The implementation of IFRS 17 (International Financial Reporting Standard 17) and emerging ESG (Environmental, Social, and Governance) requirements are putting actuaries under pressure to adapt.

   Despite ongoing modernization efforts, manual processes still persist within the actuarial function, necessitating a focus on process excellence.

   Actuaries face the challenge of understanding and implementing this complex accounting standard, which aims to improve transparency and consistency in insurance contracts.

   Resource constraints: Internal resource capacity often limits the speed of modernization initiatives. Balancing day-to-day business demands with the need for modernization remains a delicate task.

   Data sourcing and quality: Actuaries spend a significant amount of time, dealing with data issues. Improving data sourcing and quality is crucial for their efficiency and effectiveness.

   Long-term challenges: Challenges include adapting to technological advancements, managing risk, and staying relevant in a changing industry.

9. **Can generative AI help or not help actuaries?**

   Generative AI, with its predictive capabilities, can significantly assist actuaries in their work.

   Enhanced accuracy in reserving and forecasting: Generative AI can help actuarial reserving processes by improving the accuracy of loss reserve estimates.

   By analyzing historical claims data, identifying patterns, and simulating future claim scenarios, generative AI assists actuaries in more accurately forecasting future liabilities.

   Scenario generation and decision support: Generative AI suggests potential scenarios or outcomes for actuaries. It leverages historical data and patterns to provide insights, aiding decision-making.

   Efficiency gains and new capabilities: Generative AI excels at processing huge amounts of data and generating content at scale and speed.

   Actuaries can leverage it to unlock new capabilities or achieve significant efficiency gains.

   Risks associated with generative AI: Data Integrity: Ensuring accurate and unbiased data for training AI models is crucial. Partialities in data may spread in the AI system.

   Ethical consideration: Actuaries must alert proper implications when relying on AI-generated insights.

2.9.6.3 Expert 3: Mr. Raviraja Nayak, Ex-Regional Manager, ICICI Prudential Life Insurance Company Limited, Udupi

1. **What do you think actuarial science is all about?**
   Actuarial science is about assessing the risk associated with financial, insurance, and any other long-term investments.
2. **How actuarial science was used in business/insurance?**
   In insurance, the actuaries assess the financial value of the risks associated with future events and arrive at premiums to be levied. They use mathematical and statistical models to determine the near-probable values.
3. **What are the issues actuaries face today?**
   Ever-changing financial conditions across the globe that affect the outcomes beyond the original country are the biggest challenge actuaries face. The increasing interdependence of mathematical and statistical models between the countries, political, religious, and socio-economic factors, and regulatory changes all pose a threat to actuarial decision-making.
4. **Are there any pertinent traditional models that are used by actuaries?**
   Yes, actuaries still rely on several traditional models and methods in their work, alongside the incorporation of AI and advanced analytics. Some of the pertinent traditional models used by actuaries are mathematical and statistical models in actuarial decision-making.
5. **Is AI used? If used, how is it used by actuaries today?**
   Yes, AI is indeed used in actuarial work today, particularly in the insurance industry. Actuaries use AI and ML techniques to enhance various aspects of their work. AI is transforming the field of actuarial science by enabling actuaries to leverage advanced analytics and automation to better assess risk, improve decision-making, and enhance operational efficiency in the insurance industry.
6. **What changes over some time has the actuarial science undergone?**
   Actuarial science has undergone significant changes over time, driven by technological advancements, regulatory developments, shifts in demographic trends, and evolving industry practices.
7. **Was technology used in solving problems with actuaries?**
   Yes, technology has been instrumental in solving problems within the field of actuarial science. Actuaries have long relied on technology to perform complex calculations, analyze data, and develop models to address various challenges in insurance, pensions, and other areas of risk management.
8. **What are the pressing issues actuaries face today?**
   Ethical, geo-political, regulatory changes, cybersecurity, data privacy, etc. are some of the pressing issues that actuaries face today. Addressing these pressing issues requires collaboration among actuaries, regulators, policymakers, and other stakeholders to develop innovative solutions and ensure the continued relevance and effectiveness of actuarial practices in a rapidly changing world.

9. **Can generative AI help or not help actuaries?**
   Generative AI, which includes technologies like Generative Adversarial Networks (GANs) and other generative models, has the potential to both help and challenge actuaries in their work.

2.10 FINDINGS

Generative AI is not merely a replacement for underwriters, agents, brokers, actuaries, claims adjusters, or customer service representatives. Generative AI can help to streamline repetitive or manual tasks that create an opportunity for new operational efficiencies, build greater customer satisfaction, and empower employees to focus on higher value-added activities. Generative AI technology offers an instant feedback loop of information, allowing insurers to analyze customer insights or quickly solve an issue across multiple mediums including emails, website interactions, and customer service discussions. Insights can be produced in shorter timeframes – from seconds, minutes, and hours rather than multiple days or weeks. This offers a powerful co-pilot for underwriters, claim adjusters, agents, and other roles, which can supplement human expertise and help expedite complex decision-making. Many of these roles rely on a large amount of expertise that cannot be replaced by rules-based algorithms. Generative AI can help accelerate experts' analyses and assessments.

The combination of generative AI use cases to create efficiencies, "co-pilots", and personalization along with other technology, operation, and behavioral changes may lead to new opportunities for the industry. These offer the potential to reinvent the entire insurance value chain and transform the role of the insurer altogether. In the short term, the anticipation is that generative AI will materialize in more targeted areas within insurers' organizations and value chains. These focused areas need to meet a set of materiality, feasibility, and organizational readiness criteria, as well as serve as an initial beam for scaling high to more transformative solutions shortly. However, challenges persist, such as ensuring ethical use, managing privacy concerns, and maintaining regulatory compliance. The transformative impact of generative AI and ML on actuarial science is undeniable, offering a blend of opportunities and challenges that will shape the future of the insurance industry.

2.11 CONCLUSIONS

The collaboration between AI and actuarial science embraces great promise for the future of risk management and financial forecasting. Actuaries embracing AI technologies are likely to find novel opportunities for innovation and efficiency, ultimately enhancing their ability to handle the complicated domain of insurance. While the field continues to grow, a match between traditional actuarial methods and cutting-edge AI applications will be essential for ensuring powerful and ethical risk management practices. The greatest concern is that actuaries are not examining the social reinforcement of the data and what kind of social policies and practices may have embedded bias into the content that they are using in their models. Ethical AI will play a big role in the adaptation of LLMs into a niche domain like actuarial science, where data is generally sensitive. The application of generative AI will accelerate the process of getting a solution to a given situation.

REFERENCES

Adeoye, Omotayo Bukola, Chinwe Chinazo Okoye, Onyeka ChrisanctusOfodile, Olubusola Odeyemi, Wilhelmina Afua Addy, and Adeola Olusola Ajayi-Nifise. "Integrating artificial intelligence in personalized insurance products: a pathway to enhanced customer engagement." *International Journal of Management & Entrepreneurship Research* 6, no. 3 (2024): 502–511.

Amerirad, Behnaz, Matteo Cattaneo, Ron S. Kenett, and Elisa Luciano. "Adversarial artificial intelligence in insurance: from an example to some potential remedies." *Risks* 11, no. 1 (2023): 20.

Clemente, Gian Paolo, Francesco Della Corte, Nino Savelli, and Diego Zappa. "Special issue 'data science in insurance'." *Risks* 11, no. 5 (2023): 80.

Das, Vishal, Tianyi Mao, Zhicheng Geng, Carmen Flores, Diego Pelloso, and Fang Wang. "Enhancing sell-in and sell-out forecasting using ensemble machine learning method." In *International Conference on Business Forecasting and Marketing Intelligence* (2024).

du Preez, Valerie, Shaun Bennet, Matthew Byrne, AureliénCouloumy, Arijit Das, Jean Dessain, Richard Galbraith et al. "From bias to black boxes: understanding and managing the risks of AI–an actuarial perspective." *British Actuarial Journal* 29 (2024): e6.

Duval, Francis, and Mathieu Pigeon. "Individual loss reserving using a gradient boosting-based approach." *Risks* 7, no. 3 (2019): 79. https://doi.org/10.3390/risks7030079

Etzler, Sonja, Felix D. Schönbrodt, Florian Pargent, Reinhard Eher, and Martin Rettenberger. "Machine learning and risk assessment: random forest does not outperform logistic regression in the prediction of sexual recidivism." *Assessment* 31, no. 2 (2024): 460–481.

He, Rong, Zhuo Jin, and Johnny Siu-Hang Li. "Modeling and management of cyber risk: a cross-disciplinary review." *Annals of Actuarial Science* (2024): 1–40.

Laporta, Alessandro G., Susanna Levantesi, and Lea Petrella. "Neural networks for quantile claim amount estimation: a quantile regression approach." *Annals of Actuarial Science* 18, no. 1 (2024): 30–50.

Lozano-Murcia, Catalina, Francisco P. Romero, Jesus Serrano-Guerrero, and Jose A. Olivas. "An Application of a Fuzzy Multi criteria Decision Making Process for Explainable Machine Learning in the Actuarial Context." In Laszlo T. Koczy, Jesus Medina-Moreno, Eloisa Ramirez-Poussa, and Alexander Sostak (Eds.), *Computational Intelligence and Mathematics for Tackling Complex Problems* 5, pp. 67–72. Cham: Springer Nature Switzerland, 2024.

Ngwenduna, Kwanda Sydwell, and Rendani Mbuvha. "Alleviating class imbalance in actuarial applications using generative adversarial networks." *Risks* 9, no. 3 (2021): 49.

Parodi, Pietro. "Computational intelligence with applications to general insurance: a review: I–the role of statistical learning." *Annals of Actuarial Science* 6, no. 2 (2012): 307–343.

Perla, Francesca, Ronald Richman, Salvatore Scognamiglio, and Mario V. Wüthrich. "Accurate and explainable mortality forecasting with the LocalGLMnet." *Scandinavian Actuarial Journal* 2024 (2024): 739–761.

Power, Justine, Marie-Pier Cote, and Thierry Duchesne. "A flexible hierarchical insurance claims model with gradient boosting and copulas." *North American Actuarial Journal* (2024): 1–29.

Richman, Ronald, and Mario V. Wüthrich. "LocalGLMnet: interpretable deep learning for tabular data." *Scandinavian Actuarial Journal* 2023, no. 1 (2023): 71–95.

Ridzuan, Ahmad Nur Azam Ahmad, Aina Zafirah Azman, Fatin Alya Marzuki, Wan Shazmien Danieal Mohamed Faudzi, Siti Hajar Abd Aziz, and Norida Abu Bakar. "Health insurance premium pricing using machine learning methods." *Journal of Advanced Research in Applied Sciences and Engineering Technology* 41, no. 1 (2024): 134–141.

So, Banghee, Jean-Philippe Boucher, and Emiliano A. Valdez. "Synthetic dataset generation of driver telematics." *Risks* 9, no. 4 (2021): 58.

Sun, Tingting, Haoyuan Wang, and Donglin Wang. "Robust prediction intervals for valuation of large portfolios of variable annuities: A comparative study of five models." *Journal: Computational Economics* (2024): 1–22. https://doi.org/10.1007/s10614-024-10574-9

3 AI
A Revolutionary Tool for Actuarial Work in Insurance

Gurpreet Kaur, Puneet Singh, and Sachin Rawat

3.1 INTRODUCTION

The actuarial sciences are an important subset of the insurance industry as they help in assessment of risk so as to ensure financial stability of insurer (Naim 2022). By employing statistical tools, actuaries play a crucial role in decision-making by analyzing data and predicting the future (Singh and Chivukula 2020).

However, in the present scenario, the traditional actuaries are exposed to several challenges such as increased volume and complexity of data; therefore, AI acts as a tool for upgrading the actuarial work in the insurance industry (Sanwal 2021). AI with its different verticals such as predictive modeling, machine learning, and natural language processing is helpful for actuaries in extracting useful insights from data more accurately and efficiently (Richman 2024). These verticals provide enhanced mechanism for risk management (Trivedi and Malik 2024).

Machine learning algorithms can uncover complex patterns and relationships within data, allowing actuaries to make more informed decisions in areas such as risk assessment, pricing, and underwriting (Xu 2024).

In addition, Algorithmic Risk Management has shifted the paradigm for Fraud Detection, where AI algorithms can analyze claims data to identify patterns and red flags indicative of fraudulent activity and Real-Time Risk Assessment, where AI can analyze real-time data (e.g., telematics in car insurance) to dynamically adjust risk profiles and offer usage-based premiums (Gooding and Maker 2024).

AI-powered predictive models can assess the risk associated with insuring individuals based on their health profiles (Trivedi and Malik 2022a). By considering factors such as age, pre-existing conditions, lifestyle habits, and genetic predispositions, AI can accurately predict the likelihood of future medical expenses for each policyholder, enabling insurance companies to adjust premiums accordingly (Orji and Ukwandu 2024).

AI-driven insights can help insurers implement proactive measures to manage healthcare costs and promote preventive care (Malik and Trivedi 2022). By analyzing population health trends and identifying high-risk individuals, insurers can collaborate with healthcare providers to implement targeted interventions, such as wellness programs or disease management initiatives, which reduce the likelihood of costly medical procedures and improve overall health outcomes (Orji and Ukwandu 2024).

DOI: 10.1201/9781003472551-5

Building on the last point, Embedded Insurance Technology (InsurTech) is radically reshaping the industry through Seamless Integration where InsurTech platforms leverage AI to seamlessly integrate insurance coverage into everyday activities (Choudhary et al. 2023). Imagine car insurance that automatically adjusts based on driving behavior (Trivedi and Malik 2022b). This has led to Personalized Micro-Insurance, where AI can personalize insurance offerings to specific situations (e.g., temporary insurance for a rental car) (McDonald et al. 2024).

AI algorithms can process vast amounts of historical claims data more efficiently than traditional methods, enabling actuaries to identify complex patterns and correlations that may not be apparent through manual analysis (Trivedi et al. 2021). This enhanced data analysis capability allows for more accurate predictions of future claim frequencies and severities (Hoseini 2023).

AI enables insurers to segment their policyholders into more granular risk categories based on individual characteristics, behaviors, and preferences (Trivedi and Malik 2024). By tailoring predictive models to specific customer segments, actuaries can provide personalized claim forecasts that reflect the unique risk profiles of each policyholder, ultimately leading to more accurate predictions of claim frequencies and severities at the individual level (Hosein 2023).

The current paper is an attempt to study the application of AI in actuarial science. The study deals with the in-depth analysis into the process as to how AI mitigates the risk. Artificial Intelligence has emerged as the most effective and innovative technology in the present scenario (Naim 2022).

The paper is divided into different sections. Section 3.1 relates to introduction and background of the study, Section 3.2 constitutes the literature review, Section 3.3 deals with analysis and interpretation, Section 3.4 deals with conclusion and future scope of study, and Section 3.5 contains the references for the paper.

3.2 REVIEW OF LITERATURE

This research paper has explored a wide array of scholarly articles, reports, and studies to provide a comprehensive understanding of the impact of AI on actuarial services within the insurance domain. Few research studies are mentioned below.

Ahmadi (2024) explores the future impact of AI on finance, especially on insurance, predicting a revolution with diverse applications and seamless integration, while examining the convergence of Big Data and AI in the industry. Gupta and Venkataraman (2024) investigate the impact of acute and chronic climate risks on the insurance sector through literature review and a conceptual framework, aiming to identify future research needs for a resilient global insurance industry.

Kumari et al. (2024) examine the transformative role of Artificial Intelligence in the financial sector, highlighting its potential to transform challenges into learning opportunities and reshape our financial perception. Lozano-Murcia et al. (2024) explore the need for interpretable AI and machine learning systems by utilizing a fuzzy inference system and a modified MCDM model for decision-making. Harris et al. (2024) examine how deep learning advancements can improve actuarial standards in the United Kingdom and South Africa, ensuring model understand ability, reducing bias, and managing prediction variability.

Gooding and Maker (2024) explore the connection between algorithmic risk management, mental health, preventive policing, and biometric surveillance, utilizing Bernadette McSherry's predictive analytics work. Orji and Ukwandu (2024) explore machine learning's potential for medical insurance cost prediction using XGBoost, GBM, and Random Forest models, with Explainable AI methods providing deeper insights. Jawhar et al. (2024) explore the potential of AI-powered tools in enhancing the cybersecurity insurance lifecycle by analyzing existing literature on threat assessment, security awareness, and risk management.

Kanaparthi (2024b) examines the surge in interest in AI and ML in the insurance sector, highlighting its rapid growth from 2017 to 2022 and its potential impact on financial research.

Yadav et al. (2024) explore AI applications in ethical finance through a literature review, analyzing implementation challenges to promote responsible financial practices. Van Bekkum and Borgesius (2024) examine the transformation of embedded insurance technology, its potential for industry growth, insurance gap filling, and the need for balanced regulations through literature review, case studies, and legal framework analysis. Agarwal (2023) evaluates AI prediction's impact on decision-making and risk, highlighting challenges in existing processes while offering greater benefits with lower change costs.

McDonald et al. (2024) examine the dynamic nature of embedded insurance, utilizing a literature review and case studies to analyze how technology facilitates insurance partnerships between insurers and non-insurance brands. Kanaparthi (2024a) highlights five research gaps in using AI for personalized services in digital finance: explainability, trustworthiness, privacy, ethics, and credit risk management.

Rodríguez-Aguilar et al. (2024) explore the digital transformation in organizations due to COVID-19, focusing on the implementation of machine learning for patient risk forecasting in the insurance sector. Patel (2024) explores ethical issues in data-centric AI, proposing strategies to balance benefits and risks, emphasizing the need for ongoing reflection and proactive governance.

Durrani et al. (2024) highlights the Finnish Insurance Company's adoption of digitalization, including AI, NLP, and robotics, to improve service experiences and streamline processes for policyholders and insurers.

Wilkinson et al. (2023) examine the influence of big data and AI on insurance, highlighting potential benefits such as improved risk assessment, personalized marketing, and enhanced fraud detection. Tomar and Sharma () explore the growth potential of tech in embedded insurance, its role in bridging the insurance gap, and the need for balanced regulations in this evolving landscape. Hosein (2023) presents a novel model for balancing claim rate prediction accuracy for limited insurance products, demonstrating its effectiveness with real data and showcasing feature selection and parameter optimization.

Apergis (2024) examines the impact of Cognitive Digital Underwriting Assistants in medical insurance underwriting; this research utilizes literature review, case studies, and expert interviews to conclude that CDUAs can revolutionize the process.

CDUAs combine AI efficiency with human expertise, enhancing accuracy and collaboration. Kumar et al. (2019) explored AI's potential in insurance through a validated quantitative model, offering practical solutions for insurers to address customer concerns and streamline operations, which are also useful for insurance.

3.3 INTERPRETATION BASED ON LITERATURE REVIEW

Based on past research, it is evident that AI technologies are profoundly transforming various aspects of the insurance sector. AI implementation has helped in the retrieval of information relating to the potential and current clients, which is further helpful in mitigating risk in the insurance sector (Ahmad et al. 2023). The role of AI is very important and cannot replace human beings (Khalisa 2024).

The potential application of AI integration with blockchain helps in developing better models for risk assessment and mitigation (Bodemer 2023). The usage of AI-driven predictive analysis has improved risk assessment process in the insurance sector. Besides, this has effectively detected and prevented insurance claims (Komperla 2023).

TABLE 3.1
Papers with the Maximum Number of Citations

Authors Name & Year of Publication	Title of Paper	Citations
Kelley et al. (2018)	Artificial Intelligence: Implications for Social Inflation and Insurance. Risk Management and Insurance Review	65
Cappiello (2020)	The Technological Disruption of Insurance Industry: A Review	53
Ahmadi (2024)	A Comprehensive Study on Integration of Big Data and AI in Financial Industry and its Effect on Present and Future Opportunities	34
Kumar et al. (2019)	Artificial intelligence in Insurance Sector	31
Agarwal (2023)	Prediction Machines, Insurance, and Protection: An Alternative Perspective on AI's Role in Production	12
Hosein (2024)	A Data Science Approach to Risk Assessment for Automobile Insurance Policies	11
Sharma and Manhas (v2024)	The Future of Finance: Revolutionizing the Industry With Artificial Intelligence	7
Kanaparthi (2024b)	AI-Based Personalization and Trust in Digital Finance	6
Kanaparthi (2024b)	Transformational Application of Artificial Intelligence and Machine learning in Financial Technologies and Financial services: A Bibliometric Review	6

Source: Author's Compilation.

TABLE 3.2
Papers with Author's Name & Year of Publication

Authors Name & Year of Publication	Name of the Journal	Title of Paper
Agarwal (2023)	*Journal of the Japanese and International Economies*	Prediction Machines, Insurance, and Protection: An Alternative Perspective on AI's Role in Production
Ahmadi (2024)	*International Journal of Current Science Research and Review*	A Comprehensive Study on Integration of Big Data and AI in Financial Industry and its Effect on Present and Future Opportunities
Baruah and Singh (2023)	*International Conference on Advances in IoT and Security with AI*	Risk Prediction in Life Insurance Industry Using Machine Learning Techniques—A Review
Cappiello (2020)	*International Journal of Business and Social Science*	The Technological Disruption of Insurance Industry: A Review
Hosein (2024)	International Journal of Data Science and Analytics	A Data Science Approach to Risk Assessment for Automobile Insurance Policies
Jawhar et al. (2024)	In *2024 IEEE 14th Annual Computing and Communication Workshop and Conference (CCWC)*	Enhancing Cyber Resilience with AI-Powered Cyber Insurance Risk Assessment
Khalisa (2024)	*Ilomata International Journal of Management*	The Digitalization in Insurance Broker Industry: How Artificial Intelligence Affect This Industry
Kumar et al. (2019)	*Journal of the Gujarat Research Society*	Artificial Intelligence in Insurance Sector
Lozano (2024)	*Computational Intelligence and Mathematics for Tackling Complex Problems*	An Application of a Fuzzy Multi-Criteria Decision Making Process for Explainable Machine Learning in the Actuarial Context
McDonald et al. (2024)	*The Global Insurance Market and Change*	Embedded Insurance
Orji and Ukwandu (2024)	*Machine Learning with Applications*	Machine Learning for an Explainable Cost Prediction of Medical Insurance
Patel (2024)	*International Journal of Artificial Intelligence Research and Development*	Ethical Reflections on Data-Centric AI: Balancing Benefits and Risks
Prince and Taylor (2023)	*Research Handbook on International Insurance Law and Regulation*	Artificial Intelligence: Attempts at Developing an Ethical Approach for its Use in Insurance

(*Continued*)

TABLE 3.2 (*Continued*)
Papers with Author's Name & Year of Publication

Authors Name & Year of Publication	Name of the Journal	Title of Paper
Rodríguez-Aguilar et al. (2024)	*Mobile Networks and Applications*	Machine Learning for Digital Shadow Design in Health Insurance Sector
Sanwal (2021)	*Applications of Artificial Intelligence in Business and Finance*	Impact of Artificial Intelligence on the Insurance Industry
Sharma and Manhas (2024)	*Leveraging AI and Emotional Intelligence in Contemporary Business Organizations*	The Future of Finance: Revolutionizing the Industry with Artificial Intelligence
Tomar and Sharma (2024)	*Data-Driven Technologies and Artificial Intelligence in Supply Chain*	A Proposed Artificial Intelligence and Blockchain Technique for Solving Health Insurance Challenges
Wilkinson et al. (2024)	*The Global Insurance Market and Change*	Big Data, Artificial Intelligence and Insurance.
Yadav et al. (2024)	*Fintech Applications in Islamic Finance: AI, Machine Learning, and Blockchain Techniques*	Fusion of AI and Ethical Finance: Changing the Outlook of Financial Companies and Society

Source: Author's Compilation.

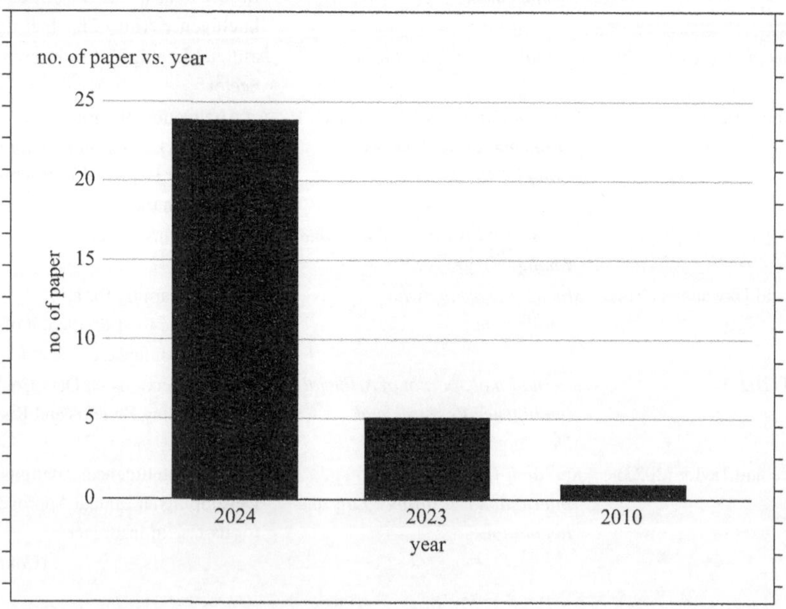

FIGURE 3.1 Years with the maximum number of publications. (Author's Compilation.)

AI has the ability to enhance the insurance industry by improvising the actuarial sciences (Kelley et al. 2018). When combined with advanced technologies like ML and DL, these powerful technologies have the potential to provide hassle-free services to the customers and speedy accomplishment of the tasks (Varadarajan 2024). Further, it has been found from past literatures that the emergence of new business models, services, and products aids in decision-making and process management (Nicoletti and Nicoletti 2021; Baruah and Singh 2023). The AI application in the insurance industry has improved the service capacity of actuarial sciences (CappiellO 2020). The risk assessment process has been streamlined, better customer services have been discharged, and fraudulent claims have been avoided.

3.4 CONCLUSION AND FUTURE SCOPE OF STUDY

The emergence of advanced technologies has led to rapid growth in the adoption of Artificial intelligence in almost all segments of the economy, one of which is the insurance industry (Trivedi 2023a). Though the usage of AI in insurance is still in its infancy stage, many initiatives have to be expanded and launched. One of the potential developments of AI system is risk assessment and management, which ensures not only accuracy but also fairness, transparency, and proper alignment (Trivedi 2024).

The key insights regarding the role of AI in transforming actuarial practices are enhanced risk assessment and underwriting (Lehmann 2020; Agarwal 2023), enhanced operational efficiency (Cappiello 2020; Harris et al. 2024), implementation of advanced predictive analytics (Baruah and Singh 2023; Hosein 2024), and fraud prevention and detection (Ahmadi 2024; Orji and Ukwandu 2024). Studies have proved that there is a positive impact of AI on the risk dimensions of banks (El-Khateeb and AL-Omari 2023). Implementing the advanced versions of AI technologies has the potential to revolutionize actuarial tasks and can bring in more avenues for innovations, value creation, and efficiency (Trivedi 2023b). Besides this, it provides transparency and interpretability to the work performed by actuaries (Richman 2024).

New advanced technologies have paved way for future researchers (Lehmann 2020). Future researchers can explore the development of AI-driven technologies that are specifically designed to foster the needs of actuaries. A collaboration between industry stakeholders, academia, and policymakers is vital to realize the potential of AI in structuring the future of actuarial services in the insurance industry.

REFERENCES

Agarwal, Shashank. "An Intelligent Machine Learning Approach for Fraud Detection in Medical Claim Insurance: A Comprehensive Study." *Scholars Journal of Engineering and Technology* 11, no. 9 (2023): 191–200.

Ahmadi, Sina. "A Comprehensive Study on Integration of Big Data and AI in Financial Industry and Its Effect on Present and Future Opportunities." *International Journal of Current Science Research and Review* 7, no. 1 (2024): 66–74.

Ahmad, Sana, Warda Gul, Imran Sadiq, and Saeed Ur Rehman. "Impact of Using AI to Manage Project Risks Including Change in Scope and Lack of Required Skills: Moderating Effect of Team Expertise in IT Industry of Pakistan." *Russian Law Journal* 11, no. 12S (2023): 753–775.

Apergis, Antonios. "The role of cognitive assistants in medical insurance underwriting." (2024).

Baruah, Prasanta, and Pankaj Pratap Singh. "Risk Prediction in Life Insurance Industry Using Machine Learning Techniques—A Review." In *International Conference on Advances in IoT and Security with AI*, Singapore, pp. 323–332. Singapore: Springer Nature Singapore, 2023.

Bodemer, Oliver. "Artificial Intelligence in Governance: A Comprehensive Analysis of AI Integration and Policy Development in the German Government." *Authorea Preprints* (2023).

Cappiello, Antonella. "The Technological Disruption of Insurance Industry: A Review." *International Journal of Business and Social Science* 11, no. 1 (2020): 1–11.

Choudhary, Vinita, Neha Kamboj, and Sonal Trivedi. "Scoping Review of Literature on the Application of Blockchain in Finance." In Sonal Trivedi, Rashmi Aggarwal, and Gurmeet Singh (Eds.), *Perspectives on Blockchain Technology and Responsible Investing*, pp. 1–28. USA: IGI Global, 2023.

Choudhary, Vinita, and Sonal Trivedi. "The Role of Internal Audit in Risk Management with a Perspective of Sustainability Development." In Kiran Sood, Simon Grima, Peter Young, Ercan Ozen, and Balamurugan Balusamy (Eds.), *The Impact of Climate Change and Sustainability Standards on the Insurance Market*, pp. 287–315, 2023.

Durrani, Christer, Matti Häikiö, Leila Mozaffari, Asif Hassan, Leila Mohammadian, Javad Khaleghi Hozhabrasa, and Reza Fattahi. "Study Report." (2024)

El-khateeb, Ahmad Ibrahim, and Omar Hani AL-Omari. "Study the Impact of Artificial Intelligence Applications on Insurance Industry: A Case of Jordan." In *The 2023 WEI International Academic Conference Proceedings*, Barcelona, Spain, October 24–26, 2023. ISSN 2167-3179, pp. 3–11 (2023).

Gooding, Piers, and Yvette Maker. "The Digital Turn in Mental Health and Disability Law: Actuarial Traditions and AI Futures of Risk Assessment From a Human Rights Perspective." In *The Future of Mental Health, Disability and Criminal Law*. Taylor & Francis, 2024.

Gupta, Aparna, and Sreekanth Venkataraman. "Insurance and Climate Change." *Current Opinion in Environmental Sustainability* 67 (2024): 101412.

Harris, Roseanne, Ronald Richman, and Mario V. Wuthrich. "Reflections on deep learning and the actuarial profession (al)." Available at SSRN 4672447 (2024).

Hoseini, Marjan. "Patient Experiences with AI in Healthcare Settings." *AI and Tech in Behavioral and Social Sciences* 1, no. 3 (2023): 12–18.

Hosein, Patrick. "A Data Science Approach to Risk Assessment for Automobile Insurance Policies." *International Journal of Data Science and Analytics* 17, no. 1 (2024): 127–138.

Jawhar, Shadi, Craig E. Kimble, Jeremy R. Miller, and Zeina Bitar. "Enhancing Cyber Resilience with AI-Powered Cyber Insurance Risk Assessment." In *2024 IEEE 14th Annual Computing and Communication Workshop and Conference (CCWC)*, pp. 435–438, 8–10 January 2024. Las Vegas, NV, USA. IEEE, 2024.

Kanaparthi, Vijaya. "AI-based personalization and trust in digital finance." arXiv preprint arXiv:2401.15700 (2024a).

Kanaparthi, Vijaya. "Transformational application of artificial intelligence and machine learning in financial technologies and financial services: a bibliometric review." arXiv preprint arXiv:2401.15710 (2024b).

Kelley, Kevin H., Lisa M. Fontanetta, Mark Heintzman, and Nikki Pereira. "Artificial Intelligence: Implications for Social Inflation and Insurance." *Risk Management and Insurance Review* 21, no. 3 (2018): 373–387.

Khalisa, Arvidhia. "The Digitalization in Insurance Broker Industry: How Artificial Intelligence Affect This Industry." *Ilomata International Journal of Management* 5, no. 1 (2024): 261–279.

Komperla, Ramesh Chandra Aditya. "The Auto Health Revolution Ai Strategies For Insurance And Healthcare." *International Neurourology Journal* 27, no. 4 (2023): 1598–1605.

Kumar, Naman, Jayant Dev Srivastava, and Harshit Bisht. "Artificial Intelligence in Insurance Sector." *Journal of the Gujarat Research Society* 21, no. 7 (2019): 79–91.

Kumari, R., K. Sharma, and R. Kumar. "Social and Ethical Implications of AI in Finance for Sustainability: Convergence of Culture in the Banking Sector After Adaptation of Artificial Intelligence". In *Social and Ethical Implications of AI in Finance for Sustainability* (pp. 141–155). IGI Global, 2024.

Lehmann, Martin. "Essays on digitalization, value of data, and efficiency in the insurance industry." (2020).

Lozano-Murcia, Catalina, Francisco P. Romero, Jesus Serrano-Guerrero, and Jose A. Olivas. "An Application of a Fuzzy Multi-criteria Decision Making Process for Explainable Machine Learning in the Actuarial Context." In M. Eugenia Cornejo, László T. Kóczy, Jesús Medina, and Eloísa Ramírez-Poussa (Eds.), *Computational Intelligence and Mathematics for Tackling Complex Problems* 5, pp. 67–72. Cham: Springer Nature Switzerland, 2024.

Malik, Reena, and Sonal Trivedi. "Blockchain Technology and Healthcare: Towards Combating COVID-19." In Kiran Sood, Rajesh Kumar Dhanaraj, Balamurugan Balusamy, and Seifedine Kadry (Eds.), *Blockchain Technology in Corporate Governance: Transforming Business and Industries*, pp. 57–74. New Jersey: John Wiley & Sons, 2022.

McDonald, Angus, Kirsty Paynter, and Ernie Van der Vyver. "Embedded Insurance." In *The Global Insurance Market and Change*, pp. 66–94. Informa Law from Routledge, 2024.

Naim, Arshi. "Market Development and Financial Stability by the Application of AI." *European Journal of Interdisciplinary Research and Development* 7 (2022): 28–39.Nicoletti, Bernardo, and Bernardo Nicoletti. "Platforms for Insurance 4.0." In *Insurance 4.0: Benefits and Challenges of Digital Transformation*, pp. 173–259. Palgrave Macmillan, 2021.

Orji, Ugochukwu, and Elochukwu Ukwandu. "Machine Learning for an Explainable Cost Prediction of Medical Insurance." *Machine Learning with Applications* 15 (2024): 100516.

Patel, Kaushikkumar. "Ethical Reflections on Data-Centric AI: Balancing Benefits and Risks." *International Journal of Artificial Intelligence Research and Development* 2, no. 1 (2024): 1–17.

Prince, Anya E. R., and Seamus Taylor. "Artificial Intelligence: Attempts at Developing an Ethical Approach for Its Use in Insurance." In Francine O'Sullivan and Daniel Mather (Eds.), *Research Handbook on International Insurance Law and Regulation*, pp. 647–673. Edward Elgar Publishing, 2023.

Richman, Ronald. "An AI vision for the actuarial profession." Available at SSRN 4758296 (2024).

Rodríguez-Aguilar, Román, José-Antonio Marmolejo-Suacedo, Miriam Rodríguez-Aguilar, and Liliana Marmolejo-Saucedo. "Machine Learning for Digital Shadow Design in Health Insurance Sector." In Imrich Chlamtac (Ed.), *Mobile Networks and Applications*, pp. 1–14. Springer Nature, 2024.

Sanwal, Ravi. "Impact of Artificial Intelligence on the Insurance Industry." In *Applications of Artificial Intelligence in Business and Finance*, pp. 203–219. Apple Academic Press, 2021.

Sharma, Poonam, and Sapna Manhas. "The Future of Finance: Revolutionizing the Industry With Artificial Intelligence." In Dipanker Sharma, Bhawana Bhardwaj, and Mohinder Chand Dhiman (Eds.), *Leveraging AI and Emotional Intelligence in Contemporary Business Organizations*, pp. 187–210. USA: IGI Global, 2024.

Singh, S. K., and M. Chivukula. "A Commentary on the Application of Artificial Intelligence in the Insurance Industry." *Trends in Artificial Intelligence* 4, no. 1 (2020): 75–79.

Tomar, Kuldeep, and Shivani Sharma. "A Proposed Artificial Intelligence and Blockchain Technique for Solving Health Insurance Challenges." In Mahesh Chand, Vineet Jain, and Puneeta Ajmera (Eds.), *Data-Driven Technologies and Artificial Intelligence in Supply Chain*, pp. 31–57. Florida: CRC Press, 2024.

Trivedi, Sonal. "Blockchain Framework for Insurance industry." *International Journal of Innovation and Technology Management* 20, no. 06 (2023a): 2350034.

Trivedi, Sonal. "Blockchain Technology and Structural Change in Financial Services." In Kiran Sood, Simon Grima, Ganga Sharma, and Balamurugan Balusamy (Eds.), *The Application of Emerging Technology and Blockchain in the Insurance Industry*, pp. 249–263. Denmark: River Publishers, 2024.

Trivedi, Sonal. "Convention of Blockchain in Financial Services: A State-of-the-Art Literature Review." In Kiran Mehta, Renuka Sharma, and Poshan Yu (Eds.), *Revolutionizing Financial Services and Markets through FinTech and Blockchain*, pp. 237–250. USA: IGI Global, 2023b.

Trivedi, Sonal, Vinita Choudhary, NehaKamboj, and Nirmaljeet Kaur Virk. "New Avenues of Opportunities and Challenges for Start-Ups, MSMEs, the Indian Financial Sector, and the Indian Insurance Sector." In Simon Grima, Shilpa Chaudhary, Kiran Sood, and Sanjeev Kumar (Eds.), *Business Drivers in Promoting Digital Detoxification*, pp. 226–250. USA: IGI Global, 2024.

Trivedi, Sonal, and Reena Malik. "Blockchain Technology as an Emerging Technology in the Insurance Market." In Kiran Sood, Rajesh Kumar Dhanaraj, Balamurugan Balusamy, Simon Grima, and R. Uma Maheshwari (Eds.), *Big Data: A Game Changer for Insurance Industry*, pp. 81–100. UK: Emerald Publishing Limited, 2022a.

Trivedi, Sonal, and Reena Malik. "Role and Significance of Data Protection in Risk Management Practices in the Insurance Market." In Kiran Sood, Balamurugan Balusamy, Simon Grima, and Pierpaolo Marano (Eds.), *Big Data Analytics in the Insurance Market*, pp. 263–273. UK: Emerald Publishing Limited, 2022b.

Trivedi, Sonal, Kiran Mehta, and Renuka Sharma. "Systematic Literature Review on Application of Blockchain Technology in E-Finance and Financial Services." *Journal of Technology Management & Innovation* 16, no. 3 (2021): 89–102.

van Bekkum, Marvin S. L., and Frederik J. Zuiderveen Borgesius. "AI, Insurance, Discrimination and Unfair Differentiation. An Overview and Research Agenda." arXiv preprint arXiv:2401.11892 (2024).

Varadarajan, Vijayakumar, and Vijaya Kumar Kakumanu. "Evaluation of Risk Level Assessment Strategies in Life Insurance: A Review of the Literature." *Journal of Autonomous Intelligence* 7, no. 5 (2024): 1–19.

Wilkinson, Dino, Alec Christie, Anthony A. Tarr, and Julie-Anne Tarr. "Big Data, Artificial Intelligence and Insurance." In Anthony A. Tarr, Julie-Anne Tarr, Maurice Thompson, and Dino Wilkinson (Eds.), *The Global Insurance Market and Change*, pp. 22–46. USA: Informa Law from Routledge, 2024.

Wilkinson,Thomas David; Wang,Mengxiao; Friedman,Jed; Prestidge,Marelize. A Framework for the Economic Evaluation of Digital Health Interventions (English). Policy Research working paper ; no. WPS 10407 Washington, D.C. : World Bank Group. http://documents.worldbank.org/curated/en/099446504122313917/IDU0f639726d0f11404a3509af8054677649dcd6

Xu, Y. (2024). Climate change and sustainability: an actuarial risk management perspective. Doctoral thesis, Nanyang Technological University, Singapore. Publisher: Nanyang Technological University https://hdl.handle.net/10356/180071. DOI: 10.32657/10356/180071

Yadav, Neelam, Ashish Mathur, and Jyoti Thanvi. "Fusion of AI and Ethical Finance: Changing the Outlook of Financial Companies and Society." In Mohammad Irfan,Seifedine Kadry,Muhammad Sharif, and Habib Ullah Khan (Eds.), *Fintech Applications in Islamic Finance: AI, Machine Learning, and Blockchain Techniques*, pp. 24–34. USA: IGI Global, 2024.

4 Explainability AI

A Key Driver for Enhanced Quality of Service in Actuarial Practices

Rama Seetha Maha Lakshmi Patibandla, Gokul Yenduri, Praveen Kumar Reddy Maddikunta, Ramalingam Murugan, and Thippa Reddy Gadekallu

4.1 INTRODUCTION

In the area of actuarial science, supreme services are significant for maintaining stakeholder expectation and facilitating valuable risk management. In order to acquire close addiction to the intricate models and supervisory measures that build up actuarial practices, explainability has developed into a crucial constituent. Professionals among backgrounds in arithmetic, statistics, and finances are notorious as actuaries, and actuarial science is vital in lots of diverse fields, as well as risk management, assurance, and economics. Designed for numerous reasons, it is decisive to afford actuarial services of an elevated pattern. Initially, these services facilitate firms composed of skilled decision, which reduces monetary risks and ensures durable solidity. Precise assessments are essential for actuaries to do their jobs suitably, which embrace pricing assurance policy and set apart reserves for hope claims. This ensures that policyholders and insurance companies mutually have their money's appeal. Besides, research by Olaoye et al. (2024) shows that stakeholders, regulators, and lawmaker must all discern that actuaries are honourable while they trail the policy and convention set away by the vocation. Auxiliary, actuaries facilitate citizens and companies with retreat scheduling and allowance sponsor supervision so that they may save, empower, and administer their resources sensibly, which restore humanity, industry, and folks as a whole.

In favour of recent industries, the altering dynamics of risk appraisal and supervisory actuarial events must integrate explainability. Apparent and interpretable models are attractive further and auxiliary crucial as expertise advances, particularly in AI and ML, prolonging the collision of numerous industries. In this sagacity, "explainability" refers to the competence to comprehend and formulate the intellect of the choices through near models or algorithms, provided that within reach

DOI: 10.1201/9781003472551-6

addicted to the reflection processes that go keen on building forecasts or suggestions. Explainability is awfully essential in actuarial measures, while exact risk appraisal is a key to maintain economic permanence and defend the security of stakeholders. Actuaries depend on multifarious models and data-driven approaches to analyse and handle risks in areas such as assurance, finance, and allowance funds (Bhuyan et al., 2022). Ensuring precision and indulgence becomes gradually more exigent as these models become elaborate and obscure. As a result, a decisive measure in tackling these issues and recuperating supervisory eminence is to integrate explainability into actuarial methods.

4.1.1 Understanding Explainability

In actuarial science, essential explainability is vital for acquiring how it contributes to managerial processes that are extra translucent and effortless to appreciate. Algorithms and models used in systematic analytics and machine learning must be capable of having their judgements implicitly and interpreted by humans. In favour of actuarial analysis to be plausible, stakeholders must be competent to appreciate it. This is where explainability comes in. Professionals in the field of risk evaluation and supervision, notorious as actuaries, use intricate models and data-driven approaches to formulate decisions in industries as assorted as insurance, banking, and pension funds. But it's not forever effortless to interpret the analysis after these models' forecasts or suggestions due to their obscurity. So, to identify explainability in actuarial science, researchers have to stature out how actuaries preserve and compose their models that are easier to value and use, so that stakeholders can ensure the fallout and make elegant choices.

To be valuable in attractive precision and conception, explainability in actuarial processes should wrap a number of critical criteria. The foremost step is to register and name every variables and assumptions that make up actuarial models and measures. If stakeholders desire to realize the reckoning based on the predictions or recommendations finished by actuaries, they must be able to pursue the sense and rationale using the models that the actuaries use. In summary, Gonaygunta (2023) sets up that explainability is achieved through sensitivity analyses and interpretable machine learning methods to prove how changes in key parameters or model assumptions affect the consequences. By utilizing interpretable models and liability warmth studies, actuaries can make their assessments more apparent and supply stakeholders with insights into how consistent and durable the conclusions are. Furthermore, explainability is extremely reliant on superior communication diplomacy. For stakeholders with changeable degrees of alertness, actuaries have to inform convoluted industrial thought in unforced terminology. Hence, in the standpoint of actuarial science, explainability earnings edifice models are noticeable and simple to recognize, and it also involves building resources ensuring that stakeholders acquire the information they require to make superior decisions.

4.1.2 Importance of Explainability in Addressing Challenges

So as to entirely snatch explainability's central role in attracting simplicity, belief, and efficacy across diverse industries, it is critical to speak on how it helps with troubles associated with dense models and managerial processes. Several stakeholders are resistant to appreciating the logic and sense after predictions or recommendations are completed by amalgamated models suitable for the massive datasets and multipart algorithms used in these sectors, predominantly healthcare, actuarial science, and finance. Stakeholders can legalize the outcome and formulate skilled decisions with a systematic seize of the issues implicated, while explainability sheds luminosity on how these models appear at their conclusions. According to Tripathy et al. (2022), the worth of explainability in actuarial science is foremost, as specific risk appraisal is crucial for maintaining monetary solidity and shielding the benefit of stakeholders. Although actuaries make decisions using multifarious models and data-driven approaches, people might mislay belief in the outcomes if the algorithms aren't apparent. To facilitate the compilation of executive processes that are more translucent and liable, actuaries can recover explainability, which helps stakeholders in recognizing multipart models.

The results are further consistent and vigorous, and explainability is elevated as it reduces the brunt of biases and errors that are intrinsic to multifarious models. There are numerous probable causes of bias in multifarious models, including individual decision, algorithmic advice, and statistics assortment. Meagre management might arise if these biases cause the source community to formulate untrue forecasts or suggestions. By providing insights into the replica preparation procedure, facet weighting, and supervisory measures, explainability enables stakeholders to discover and tackle biases. Stakeholders are capable of recovering the exactness and dryad of the outcome with the use of explainability, which permits them to adjust their models and measures by recognizing biases and inaccuracies. By illuminating the models' strength and consistency to stakeholders, explainability also promotes conviction and assurance in managerial processes. By using explainability, actuaries can ensure that their assessments are exact, which helps stakeholders hope for the results and makes it easier to make up-to-date decisions. As a result, explainability is critical for addressing troubles with dense models and administrative processes since it can recover consistency, precision, and answerability, which in turn increases the worth of results in several unusual industries.

4.2 RISK MANAGEMENT

In order to entirely seize explainability's critical task in enhancing precision, hope, and efficacy across dissimilar industries, it is crucial to speak on how it helps with troubles associated with complex models and executive processes. Several stakeholders resist understanding the interpretation and reason after the predictions or recommendations through multifaceted models due to the gigantic datasets and intricate algorithms used in these sectors, mostly healthcare, actuarial science, and finance. Stakeholders may authorize the consequences and construct skilled decisions with a systematic seize of the issues implicated, while explainability sheds light on how these models disembark at their conclusions. According to Tripathy et al. (2022), the connotation of explainability in actuarial science is dominant, as exact risk estimation is critical for maintaining financial solidity and caring the benefit of stakeholders. Even though actuaries make decisions with multifaceted models and data-driven approaches, people may drop assurance in the outcomes if the algorithms aren't clear. With the intention of crafting administrative processes that are clearer and more responsible, actuaries can recover explainability, allowing stakeholders to realize multifaceted models.

The results are further dependable and strong when explainability is elevated as it reduces the collision of biases and errors that are innate to multifaceted models. There are numerous latent causes of bias in compound models, including human being decision, algorithmic design, and data collection. Reduced executive may proceed if these biases cause the source community to craft wrong forecasts or suggestions. As long as they have insights into the model guidance procedure, feature weighting, and decision-making procedures, explainability enables stakeholders to uncover and address biases. Stakeholders are able to recover the exactness and equality of the outcome through the use of explainability, which permits them to acclimatize their models and measures by recognizing biases and inaccuracies. By informing the models' sturdiness and constancy to stakeholders, explainability also promotes hope and poise in decision-making processes. By using explainability, actuaries can ensure that their assessments are exact, which helps stakeholders convict the consequences and makes it easier to make up-to-date decisions. Thus, explainability is essential for addressing troubles with dense models and managerial processes as it can recover consistency, simplicity, and responsibility, which in turn raises the excellence of outcomes in a variety of industries.

4.3 TECHNIQUES FOR ACHIEVING EXPLAINABILITY

Abusing numerous tactics to attain explainability in actuarial performance highlights the variability of campaigns existing for making multifaceted replicas and policymaking procedures informal to appreciate and effort with.

4.3.1 Model Transparency

One approach is model transparency, which means that investors can perceive all of the efforts, variables, and procedures used by actuarial replicas. Actuaries permit investors to drop cognitive and logic due to twisted forecasts or endorsements by authenticating the causal influences and expectations privileged by the models (Bhuyan et al., 2023). Investors are able to authenticate the consequences and appreciate the reasons that group them to model transparency, which endorses accountability and faith. Machine learning models intended to produce results that are informal for investors to comprehend and investigate are an additional decision. For the sake of interpretability, these replicas usually sacrifice some forecast exactness in favour of easiness and sincerity. Actuaries can make them more translucent and comprehensible by consuming explainable machine learning models. This will help investors make decisions based on visions that are clear and easy to grasp.

4.3.2 Sensitivity Analysis

According to further supporting tool for creation of actuarial actions that are extra translucent, sympathy analysis permits stakeholders to measure the consistency and strength of actuarial models by looking at the possessions of altering input restrictions or model expectations on assumptions. Actuaries can aid stakeholders comprehend what variables' strength disturbs the effects' precision and reliability through performance compassion revisions, which help them classify the key causes of risk and ambiguity. As actuaries are answerable for explaining intricate procedural concepts to stakeholders with diverse stages of data, Zeinali et al. (2022) initiate that respectable communication practices are decisive to attain explainability in actuarial observations. Actuaries are controllers at collaborating with the cognitive overdue their instructions and creation, ensuring that stakeholders appreciate the penalties of the answers through humble linguistic, visual aids, and other statement approaches. To reiterate, the numerous approaches used to make various actuarial functions extra explicable highlight the reputation of being open, humble, and unrestrained so as to help stakeholders appreciate intricate models and managerial measures.

4.3.3 Machine Learning Models

It is crucial to designate how explainable machine learning models can expand empathetic and transparency in intricate risk valuation and policymaking procedures by familiarizing these models and participating them into actuarial situations. When stakeholders in an industry necessitate clear visions into the essentials affecting predictions or endorsements, explainable machine learning replicas are an excellent fit due to their prominence on ease and transparency. There are substantial aids to consuming explainable machine learning models in actuarial measures where liability risk calculations exactly are serious for preserving monetary constancy and protecting the comforts of stakeholders. Decision trees, linear models, and rule-based systems are instances of explainable machine learning models that produce results that stakeholders can further effortlessly appreciate and make sense of, as divergent to traditional black box methods. By providing vision into the decision-making process, these replicas help stakeholders appreciate the cognitive and logic causes of predictions or recommendations. According to Nguyen et al. (2021), actuarial assessments can be made more effective and clearer with explainable machine learning models as they rise transparency and grasp, which in turn lets stakeholders to make improved decisions with more comprehensible visions.

Moreover, actuaries can classify serious causes of risk and ambiguity with the help of explainable machine learning models, which offer significant visions into the associates among input issues and results. In order to make more precise and responsible predictions, actuaries are essential to appreciate what variables influence the results. Individual formerly progressed their models and measures. Model authentication and confirmation are both completed easily with explainable ML models since stakeholders can measure the models' strength and presentation more precisely. This aids actuaries' treasure and fixes any faults or biases in the replicas, which makes their analyses more consistent. As soon as they are applied to actuarial sceneries, explainable machine learning models have the prospect to significantly recover the sincerity, accountability, and efficiency of risk assessment and decision-making.

4.3.4 Importance of Sensitivity Analysis

The conversation concerning the implication of sensitivity analysis and competent communication policies in achieving explainability highlights two key impacts in enlightening transparency and grasp in elaborate models and decision-making procedures. Sensitivity analysis plays a vigorous role in appraising the asset and reliability of actuarial replicas by inspecting the possessions of distinctions in input parameters or model norms on the results. Actuaries conduct sensitivity analyses to identify the main drivers of risk and indecision, consenting stakeholders to hold the aspects inducing the reliability and exactness of the results. By measuring the model productions' sensitivity to changes in input variables, sensitivity analysis provides stakeholders with visions into possible causes of difference in forecasts or references made. Additionally, sensitivity analysis authorizes actuaries to assess the impacts of diverse setups or conventions on results, facilitating more knowledgeable decision-making and risk management methods. Hence, Bhuyan et al. (2023) interpret the implication of sensitivity analysis in realizing explainability deceits in its dimensions to enhance the transparency, reliability, and flexibility of actuarial models, finally appealing to stakeholders' understanding of the allied risks and uncertainties.

Similarly, dynamic communication policies remain effective in attaining explainability, as actuaries are tasked with enunciating multifaceted practical notions in an articulate and reachable method to stakeholders at various stages of proficiency. Actuarial analyses repeatedly comprise complicated procedures and sophisticated precise models, which may pose challenges for entities with deficient technical proficiency. Thus, actuaries must use basic language, visual aids, and other communication tools to convey the validation overdue their analyses efficiently and confirm stakeholders grasp the inferences of the results. By offering the discoveries in a logical and clear manner, actuaries enable discourse and alliance among stakeholders, nurturing transparency and assurance in decision-making procedures. Additionally, actual communication policies allow actuaries to solicit response and discuss our stakeholders' anxieties, confirming that analyses are in line with their necessities and prospects. Overall, Kulesza et al. (2012) recommended that the implication of actual communication policies in attaining explainability deceits in their capacity to bridge the gap between complex procedural analyses and stakeholders' grasp, thereby attracting the eminence and efficiency of actuarial performs.

4.4 BENEFITS OF INTEGRATING EXPLAINABILITY

4.4.1 Exploration of Benefits

Analysing the recompense associated with incorporating explainability addicted to actuarial processes uncovers abundant payback that contributes to bolstering simplicity, trust, and efficacy in decision-making. A major benefit is the augmentation of stakeholder faith and assurance. Bhuyan et al. (2023) explained that by detaching glow from the central works of multifaceted models, explainability enriches stakeholders' grasp of the factors routing predictions or recommendations, thereby bolstering their trust in the outcomes. Actuarial analysis regularly entails crucial decisions distressing individuals, businesses, and humanity at large. During the amalgamation of explainability into actuarial processes, actuaries can encourage stakeholders to base their analyses on strong methodologies and clear decision-making frameworks, thereby refining faith and assurance in the fallout consistency and authority. Moreover, explainability empowers stakeholders to validate the outcomes and seize the assumptions and confines of the models, allowing them to make knowledgeable decisions based on logical and explicable insights. As a result, the amalgamation of explainability into actuarial processes amplifies stakeholder belief and assurance, finally distilling the excellence and efficacy of decision-making.

Another prominent assistance associated with incorporating explainability into actuarial processes is the augmentation of risk management practices. According to Barongo et al. (2024), actuaries play a key role in evaluating and explaining risks in diagonally varied industries, encircling insurance, finance, and pension funds. By furnishing insights into the drivers of prediction or recommendations, explainability enables stakeholders to expand a deeper perceptive of the allied risks and suspicions, thereby facilitating more expert risk management strategies. Actuaries can persuade explainability to detach feasible biases or inexactness in models, allowing them to perfect their methodologies and enhance the meticulousness and constancy of their predictions. Furthermore, explainability streamlines the constant monitoring and rationale of models, empowering actuaries to measure the models' concert and strength over time and realize required tuning to make certain finest outcomes. Hence, Bhuyan et al. (2023) investigated the amalgamation of explainability into actuarial processes, which fortifies risk executive practices by providing stakeholders with insights into the determinants of risk and uncertainty, finally enabling more informed decision-making and higher outcomes.

4.4.2 Explainability Analysis

By analysing its effect on confidence, transparency, and risk management, explainability demonstrates how decisive it is for building assurance and facilitating superior decision-making. Augmented assurance is an outcome of explainability's skill to discard radiance from the essential mechanism of intricate models, allowing stakeholders to recognize what goes into making forecasts or recommendations. Research by Orji and Ukwandu (2024) establishes that stakeholders can be secure of the strength of actuarial analyses by incorporating explainability into their processes. This is due to the fact that actuarial decisions can have a momentous surprise on individuals, businesses, and society as a whole. This, in turn, encourages reliance in the results' honesty and consistency. Formulate skilled decisions based on clear and available insights with explainability. Stakeholders may confirm outcomes and understand the assumptions and restrictions innate in the models. This investigation shows how explainability is significant for actuarial procedures to be more responsible and apparent, which improves decision-making eminence and efficiency.

By serving stakeholders with enhanced grasp of the risks and suspicions allied with decision-making, explainability in addition helps to progress risk management measures. In several diverse fields, such as pension funds, insurance, and banking, actuaries are liable for assessing and sinking risk. With the help of explainability, stakeholders may better appreciate the essentials that control forecasts or recommendations. This, sequentially, allows them to stain any biases or flaws in the models, which in turn allows them to recover their techniques and make more consistent predictions. In addition, actuaries can appraise the concert and strength of models over instance and construct any requisite adjustments for finest results, as explainability allows for fragmentary monitoring and rationale of models. The work by Bhuyan et al. (2023) highlights the importance of explainability in risk supervision and shows how stakeholders can benefit from considering risk drivers and suspicions, which leads to enhanced decision-making and better results.

Investigating the payback that comprises explainability in actuarial measures reveals many recompense that helps to recover decision-making sincerity, constancy, and competence. The augmentation of assurance and confidence among stakeholders is a remarkable assistance. Stakeholders' confidence in the results is superior when explainability sheds illumination on the intricate models' central mechanism, allowing them to enhance appreciation of the rudiments impacting predictions or recommendations. According to research by Bachute and Subhedar (2021), actuaries can encourage stakeholders that their analyses pursue concrete methodologies and transparent decision-making frameworks when they integrate explainability into their processes. This builds expectation and assurance in the strength and precision of the results, which is imperative for actuarial assessments because they absorb major decisions that concern individuals, start-ups, and humanity as a whole. Stakeholders are able to make skilled decisions based on clear and reasonable insights when models are explainable, which allow them to inspect results and recognize assumptions and constraints. Decisions are prepared with further precision and belief by stakeholders when explainability is integrated into actuarial measures. Cultivating risk management strategies is just an extra perquisite with explainability in actuarial processes. Insurance, banking, and pension funds are just a few of the numerous industries that rely on actuaries to measure and diminish risk. Stakeholders can enhance grasp of the risks and suspicions engaged in risk managing strategies when explainability provides insights into the variables' energetic predictions or recommendations. With the use of explainability, actuaries can locate wherever their models can be defective, which will permit them to recover their methods and make further precise forecasts. Actuaries can measure the concert and elasticity of models over instance and create any essential adjustments to attain the most favourable outcomes, as explainability allows for partial monitoring and justification of models. According to Wickramasinghe (2022), stakeholders can increase an improved indulgence of risk drivers and suspicions when explainability is included in actuarial methods. This, in turn, allows for enhanced decision-making and superior outcomes in risk management.

The vital importance of explainability in establishing assurance and enabling thriving decision-making processes is highlighted by investigating its assistance in reinforcement belief, simplicity, and risk management. Explainability, according to Bhuyan et al. (2023), fosters dependence by leasing stakeholders realize the variables energetic predictions or recommendations by providing insights into the intricate models' internal procedure. By incorporating explainability into their measures, actuaries can encourage stakeholders that their analyses are based on solid methodologies and obvious decision-making frameworks. This is essential because actuarial decisions can have extensive possessions on individuals, businesses, and humanity as a whole. As an impact, all parties concerned can have confidence in the results since they are reliable and genuine. In addition, stakeholders can observe the results and grasp the models' assumptions and constraints with the help of explainability, which helps them make knowledgeable decisions based on apparent and explicable insights. The exploration highlights the importance of explainability in recovering decision-making by escalating belief and simplicity in actuarial methods. In addition, stakeholders are able to enhance their ability to seize the consistent risks and suspicions in decision-making processes when explainability is recent, which helps to recover risk management techniques. In many dissimilar industries, as well as pension funds, insurance, and banking, actuaries are accountable for assessing and dropping risk. Stakeholders are able to recover tactics and increase the accuracy and reliability of predictions when explainability helps them to realize probable biases or errors within models by informing the variables of dynamic forecasts or recommendations. Additionally, actuaries can appraise the concert and strength of models over time and build the required adjustments to realize best outcomes since explainability allows for constant monitoring and rationale of models. Hence, according to Mallick et al. (2021) research, stakeholders are able to make healthier decisions and accomplish enhanced results when explainability enhances risk management practices by providing insights into risk drivers and suspicions.

4.4.3 Role of Explainability

In order to attain inflexible authoritarian values and assure decent behaviour, it is significant to consider the task of explainability in secondary dictatorial obedience in actuarial dealing. Abundant rules and policy are in position to make certain the security of clients, the security of the financial system, and the endorsement of principled behaviour in actuarial operations. Actuaries can exhibit conformity with authoritarian requests by giving stakeholders a superior perceptive of the variables that went into building predictions or recommendations during the explainability structure they employ in their work. This improves decision-making sincerity and answerability by hiring stakeholders (such as clients, legislators, and regulators), who appreciate the reason behind primary actuarial assessments and authenticate the results. Actuaries can recover their slant and certify observance with rigid principles by utilizing explainability, which, according to Mohanty et al. (2023) research, enables stakeholders to recognize probable biases or errors in models. By using explainability, actuaries can afford a clear appraisal track that demonstrates observance with dogmatic desires and moral principles by documenting the basics and assumptions that sustain their models. As a result, the symposium highlights how significant explainability is for ensuring observance with policy in the actuarial field, which protects the authority and exactness of actuarial analyses.

Also, by allowing for unvarying model monitoring and confirmation, explainability provides actuaries with the tools they need to better supervise the continuously growing rigid situation. Market trends, new dangers, and expertise developments all contribute to the progression of authoritarian desires in the actuarial sphere. Actuaries can measure how novel policy will shape their models and build the obligatory changes to continue in observance by providing stakeholders with information on the essentials that influence predictions or recommendations. In addition, stakeholders are better capable of recognizing the models' assumptions and constraints when explainability is present, which improves transparency and responsibility in authoritarian disclosures. To make sure that stakeholders comprehend the results and can craft conversant decisions, actuaries can use explainability to describe their analyses in a mode that is effortless for each one to realize. Subsequently, the magnitude of explainability in selecting the actuarial area that adheres to policy that is tinted in the symposium. This will consent to actuaries to better navigate the authoritarian setting while maintaining the premier levels of veracity and beliefs.

4.5 CHALLENGES AND LIMITATIONS

Actuaries have a host of challenges when it comes to recover decision-making transparency and consideration, and these challenges become extra deceptive as they reflect the limits and hurdles allied with integrating explainability into actuarial actions. Due to their complexity, actuarial models and actions are substantial impediments. It is a mutual exercise for actuaries to use erudite statistical procedures and machine learning algorithms to investigate huge datasets and make predictions about the imminent. Transparency and interpretability are two areas where these replicas may fall short, reducing their probability of amended estimate precision. As soon as stakeholders have assorted steps of practice and the models comprise intricate mathematical values or exclusive algorithms, it can be tough to explain how the models function. The intricacy of approving explainability is extra augmented by the ever-changing permissible necessities, market dynamics, and commercial sceneries that describe the lively environment of actuarial processes. According to Vijayaraj et al. (2023), preserving sincerity and constancy in decision-making procedures inspires actuaries since they are essential to continuously adjust their models and measures to encounter altering desires and adhere to supervisory ethics.

The trade-offs between exactness and explainability are not shorn of their limitations, yet. Every so often, with the purpose of making intricate models further explainable, researchers have to give up roughly predicted accuracy. Actuaries need to strike a happy medium between reality being too mysterious and existence being too expected for their models to be comprehensible and trustworthy. Additional possessions and familiarity may be essential to attain explainability, mostly for multifaceted models that are essential to be modernized or improved with interpretability-enhancing methods. Gaining investor buy-in can be interesting for actuaries, especially when dealing with challenging areas or logistic hostility to change.

Moreover, actuaries' essential decent communication skills and approaches to make sure that the descriptions they stretch are strong, brief, and comprehensible by stakeholders at dissimilar stages of proficiency. Consequently, it is critical that researchers work together to overcome the restraints and confines of integrating explainability into actuarial performs so that decision-making procedures are transparent and easy to comprehend.

Risk assessment and decision-making in actuarial achieve make use of classic processes and instruments, as can be revealed by delving into the complexities of actuarial models. So as to serve huge datasets and craft resonance predictions about what's to come, actuaries occupy an ample diversity of algebraic methods, numerical models, and predictive analytics. In order to discover trends, patterns, and correlations in the data, these models regularly fit in complicated algorithms, such as machine learning algorithms. However, attaining explainability is delayed by the intricacy of these models. It can be tricky to comprehend the calculation and logic after the predictions or recommendations completed by actuarial models since the huge number of variables, nonlinear relationships, and relations may be implicated. Efforts to accomplish simplicity and conception are auxiliary intricate when actuarial models rely on proprietary algorithms or data sources. As a result, it is essential to extend innovative approaches and tactics to improve the explainability of actuarial models so that stakeholders can trust and comprehend the fallout of these assessments.

Broader concerns about sincerity, accountability, and assurance are encompassed by the implications of the industrial challenges associated with actuarial models for attaining explainability. To ensure that certain stakeholders appreciate the logic behind the predictions or recommendations their models fabricate, actuaries should locate a well poise amid accuracy and interpretability. To make certain models explainable, actuaries should trace all applicable specifics and assumptions, afford a framework for decision-making, and evidently express the outcomes' consequences to persons who need to know. Furthermore, actuaries, data scientists, and extra concerned parties may need to work together to extend narrative approaches that amplify simplicity and conception in order to conquer explainability. Decisions in the actuarial province can be ended more consistently and efficiently when actuaries take the time to clarify their models and switch the complexities implicated. This builds faith and poise among stakeholders.

The multifaceted complementary action that actuaries must take to act upon linking sincerity and prognostic capability is enriched by the debates over the trade-offs involving explainability and precision in actuarial measures. Explainability is imperative for stakeholders to comprehend why actuarial model forecasts or recommendations are completed, but it can intermittently diminish the precision of those projections. While intricate models with classy algorithms and approaches may fabricate further exact forecasts, they can be complicated to appreciate and clarify to those who have a concern in the conclusion. When creating and using actuarial models, actuaries should suspiciously believe the profit and drawbacks of explainability and precision to discover a content standard that meets the desires of stakeholders exclusive of sacrificing prognostic concert. In addition, actuaries can deal with the difficulties allied with these trades-offs by using interpretable machine learning models, simplifying complex models, or adding post hoc explanations to black box models. Actuaries can expand stakeholders' confidence and poise by civilizing explainability without compromising predictive precision through this diplomacy.

The challenges caused by the trade-offs between precision and explainability capacity can be narrowed by using superior communication diplomacy. To make certain that stakeholders with diverse levels of familiarity appreciate the interpretation after actuarial model forecasts or recommendations, actuaries should plainly and succinctly speak the implications of their result. To assist stakeholders in making decisions based on apparent and explicable insights, actuaries might use communication strategies like basic language and visual aids to clarify intricate industrial topics in a mode that anyone can grab. In addition, actuaries can discover ways to recover their models and better convene stakeholders' desires by involving stakeholders in decision-making and asking for their guidance. The decision-making processes in the actuarial vicinity can be elevated in quality and efficacy by prioritizing effective communication tactics, which in turn lead to large transparency and conception.

The employment of explainability in actuarial procedures has mutual prospects and restraints that must be acknowledged:

- Exploring the implications for determination of explainability in light of the intricacy of actuarial replicas.
- An appraisal of the complications related to amplification multifaceted notions and approaches for corresponding explainability and precision.

4.6 ILLUSTRATIVE CASE STUDIES AND EXAMPLES

At this point, we provide tangible samples of how actuarial performs have used explainability to recover provision superiority, signifying how extra sincerity and empathy have enhanced policymaking. An assurance concern that uses explicable machine learning models to measure the risk shapes of policyholders is one sample of this category of case study. Policyholders were able to appreciate the cognitive overdue their finest and exposure conclusions as actuary's castoff explainable algorithms, such as decision trees and linear models, to obviously clarify the essentials of artificial risk valuations. Amended client retention charges and progressive stages of gratification were results of this extra open and assumed approach to policyholder communication. Furthermore, actuaries were able to classify and pinpoint biases or errors in the risk valuation procedure appreciations to the open models, which resulted in improved risk management strategies and more precise prognoses. On the whole, this case study establishes how actuarial methods can profit from explainability by emphasizing decision-making accuracy, responsibility, and transparency.

Exploring the customs in which explainability progresses policymaking and facility conveyance exposes the substantial inspiration that empathy and directness have on actuarial measures. Decisions can be made more competently as soon as they are founded on strong and understandable visions, as explainability affords. Stakeholders can then make conversant adoptions based on these perceptions. Actuaries use explainability to authorize results with stakeholders, explicate the perceptive overdue their evaluation, and plan the expectations and confines of their models.

Improved policymaking is imaginable when stakeholders are more assured in one alternative and can make an effort to have obligations to explainability's importance on simplicity and morality. The exactness and accuracy of the estimates or approvals given are certain by actuary's existence that is able to classify and fix model biases or errors to explainability. As long as investors with applied intuitions that sustenance exertions to obey the rules, recover risk management, and strategy intentionally, this expands the complete eminence of the service.

Additionally, stakeholders are acceptable to measure the implications of numerous situations and make informed decisions based on the results of actuarial valuations following explainability. To benefit stakeholders and appreciate the risks and uncertainties of policymaking, actuaries use tools like sensitivity analysis to govern how variations to key aspects disturb results. Explainability recovers actuarial exercise provision conveyance by allowing stakeholders see the decision-making process, which increases concern and assurance. In order for stakeholders to appreciate the results and make sophisticated decisions, it is critical to employ authentic communication strategies. For stakeholders to appreciate the inferences of the results and take suitable accomplishment, actuaries must connect complex methodical themes in an amicable way with modest language and visual aids. This analysis illustration shows how actuarial measures can assist in explainability in managerial and service conveyance by increasing stakeholder assurance, liability, and sincerity.

- Illustration of the significance and inspiration of explainability on facility eminence in actuarial performs over the performance of case studies and samples.
- An appraisal of the behaviours in which explainability improves policymaking and service eminence commonly.

4.7 CONCLUSION AND FUTURE DIRECTIONS

This chapter emphasizes the significance of explainability in actuarial practices, with a focus exclusively on how it encourages progression in clearness, consistency, and competence. The importance of explainability in executive and tune condition is tinted by looking at numerous methodologies such as interpretable machine learning models, efficient communication strategy, compassion scrutiny, and replica lucidity. In general, the tune superiority in actuarial practices is enhanced when stakeholders are expected to exert mutually, recognize liability, and believe one another more during explainability, which provides insights into the rudiments that influence predictions or recommendations.

The prospect of explainability in actuarial science is intense, with imminent trends focusing on identical frameworks for assessing and communicating model simplicity and interpretability, as well as integrating AI approaches and classy analytics. Given that there are desires in the indemnity trade, actuaries will be looking for novel behaviour to create forecasts and recommendations with machine learning algorithms and models that are simple to recognize and realize. Furthermore, actuaries will be capable to convene their rigid errands and amplify stakeholder hope and poise by adopting identical frameworks, which will abridge and reinforce explainability efforts. All in all, the technique explainability is caption in actuarial practices that might really recover managerial by making it more release, responsible, and proficient. This would make sure that stakeholders are receiving services that address their varying desires.

REFERENCES

Bachute, Mrinal R., and Javed M. Subhedar. "Autonomous driving architectures: Insights of machine learning and deep learning algorithms." *Machine Learning with Applications* 6 (2021): 100164.

Barongo, Rweyemamu Ignatius, and Jimmy TibangayukaMbelwa. "Using machine learning for detecting liquidity risk in banks." *Machine Learning with Applications* 15 (2024): 100511.

Bhuyan, Hemanta Kumar, Vinayakumar Ravi, Biswajit Brahma, and Nilayam Kumar Kamila. "Disease analysis using machine learning approaches in healthcare system." *Health and Technology* 12, no. 5 (2022): 987–1005.

Bhuyan, Hemanta Kumar, M. Saikiran, Murchhana Tripathy, and Vinayakumar Ravi. "Wide-ranging approach-based feature selection for classification." *Multimedia Tools and Applications* 82, no. 15 (2023): 23277–23304.

Gonaygunta, Hari. "Factors influencing the adoption of machine learning algorithms to detect cyber threats in the banking industry." PhD diss., ProQuest University (Demo), 2023.

Mallick, Arpit, Subhra Dhara, and Sushant Rath. "Application of machine learning algorithms for prediction of sinter machine productivity." *Machine Learning with Applications* 6 (2021): 100186.

Mohanty, Ricky, Hemanta Kumar Bhuyan, Subhendu Kumar Pani, Vinayakumar Ravi, and Moez Krichen. "Bird species recognition using spiking neural network along with distance based fuzzy co-clustering." *International Journal of Speech Technology* 26, no. 3 (2023): 681–694.

Nguyen, Binh, Yves Coelho, Teodiano Bastos, and Sridhar Krishnan. "Trends in human activity recognition with focus on machine learning and power requirements." *Machine Learning with Applications* 5 (2021): 100072.

Olaoye, Favour, Kaledio Potter, and Lucas Doris. Explainable AI: Interpreting and understanding machine learning models. No. 12571. EasyChair, 2024.

Orji, Ugochukwu, and Elochukwu Ukwandu. "Machine learning for an explainable cost prediction of medical insurance." *Machine Learning with Applications* 15 (2024): 100516.

Tripathy, Murchhana, SantilataChampati, and Hemanta Kumar Bhuyan. "Knowledge discovery in a recommender system: The matrix factorization approach." *Journal of Information & Knowledge Management* 21, no. 04 (2022): 2250051.

Vijayaraj, A., Hemanta Kumar Bhuyan, P. T. Vasanth Raj, and M. Vijay Anand. "Congestion avoidance using enhanced blue algorithm." *Wireless Personal Communications* 128, no. 3 (2023): 1963–1984.

Wickramasinghe, Indika. "Applications of machine learning in cricket: A systematic review." *Machine Learning with Applications* 10 (2022): 100435.

Zeinali, Yasser, and Seyed Taghi Akhavan Niaki. "Heart sound classification using signal processing and machine learning algorithms." *Machine Learning with Applications* 7 (2022): 100206.

5 Explainability of AI in Improving the Quality of Service in the Actuarial Industry

Anita Tanwar, Rashmi Aggarwal, and Arvinder Kaur

5.1 INTRODUCTION

The word AI is a method wherein a system or machine imitates the intelligence of human being to perform the work in real world. AI helps to identify and solve different challenges in solving the problem through the trained data. This AI system uses improvisation in information as and when required as well as it works intuitively (Choudhary and Trivedi, 2023). There are some examples of AI such as advanced search system in the internet, automated games, automated vehicles, advanced recognition system, and healthcare system. The concept of AI evolved around the year 1950s in the area of computer science. The main aim of this evolvement was to make the robots that could learn and perform different tasks based on the input information given to it and work like a human brain (Exarchos et al. 2021). Over the years, the usage of AI machines has increased that results in advances in the area of medical treatment, natural language processing, and different scientific researches (Shi et al. 2020). To enhance the performance of AI machines, different AI robots have been skilled or trained based on their previous experiences that help in solving the problem (Tomsett et al. 2020).

Three primary drivers have been identified that are important for the development of XAI. First, there is a requirement of a simple model; second, there is a requirement of specialized techniques that help humans to communicate with the model; third, the checking of reliability of the results withdrawn from these prototypes identified by Došilović et al. (2018) and Mullins et al. (2021). Some researchers (Biran and Cotton, 2017; Hoffman et al., 2018) have identified that AI can provide benefits to different decision-makers if they know how to use it and make better decisions. AI is a system that uses human intelligence in machines to help with different predictions, real or virtual decisions, and recommendations that help to operate and solve human problems in an automated way (Krafft et al. 2020). XAI is also called as explainable artificial intelligence that helps to understand the processes and methods for

DOI: 10.1201/9781003472551-7

models of deep learning (Scholbeck et al., 2019). The aim of XAI provides reliable and understandable explanations of deep learning systems. In Europe, the General Data Protection Regulation has been introduced by Richman (2021) for introducing laws and regulations for XAI. These laws include reliability, understanding, trust, and ethical considerations (Arrieta et al. 2020; Regulation GDP 2018; Bostrom & Yudkowsky 2018; Weld & Bansal 2019; Das & Rad 2022).

The purpose of XAI, which is a part of AI, helps in making understandable AI model by clear explanations, transparency, and interpretation (Adadi and Berrada 2018; Floridi et al. 2018). Insurance researches require more focus on understandability, explanations, and comprehensibility in the area of the insurance industry. This research is a comprehensive examination of significance of XAI in providing quality services to the insurance industry (Burrell 2016; Ribeiro et al. 2016).

The recent history of XAI is deeply based on AI, with the advancements in clarity and visibility being the main factors that have allowed XAI to thrive. Different sources define explainability differently; one defines it as a "interpretable approximation of the original complex [AI] model," and the other defines it as a "local approximation of a complex model (by another model)" (Lundberg and Lee 2017; Al-Shedivat et al. 2020). It is evident from the surge in AI-related studies since the latter part of 2010 that the concept of comprehensibility did not undergo a radical transformation; researchers are still asking the same concerns about AI. Considerations such as these pertain to AI fairness, decision pathway transparency, and end-user explanation. Importantly, XAI is just the method by which AI's deeds, suggestions, and decisions can be comprehended by humans (Anjomshoae et al. 2019). There is no imminent danger of machine-led moral judgments or comprehension in AI or XAI (Ford 2018). The fundamental concerns of (X)AI, which revolve around humans,

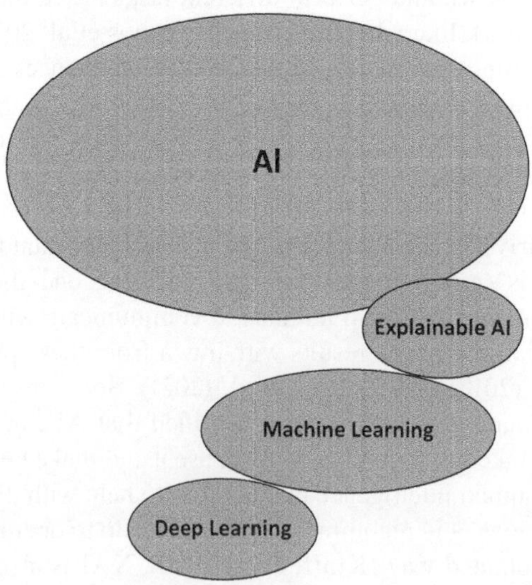

FIGURE 5.1 Deep learning, machine learning, AI, and explainable AI. (Authors Compilation.)

include prejudice and fairness. This part provides an overview of the latest XAI research and how it is influencing AI studies.

Figure 5.1 represents deep learning, machine learning, AI, and Explainable AI. It is still debatable whether black box AI models are appropriate for insurance operations, despite predictions that AI revenues in insurance would increase 23% to $3.4 billion from 2019 to 2024 (Bean & Melzer 2021; Chen et al. 2019; Global Data 2021). Financial services, insurance in particular, are undergoing a revolutionary shift due to the rise of AI as a methodology for smart decision-making capable of performing complicated computational tasks. Financial services companies view data as a key strategic resource and a competitive differentiator; using AI models to make use of this data has several benefits (Zappa et al. 2023). Improved identification of fraud in claims handling, more granularity and individualization in insurance premium pricing, smart contract creation, legal document analysis, chatbots, and administrative tasks are some of the benefits of AI utilized by the insurance sector (European Commission. 2021; Falco et al. 2021; McFall et al. 2020; Ngai et al. 2011; Apergis & Poufinas, 2020; Riikkinen et al. 2018; Zarifis et al. 2020; Dangwal et al. 2023). AI is the combination of different technologies that helps to solve problems and make decisions on different issues in human life Chi and Wei (2020). It provides analytical decision-making to solve the complicated problems. Black Box thinking is also developed to solve the complex problems (Adadi and Berrada 2018; Carabantes 2020). Clients, process, and strategies are the three main focuses of AI usage in banking institutions as per a comprehensive analysis (Owens et al. 2021) that stressed around the area of bank. This framework of AI helps banks to make strategic decisions and improve the value chain system and performance of banks. Turning our attention to the role of the actuary, the research in Nor et al. (2021) demonstrates how the field of actuarial science can change and progress over the next few years to include AI methods and approaches.

In the insurance industry, the value chain system highly relies on AI-driven system to provide valuable solutions (Eling et al. 2021). The explainability of XAI is the main focus of this research to identify the importance, implication, and limitation.

5.2 SIGNIFICANCE OF XAI IN ACTUARIAL BUSINESS

In numerous sectors of the economy, the actuarial business plays a crucial role in the management of risk and uncertainty, as shown in Figure 5.2. Figure 5.2 shows the significant role of XAI in the actuarial business, as mentioned below (Owens et al. 2021):

1. Evaluation and Risk Control

   The identification, evaluation, and control of the risk is performed by Actuaries. Different financial complications in the future that are unpredictable can be identified and solved through different approaches such as statistical, mathematical, and financial approaches. It helps an organization to make better decisions for risk management and build a strong financial system.
2. Evaluation of Financial Reserves

   In the insurance sector, actuary's role is very important and significant in maintaining financial reserves. It helps in the development and

FIGURE 5.2 Significance of XAI in actuarial business. (Authors Compilation.)

determination of appropriate rates, the framing of different policies of insurance and the analysis of the future financial requirement to cope the future financial needs. It provides the guarantee of financial growth, ability and stability of different insurance companies, while coping up with the needs of their policyholders.

3. Formulation and Administration of Pension Systems

   XAI plays a significant role in the formulation, administration, and overall management of pension system in the insurance sector. It identifies an insurance organization's financial requirement, future legal obligation, and also analyzes the financial health of different pension funds of an insurance organization. This is very important as population is growing and to cope up with insurance requirement of population.

4. Risk Management

   XAI helps insurance sector companies to manage their financial risk, investment risk, credit risk, and liquidity risk. It helps an organization to make their strategic decision in a better way, maximize their returns, and reduce their cost.

5. Healthcare

   XAI also plays a significant role in healthcare system such as management of expenses, identification of insurance premium, and framework of the healthcare system. This technological system helps different health insurance firms in analyzing the financial requirements of medical interventions, identifying the future healthcare patterns, and managing the cost efficiently.

6. Government Policies and Regulations
   It also plays a crucial role in the management of pension funds following the government policies and mentioned regulations.
7. Data Analysis and Modeling Approaches
   XAI plays a significant role in the analysis of data and modeling techniques, which is very much important in today's data world. This system uses different statistical methods and techniques to analyze a huge dataset, predict the constructive model, and measure the risk.
8. Facilitate Strategic Decision-Making
   It helps in making strategic decisions to cope up with the challenges coming from different companies. It provides helpful and effective team management. It supports different executives and stakeholders in different areas like the selection of investment avenues and the effect of mergers and acquisitions in an organization. It provides a strong survival system for an organization to survive in turbulent conditions.

5.3 IMPLICATIONS OF XAI FOR THE INSURANCE INDUSTRY

Concerns about non-life and health-related hazards were associated with four important machine learning applications, as shown in Figure 5.3. Figure 5.3 depicts the implications of XAI in order of the restrictions found in corporate use of these approaches and the degree of their application (Langer and Landers 2021; Bhargave and Tandon 2023):

1. Advertising, Developing, and Manufacturing Products for Sale
   Due to the lack of clear guidelines for the application of AI in certain tasks, they find widespread usage. Businesses may be hesitant to employ this method due to the difficulty in communicating the findings to upper management and decision-makers. Enhancing process development,

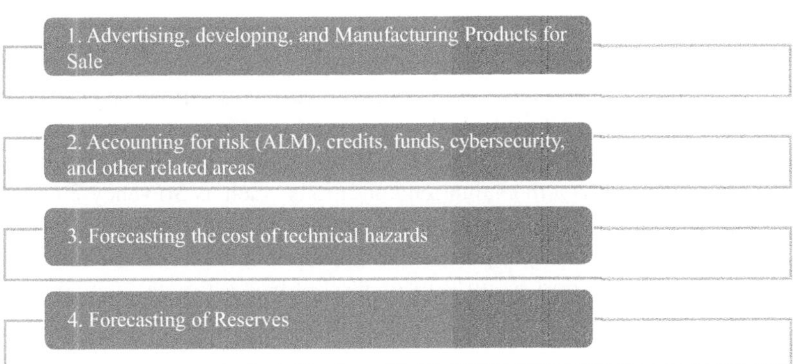

FIGURE 5.3 Implications of XAI for the insurance sector. (Author Compilation.)

interpreting findings into an accepted language, and comprehending relationships are benefits from XAI applications.

2. Accounting for Risk (ALM), Credits, Funds, Cybersecurity, and Other Related Areas

   AI methods are highly beneficial for recognizing risks, forecasting, administration, and making choices because comprehensive risk management necessitates the creation of intricate models that enable the identification of objectives or trade-offs through the interplay of several variables. But these methods face hardware limits when it comes to processing massive amounts of data and transforming it using algorithms. A lot of these procedures also need supervisory permission and trust from external as well as internal auditors. Decision-makers also need to know what goes on inside the models, what risks are associated with implementing and interpreting the results, and the best way to incorporate prescriptive models. When it comes to managing specific risks, including cybercrime or fraud, while also comprehending existing relationships, XAI approaches could simplify audit processes instead of replicating models.

3. Forecasting the Cost of Technical Hazards

   Forecasting the cost of technical hazards taking external as well as internal surcharges into account: Here is where integrating AI approaches, such as data cleansing and processing, expense and risk categorization, and models for prediction, would be most useful. But there are a lot of rules for this app, like not discriminating on the basis of gender or well-being, which includes things like the regulation of oncological insignificance, adherence to transparency in simulation of risk, and the ability to audit and trace these processes—all of which are necessary for efficient model administration but don't take into account the limits of processing speed and capacity. The use of XAI approaches enables model debugging, auditing processes, and traceability, comprehension, and overall improvement in modeling governance. This is in an effort to decrease a number of parameters that are extraneous to the techniques.

4. Forecasting of Reserves

   The forecasting of reserves (pure potential technical risk) presents the same opportunities and challenges as the pricing procedures, but with significantly stricter regulations. Companies also face a multiplicity of notifications and evaluation conditions, such as Solvency 2 and the International Financial Reporting Standards 17, all of which work together to complicate financial reporting. To make matters worse, each financial and accounting report requires its own set of best estimates, which necessitate analysis and justification of any discrepancies found.

5.4 LIMITATIONS OF XAI

When deciphering the reasoning behind AI system actions and outputs is of the utmost importance, XAI becomes an important focus of study. But XAI isn't perfect; no technology is represented in Figure 5.4. Here are a few examples of these limitations (Challen et al. 2019; Koster et al. 2021; Kaur and Tanwar 2024):

It's not uncommon for models to have compromise between being very accurate or performing well and being very explainable. Deep neural networks and other complicated models may provide more accuracy at the expense of interpretability, while decision trees and other simpler models may be simpler to comprehend but may have less predictive power.

As shown in Figure 5.4, the explanations are as follows:

1. Transparency cannot be same as interpretability

   The goal of XAI techniques is to create AI easier to understand and use; however, transparency cannot be necessarily the same as interpretability. Particularly with more complicated deep learning designs, explaining AI systems doesn't always show all their inner workings.
2. Relevance to the situation

   The audience and setting dictate the amount of detail required. An adequate response for a user or industry expert may not be enough for another. In order to meet a variety of needs, XAI approaches must be versatile.
3. Restrictions on specific models

   The intricacy and nonlinearity of certain AI models make them inherently hard to clarify. This is particularly true for the deep learning models. Some of the algorithm's choices may remain hidden from view when using methods such as maps of saliency or layer-wise significance transmission.

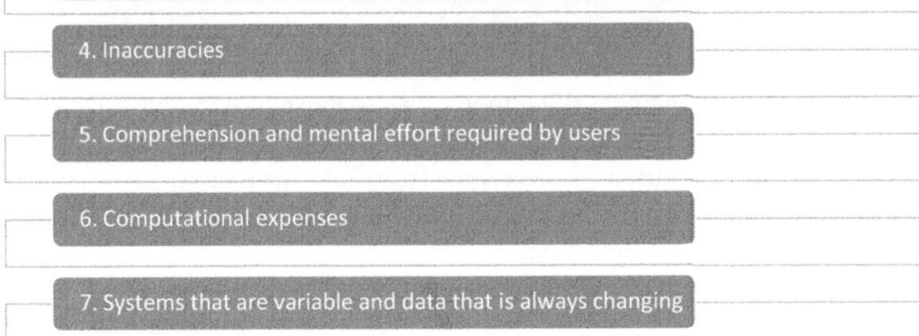

FIGURE 5.4 Limitations of XAI. (Author Compilation.)

4. Inaccuracies

   Similar to how AI models can pick up inaccuracies in their initial training data, XAI systems might produce explanations that are skewed or deceiving. This may occur if the validating procedures for the clarifications are inadequate or if that XAI methods used are prejudiced.
5. Comprehension and mental effort required by users

   Just because you explain things doesn't mean they'll fully grasp them. Complex Artificial judgments could be difficult to understand for people without extensive knowledge of the relevant subject or the techniques used to make them.
6. Computational expenses

   The computational expense of generating clarifications, particularly for enormous scale or applications that operate in real time, poses a challenge to both efficiency and scalability. Particularly in settings with limited resources, striking a balance between the requirement for description and the effectiveness of computation is not an easy task.
7. Systems that are variable and data that is always changing

   XAI techniques may have difficulty explaining AI systems that are working in surroundings that are variable and where the distributions of data are constantly shifting. To account for these shifts, existing explanations may need revising or updating.

   To overcome these constraints, XAI development and research must continue to concentrate on making AI models more interpretable without lowering its efficiency or scalability. In addition, to create reliable XAI systems, specialists in AI, interaction between humans and computers, cognitive psychology, and related domains must work together across disciplines.

5.5 CONCLUSION

On the basis of the above analysis, it can be concluded that XAI, a part of AI, helps in making understandable AI model by clear explanations, transparency, and interpretation. XAI helps an organization to make better decisions for risk management and build a strong financial system. XAI approaches enable model debugging, auditing processes, and traceability, comprehension, and overall improvement in modeling governance. When it comes to managing specific risks, including cybercrime or fraud, while comprehending existing relationships, XAI approaches could simplify audit processes instead of replicating models. Moreover, it provides helpful and effective team management. It supports different executives and stakeholders in different areas like the selection of investment avenues and the effect of mergers and acquisitions in an organization. To overcome from XAI limitation, XAI development and research must continue to concentrate on making AI models more interpretable without lowering its efficiency or scalability.

REFERENCES

Adadi, Amina, and Mohammed Berrada. "Peeking inside the black-box: a survey on explainable artificial intelligence (XAI)." *IEEE Access* 6 (2018): 52138–52160.

Al-Shedivat, Maruan, Jennifer Gillenwater, Eric Xing, and Afshin Rostamizadeh. "Federated learning via posterior averaging: A new perspective and practical algorithms." *arXiv preprint arXiv*:2010.05273 (2020).

Anjomshoae, Sule, Amro Najjar, Davide Calvaresi, and Kary Främling. "Explainable agents and robots: Results from a systematic literature review." In *18th International Conference on Autonomous Agents and Multiagent Systems (AAMAS 2019)*, Montreal, Canada, May 13–17, 2019, pp. 1078–1088. International Foundation for Autonomous Agents and Multiagent Systems, 2019.

Apergis, Nicholas, and Thomas Poufinas. "The role of insurance growth in economic growth: Fresh evidence from a panel of OECD countries." *The North American Journal of Economics and Finance* 53 (2020): 101217.

Arrieta, Alejandro Barredo, Natalia Díaz-Rodríguez, Javier Del Ser, Adrien Bennetot, Siham Tabik, Alberto Barbado, Salvador García et al. "Explainable Artificial Intelligence (XAI): Concepts, taxonomies, opportunities and challenges toward responsible AI." *Information Fusion* 58 (2020): 82–115.

Bhargave, Harshita, and Dinesh Tandon. "How does Tobin's Q respond to merger and acquisition announcements: Evidence of listed Indian firms." *International Journal of Professional Business Review* 8, no. 2 (2023): e01295–e01295.

Bean, John C., and Dan Melzer. *Engaging ideas: The professor's guide to integrating writing, critical thinking, and active learning in the classroom*. John Wiley & Sons, 2021.

Biran, Or, and Courtenay Cotton. "Explanation and justification in machine learning: A survey." *IJCAI-17 Workshop on Explainable AI (XAI)* 8, no. 1 (2017): 8–13.

Bostrom, Nick, and Eliezer Yudkowsky. "The ethics of artificial intelligence." In William Ramsay and Keith Frankish (Eds.), *Artificial intelligence safety and security*, pp. 57–69. Chapman and Hall/CRC, 2018.

Burrell, J. "How the machine 'thinks': Understanding opacity in machine learning algorithms." *Big Data & Society*, 3, no. 1 (2016). https://doi.org/10.1177/2053951715622512.

Carabantes, Manuel. "Black-box artificial intelligence: An epistemological and critical analysis." *AI & Society* 35, no. 2 (2020): 309–317.

Challen, Robert, Joshua Denny, Martin Pitt, Luke Gompels, Tom Edwards, and Krasimira Tsaneva-Atanasova. "Artificial intelligence, bias and clinical safety." *BMJ Quality & Safety* 28, no. 3 (2019): 231–237.

Chen, Gang, Peihong Xie, Jing Dong, and Tianfu Wang. "Understanding programmatic creative: The role of AI." *Journal of Advertising* 48, no. 4 (2019): 347–355.

Chi, Y., and W. Wei. "Optimal insurance with background risk: An analysis of general dependence structures." *Finance and Stochastics* 24, no. 4 (2020): 903–937.

Choudhary, Vinita, and Sonal Trivedi. "The role of internal audit in risk management with a perspective of sustainability development." In Kiran Sood, Simon Grima, Peter Young, Ercan Ozen, Balamurugan Balusamy (Eds.), *The Impact of Climate Change and Sustainability Standards on the Insurance Market*, pp. 287–315. NJ: Wiley 2023.

Dangwal, A., M. Kukreti, M. Angurala, R. Sarangal, M., Mehta, and P. Chauhan, A Review on the role of artificial intelligence in tourism. In *2023 10th International CVonference on Computing for Sustainable Global Development (INDIACom)* (pp. 164–168). IEEE, 2023, March.

Das, Arun, and Paul Rad. "Opportunities and challenges in explainable artificial intelligence (xai): A survey." *arXiv preprint arXiv*:2006.11371 (2020).

Došilović, Filip Karlo, Mario Brčić, and Nikica Hlupić. "Explainable artificial intelligence: A survey." In *2018 41st International Convention on Information and Communication Technology, Electronics and Microelectronics (MIPRO),* Opatija, Croatia, 21–25 May 2018, pp. 210–215. IEEE, 2018.

Eling, M., O. Ghavibazoo, and K. Hanewald. "Willingness to take financial risks and insurance holdings: A European survey." *Journal of Behavioral and Experimental Economics* 95 (2021): 101781.

European Commission. "European approach to artificial intelligence." Retrieved on 13th April2024.https://digital-strategy.ec.europa.eu/en/policies/european-approach-artificial-intelligence

Exarchos, Konstantinos P., Agapi Aggelopoulou, Aikaterini Oikonomou, Theodora Biniskou, Vasiliki Beli, Eirini Antoniadou, and Konstantinos Kostikas. "Review of artificial intelligence techniques in chronic obstructive lung disease." *IEEE Journal of Biomedical and Health Informatics* 26, no. 5 (2021): 2331–2338.

Falco, Gregory, Ben Shneiderman, Julia Badger, Ryan Carrier, Anton Dahbura, David Danks, Martin Eling et al. "Governing AI safety through independent audits." *Nature Machine Intelligence* 3, no. 7 (2021): 566–571.

Floridi, Luciano, Josh Cowls, Monica Beltrametti, Raja Chatila, Patrice Chazerand, Virginia Dignum, Christoph Luetge et al. "AI4People—An ethical framework for a good AI society: opportunities, risks, principles, and recommendations." *Minds and Machines* 28 (2018): 689–707.

Ford, Martin. *Architects of intelligence: The truth about AI from the people building it*. Packt Publishing Ltd, 2018.

Global Data 2021. Global market size of artificial intelligence (2019–2021, $ Billion). Retrieved on March 17, 2024. https://www.globaldata.com/data-insights/technology--media-and-telecom/global-market-value-of-artificial-intelligence/#:~:text=That%20said%2C%20as%20per%20GlobalData,it%20is%20difficult%20to%20estimate.

Hoffman, Robert R., Shane T. Mueller, Gary Klein, and Jordan Litman. "Metrics for explainable AI: Challenges and prospects." *arXiv preprint arXiv*:1812.04608 (2018).

Kaur, Arvinder, and Anita Tanwar. "Adoption Potential and Challenges of Artificial Intelligence in Banking." In Sanjay Taneja, Pawan Kumar, Simon Grima, Ercan Ozen, Kiran Sood (Eds.) *Sustainable Investments in Green Finance*, pp. 271–293. USA: IGI Global, 2024.

Koster, Olivier, Ruud Kosman, and Joost Visser. "A checklist for explainable AI in the insurance domain." In *International Conference on the Quality of Information and Communications Technology, 14th International Conference*, QUATIC 2021, Algarve, Portugal, 8–11 September 2021, proceedings, pp. 446–456. Cham: Springer International Publishing, 2021.

Krafft, Peaks, Meg Young, Michael Katell, Karen Huang, and Ghislain Bugingo. "Defining AI in policy versus practice." In *Proceedings of the AAAI/ACM Conference on AI, Ethics, and Society*, AIES '20: AAAI/ACM Conference on AI, Ethics, and Society, New York, NY, USA, 7–9 February 2020, pp. 72–78. 2020.

Langer, Markus, and Richard N. Landers. "The future of artificial intelligence at work: A review on effects of decision automation and augmentation on workers targeted by algorithms and third-party observers." *Computers in Human Behavior* 123 (2021): 106878.

McFall, Liz, Gert Meyers, and Ine Van Hoyweghen. "The personalisation of insurance: Data, behaviour and innovation." *Big Data & Society* 7, no. 2 (2020): 2053951720973707.

Mullins, Martin, Christopher P. Holland, and Martin Cunneen. "Creating ethics guidelines for artificial intelligence and big data analytics customers: The case of the consumer European insurance market." *Patterns* 2, no. 10 (2021): 100362.

Ngai, Eric W.T., Yong Hu, Yiu Hing Wong, Yijun Chen, and Xin Sun. "The application of data mining techniques in financial fraud detection: A classification framework and an academic review of literature." *Decision Support Systems* 50, no. 3 (2011): 559–569.

NIPS'17: Proceedings of the 31st International Conference on Neural Information Processing Systems. (NIPS 2017), Long Beach, CA, USA. Pages 4768 – 4777 Date of conference - 4 dec to 9 dec, 2017, vol. 30 (2017).

Nor, Ahmad Kamal Mohd, Srinivasa Rao Pedapati, Masdi Muhammad, and Victor Leiva. "Overview of explainable artificial intelligence for prognostic and health management of industrial assets based on preferred reporting items for systematic reviews and meta-analyses." *Sensors* 21, no. 23 (2021): 8020.

Owens, E., B. Sheehan, M. Mullins, M. Cunneen, J. Ressel, and G. Castignani. "Explainable Artificial Intelligence (xai) in insurance." *Risks* 10, no. 12 (2022): 230.

Regulation, General Data Protection. "General data protection regulation (GDPR). ntersoft Consulting." https://www.epsu.org/sites/default/files/article/files/GDPR_FINAL_EPSU.pdf (2018).

Ribeiro, Marco Tulio, Sameer Singh, and Carlos Guestrin. "Model-agnostic interpretability of machine learning." *arXiv preprint arXiv*:1606.05386 (2016).

Richman, Ronald. "AI in actuarial science—A review of recent advances–part 1." *Annals of Actuarial Science* 15, no. 2 (2021): 207–229.

Riikkinen, Mikko, Hannu Saarijärvi, Peter Sarlin, and Ilkka Lähteenmäki. "Using artificial intelligence to create value in insurance." *International Journal of Bank Marketing* 36, no. 6 (2018): 1145–1168.

Scholbeck, Christian A., Christoph Molnar, Christian Heumann, Bernd Bischl, and Giuseppe Casalicchio. "Sampling, intervention, prediction, aggregation: a generalized framework for model-agnostic interpretations." In *Machine Learning and Knowledge Discovery in Databases: International Workshops of ECML PKDD 2019*, Würzburg, Germany, September 16–20, 2019, Proceedings, Part I, pp. 205–216. Springer International Publishing, 2020.

Shi, Feng, Jun Wang, Jun Shi, Ziyan Wu, Qian Wang, Zhenyu Tang, Kelei He, Yinghuan Shi, and Dinggang Shen. "Review of artificial intelligence techniques in imaging data acquisition, segmentation, and diagnosis for COVID-19." *IEEE Reviews in Biomedical Engineering* 14 (2020): 4–15.

Tomsett, Richard, Alun Preece, Dave Braines, Federico Cerutti, Supriyo Chakraborty, Mani Srivastava, Gavin Pearson, and Lance Kaplan. "Rapid trust calibration through interpretable and uncertainty-aware AI." *Patterns* 1, no. 4 (2020): 100049.

Trivedi, Sonal, and Reena Malik. "Blockchain technology as an emerging technology in the insurance market." In Kiran Sood, Rajesh Kumar Dhanaraj, Balamurugan Balusamy, Simon Grima, R. Uma Maheshwari (Eds.) *Big Data: A Game Changer for Insurance Industry*, pp. 81–100. Emerald Publishing Limited, 2022a.

Trivedi, Sonal, and Reena Malik. "Role and significance of data protection in risk management practices in the insurance market." In Kiran Sood, Balamurugan Balusamy, Simon Grima, Pierpaolo Marano (Eds.) *Big Data Analytics in the Insurance Market*, pp. 263–273. Emerald Publishing Limited, 2022b.

Weld, Daniel S., and Gagan Bansal. "The challenge of crafting intelligible intelligence." *Communications of the ACM* 62, no. 6 (2019): 70–79.

Zappa, Diego, Gian Paolo Clemente, Francesco Della Corte, and Nino Savelli. "Editorial on the special issue on insurance: Complexity, risks and its connection with social sciences." *Quality & Quantity* 57, no. Suppl 2 (2023): 125–130.

Zarifis, A., P. Kawalek, and A. Azadegan. "Evaluating if trust and personal information privacy concerns are barriers to using health insurance that explicitly utilizes AI." *Journal of Internet Commerce* (2020): 1–19. https://doi.org/10.1080/15332861.2020.1832817 (open access)Zheng, Nanning, Shaoyi Du, Jianji Wang, He Zhang, Wenting Cui, Zijian Kang, Tao Yang et al. "Predicting COVID-19 in China using hybrid AI model." *IEEE Transactions on Cybernetics* 50, no. 7 (2020): 2891–2904.

6 AI Transformation of the Insurance Industry

A Systematic Review of Progress and Possibilities

Pravin Chavan, Dhanashri Sanadkumar Havale, Hrishikesh G. Kokate, Subrata Chowdhury, and Wing-Keung Wong

6.1 INTRODUCTION

The integration of artificial intelligence (AI) into the insurance industry represents a transformative shift that has the potential to reshape the landscape of risk management and financial services.

The growth of AI is impacting several businesses, including the insurance industry. As other industries, the insurance sector is now experiencing a significant change, influenced by the revolutionary capabilities of AI. Traditionally, the insurance industry is human capital-driven industry that highly relied on manual processes. Besides, the industry functions on a set of rules, regulations, and policies that are highly based on subjective assessments. The historical data for risk evaluation and decision-making was the embedded part of the insurance industry's decision-making process (Han et al. 2023). The high dependencies on manual tasks often resulted in inefficiencies, delays, and inconsistencies. However, AI is piloting a new era of data-driven insights and automation, enabling the insurers to function with greater precision, speed, and efficiency (Wamba-Taguimdje et al. 2020).

The journey of AI in insurance has evolved from basic automation, data analysis to most advanced predictive modeling that provides personalized customer experiences (Soori et al. 2023). In its early phase, AI was used as a simple algorithm for data sorting and pattern recognition. However, the past decade has witnessed a paradigm shift in AI integration in the insurance industry. This shift is driven by advanced AI technologies, including machine learning (ML), natural language processing, and robotic process automation, significantly enhancing efficiency and accuracy (Soori et al. 2023).

Today, AI is playing multifaceted role in the insurance industry. In claim processing, AI aids in automating and streamlining operations, reducing human error and fraud (Mashrur et al. 2020). In underwriting and risk assessment, predictive models and analytics provide more precise evaluations (Alotaibi 2023). Customer interaction

DOI: 10.1201/9781003472551-8

has been revolutionized by AI through chatbots and virtual assistants, offering 24/7 service and tailored advice (Li & Zhang 2023).

The AI technology, with its capabilities to analyze huge datasets, facilitate to identify complex hidden patterns in the data, and automate tasks with remarkable accuracy, enables reshaping various sectors within the industry (Christopoulos et al. 2022). AI technology has a profound impact across the entire insurance value chain. The various operations in the insurance industry from underwriting and claims processing to fraud detection and customer service and positively influenced by the AI technology (Eling et al. 2022).

Underwriting is one of the very core operation in the insurance industry that is undergoing a path-breaking change as a result of AI integration. AI algorithms have a power to analyze huge amounts of data, which include medical records, driving history, and even social media usage, to reveal a more comprehensive picture of an individual's risk profile (Miranda et al. 2024). This facilitates insurers to offer personalized pricing and coverage options, resulting in fairer and more competitive offerings. Timely claim processing is essential for the insurer to satisfy their customer and comply with the regulatory guidance. However, the claims processing operation of the insurer is burdened by paperwork. ML algorithms can analyze claims documents, identify fraudulent patterns, and even suggest settlement amounts, resulting in significantly reducing processing times and costs (Alam & Prybutok 2024).

As a result of advancement in digital technology, the insurance industry is exposed to fraudulent practices. Now AI offers the sophisticated algorithms that can analyze transaction patterns, identify anomalies, and detect the suspicious activity in real time. This will prevent significant financial losses for the insurer (Rukhsar et al. 2022).

Customer service is the face of the insurance industry, and efficient customer service offers a competitive edge for the insurance company. AI has the potential to transform the insurance industry substantially. The chatbots and virtual assistance offer the real-time customer support. These intelligent systems have not only enabled to answer customer questions, but also resolve basic issues of customers and even personalize interactions, which offer 24/7, hassle-free customer support (Sousa et al. 2019).

As the AI technology has revolutionized the insurance industry, it is the thrust area of researcher scholars to explore the possibilities of application of AI in the insurance sector and analyze its impact through continuous research. This chapter intends to take a stock of research in the field of AI application in the insurance industry. The chapter aims to provide a comprehensive analysis of the current research in applications, challenges, and future possibilities of AI in the insurance industry. The chapter will provide valuable insights for policymakers, industry stakeholders, and researchers, fostering an understanding of AI's transformative potential in reshaping the insurance sector.

6.1.1 Research Methods

This study was conducted using theme-centric review methodology. Under this approach, the researcher guides the reader on how prior publications have contributed to the development of themes, concepts, or phenomena of interest. The initial phase of the study focused on selecting a research theme that aimed to examine the research progress on the AI and its application in the insurance industry. To examine the present status of the research on AI application in the insurance industry, the Scopus research database was used to gather comprehensive and representative research studies. Following the assessment of the selected papers, a co-word analysis method was applied to gain insight into the interconnectedness among the prevailing research themes. VOSviewer, a computer program for bibliometric mapping and biblioshiny functions in the bibliometrix package in R, was used for the analysis.

6.1.1.1 Criteria for Article Inclusion

- Records within the year range 2010–2023 (refer Figure 6.1).
- Publications classified as "Articles."
- Documents written in English language.
- Documents directly relating to application of AI in the insurance and actuarial practices.

6.1.1.2 Criteria for Article Exclusion

- Records outside the year range 2010–2023.
- Non-article publications.
- Documents written in non-English language.
- Documents that are not directly relating to the AI and its application in insurance. And actuarial practices.

6.1.2 Data Collection

We used the Scopus Database to search for relevant articles for bibliometric analysis. To search the relevant articles, we used Boolean search techniques. Boolean keywords such as "Artificial Intelligence and Insurance" and "AI and Insurance" and "Artificial Intelligence and Actuarial Practices" and "AI and Actuarial Practices" were used. If an article had a specific search term in its title, abstract, or keyword, it was selected for analysis.

Figure 6.1 illustrates article inclusion and exclusion criteria used to select the documents for this study. By using the given syntax or initial search result obtained 1635 articles. The study of AI gained significant momentum in the late 1990s and experienced a period of rapid advancement between 2010 and 2023. We excluded the articles published prior to the year 2010, resulting in the availability of 1439 articles for further analysis. In the next step, by limiting the publication type as Article, we yield 525 documents. At this stage, we excluded 914 documents that were published as conference papers, reviews, and book chapters and editorials. Next, by limiting the articles published in the English language, we obtained the 512 documents. In the last stage, we evaluated each article, its title, and abstract, and retained only those documents that were relating to Artificial Intelligence and its application insurance and actuarial practices. This rigorous analysis yields a total of 113 articles, which were used for the bibliomterix analysis and systematic review.

6.1.3 Data Analysis

In this section of the chapter, we have presented the bibliomterix analysis and systematic review of the research articles selected for this study.

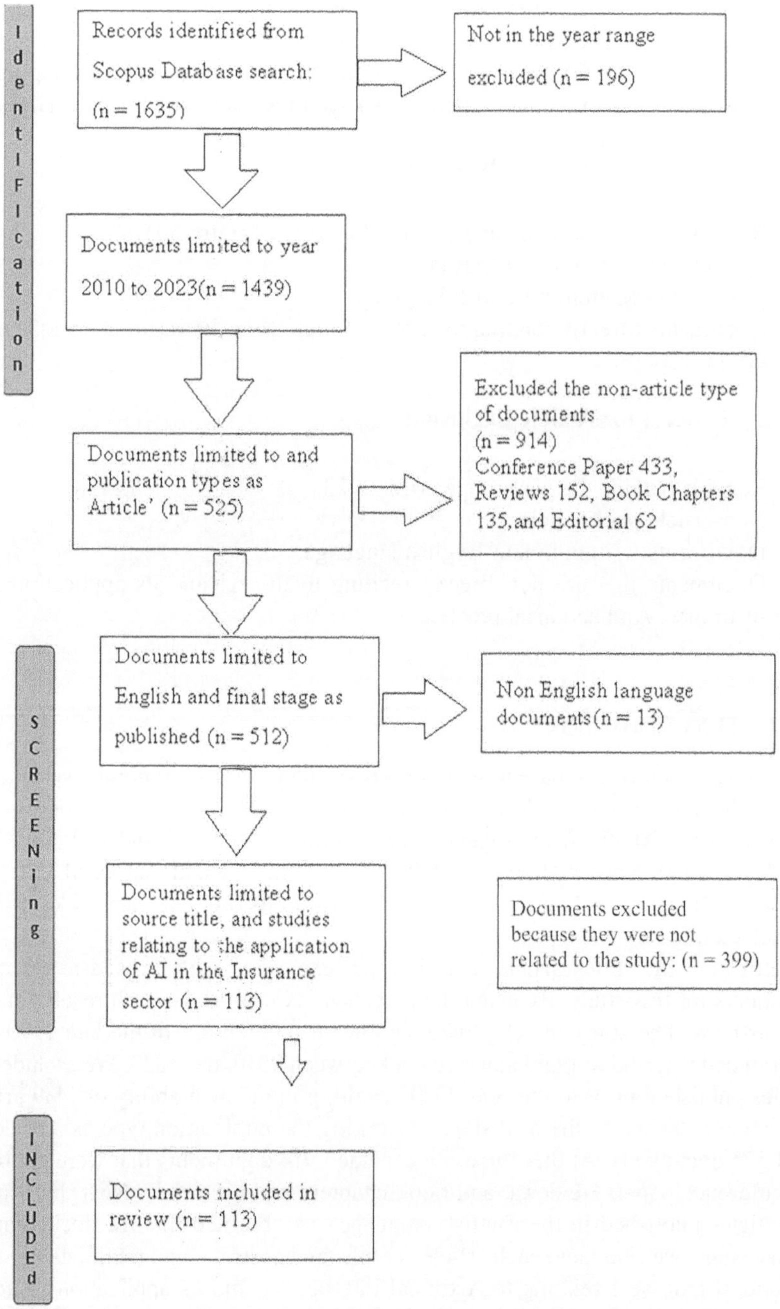

FIGURE 6.1 Article screening process. (Author Compilation.)

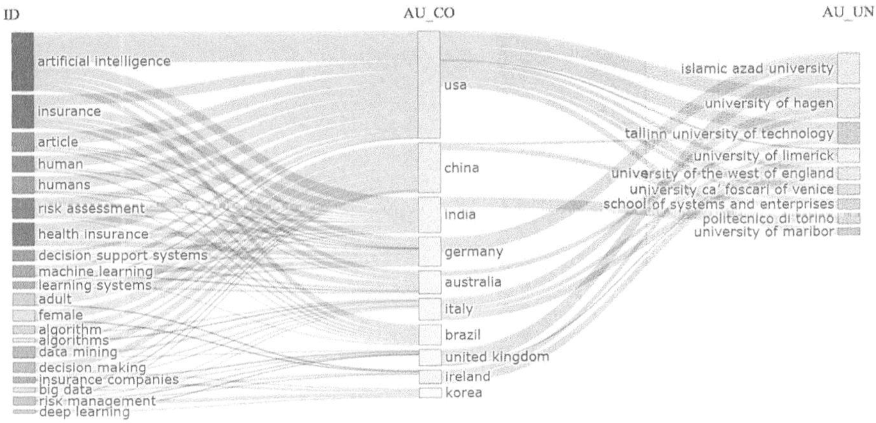

FIGURE 6.2 Three-plot graph. (Developed by Author.)

6.2 THREE-PLOT GRAPH ANALYSIS

In Figure 6.2, a three-plot graph shows the relationship between key terms (ID), countries (AU_CO), and universities (AU_UN) in the context of AI in insurance and actuarial science research. The left field (ID) represents thematic terms extracted from the literature, with "artificial intelligence" and "insurance" being the most prominent, indicating their strong presence in the research. The middle field (AU_CO) shows countries, with the United States, China, and India appearing to be the most involved in this research area, suggesting that a significant portion of the work on AI in insurance comes from these countries. The right field (AU_UN) lists universities that contribute to this research. Islamic Azad University and the University of Hagen seem to have a strong association with the thematic terms, indicating active research or publication in the field from these institutions.

6.3 TREE PLOT ANALYSIS

In Figure 6.3, a tree plot of the bibliometric analysis shows the distribution of research articles across various subject areas related to AI applications in insurance. The key observations from the tree map are presented below:

Distribution of research: The tree map reveals that a significant portion of the research focuses on "machine learning" (34%) within the domain of AI applications in insurance. Furthermore, it is followed by decision-making (29%) and health insurance (12%). ML techniques seem to be far more common when investigating AI applications for insurance, particularly in decision-making processes and in health insurance.

Exploration of a specific areas: In terms of "machine learning," the tree map shows the areas where more input could be considered for future research such as "algorithm" (18%), the way of "data mining" (8%), and "prediction" mode (7%). This refers to the fact that numerous types of ML algorithms, data mining methods, and constructing predictive models for different use cases of insurance received consideration.

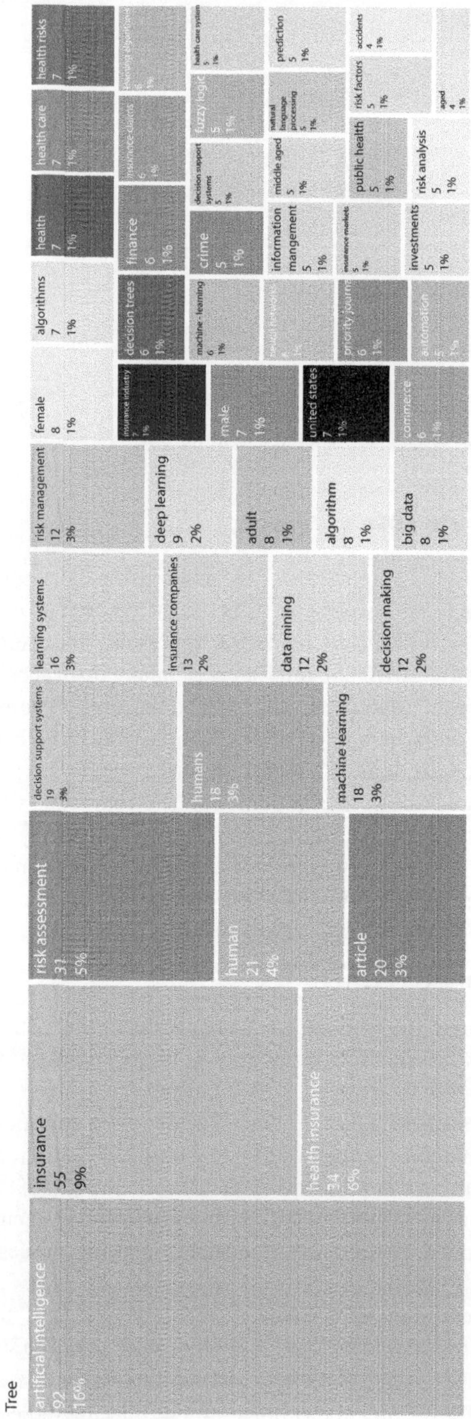

FIGURE 6.3 Tree plot. (Developed by Author.)

Other important fields: In addition, the tree plot also showed other category of research areas that are explored by the insurance researchers. It mainly includes "deep learning" (2%), "risk assessment" (6%), "insurance claim" (1%), and "insurance fraud detection" (1%). These findings reveal that scientists are investigating different AI methods apart from ML such as deep learning (DL) for diverse insurance applications including risk evaluation, claims processing, and fraud detection.

6.4 THEMATIC MAP ANALYSIS

In Figure 6.4, a thematic map depicts the key research area on AI and its application in the insurance industry. The thematic map is a two-dimensional plot, and the dimensions are relevance (centrality) and development (density).

- **Relevance (Centrality):** The relevance is the indicator that explains how the theme is central in the specified research field. Higher centrality signifies the theme fundamental that has many connections with other research areas.
- **Development (Density):** The development reflects how well the theme is developed; to assess whether the theme is developed, the parameters such as the number of publications or the internal links between the keywords within that theme are used.

Based on these dimensions, the application of AI research insurance industry is categorized into four quadrants:

- **Motor themes:** Motor theme is a theme that has high centrality and high density. The topics under this theme are well-developed and crucial topics within the research field. In this diagram, the term "health insurance" is a motor theme, suggesting that it is a mature area of study with significant research activity and it is central to the domain of AI in insurance.
- **Niche themes:** Niche theme is about high density but low centrality. These are specialized, well-developed topics that are not central to the field. They

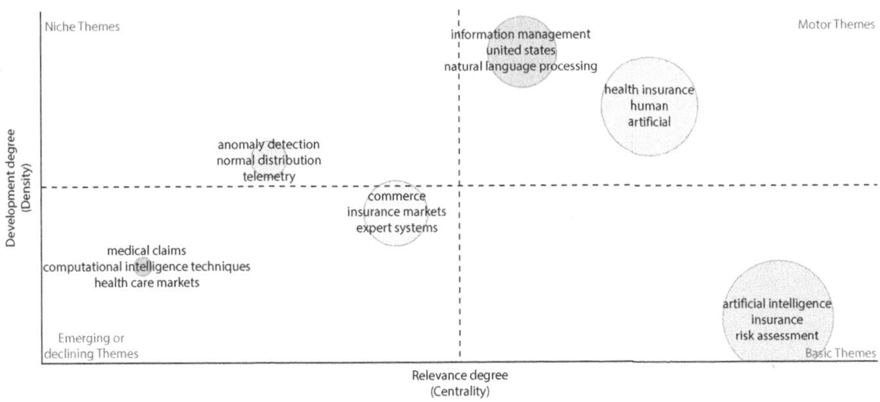

FIGURE 6.4 Thematic map. (Developed by Author.)

might be emerging or declining areas of research or specialized niches. Here, terms like "anomaly detection" and "telemetry" fall into this category, indicating that while they are developed topics, they are not as central to the AI in insurance research theme.

- **Basic themes**: Basic themes are about high centrality but low density. These are fundamental to the research field but not as well-developed. They often represent the foundational concepts upon which the field is built. In your diagram, "artificial intelligence," "insurance," and "risk assessment" are basic themes, indicating that they are central concepts with wide-ranging connections to other research areas but are perhaps not as deeply explored as motor themes.
- **Emerging or declining themes:** These are about low centrality and low density. These might be either new areas of research that are just starting to develop or old ones that are losing relevance. "Medical claims," "computational intelligence techniques," and "healthcare markets" are in this quadrant, which may suggest that these are newer or less explored in the context of AI in insurance.

6.5 WORD CLOUD ANALYSIS

In Figure 6.5, word cloud of the bibliometric data on the theme of AI application in insurance analysis covers various aspects of AI in insurance, with particular emphasis on risk assessment and health insurance. It also touches upon the human element and specific AI techniques such as ML and DL. The presence of terms like "decision support systems" hints at the practical applications of AI in facilitating decision-making processes in the insurance sector. Overall, the word cloud suggests that AI is having a significant impact on the insurance industry, and that there is a growing body of research on this topic.

6.6 CO-WORD ANALYSIS

Figure 6.6 depicts a network visualization from a co-word analysis that identifies and analyzes the relationships between different concepts within a body of literature. Furthermore, the co-word analysis revealed four significant clusters of keywords.

FIGURE 6.5 Word cloud. (Developed by Author.)

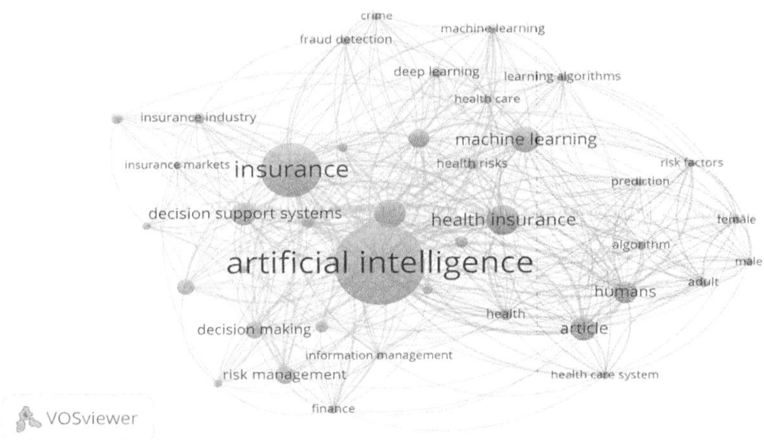

FIGURE 6.6 Co-word analysis. (Developed by Author.)

The co-word analysis facilitates the identification of the research focus of those articles. Using keyword and the identified research focus, each cluster is named that indicate the focus of the research theme of those articles. Additionally, using the keyword and the identified research focus, we have prepared the composite conceptual framework (Figure 6.7) that depicts the key focus of the research in the insurance industry using AI.

6.7 CONCEPTUAL FRAMEWORK DISCUSSION

6.7.1 AI-Driven Innovations in Insurance and Actuarial Sciences

AI-driven innovations in insurance and actuarial sciences are revolutionizing the industry by improving efficiency, accuracy, and customer experience. Insurers are leveraging AI technologies such as ML, big data analysis, and predictive modeling to enhance various aspects of their operations. These include data preparation and analysis for reinsurance treaties (Sriram et al. 2022), claims processing and settlement through image recognition and language processing (Sriram et al. 2022), which also enables personalized insurance services, precise marketing, and one-click and underwriting processes with AI-based risk intelligence models (Richman 2021). The integration of AI in insurance reporting for policyholders (Richman 2021). Explainable AI (XAI) models are being used to ensure transparency and understandability in the relationship between humans and machines, particularly in claims management, underwriting, and actuarial pricing practices (Richman 2021). These advancements in AI-driven technologies are transforming the insurance industry, improving risk assessment, decision-making, and overall risk management.

Integrative applications of AI in risk and healthcare finance can transform risk and healthcare finance sector (Ahanin et al. 2022). AI is being implemented in order to create intelligent tools, which are capable of solving real-world problems and increasing customer satisfaction in the insurance industry. ML such as neuro

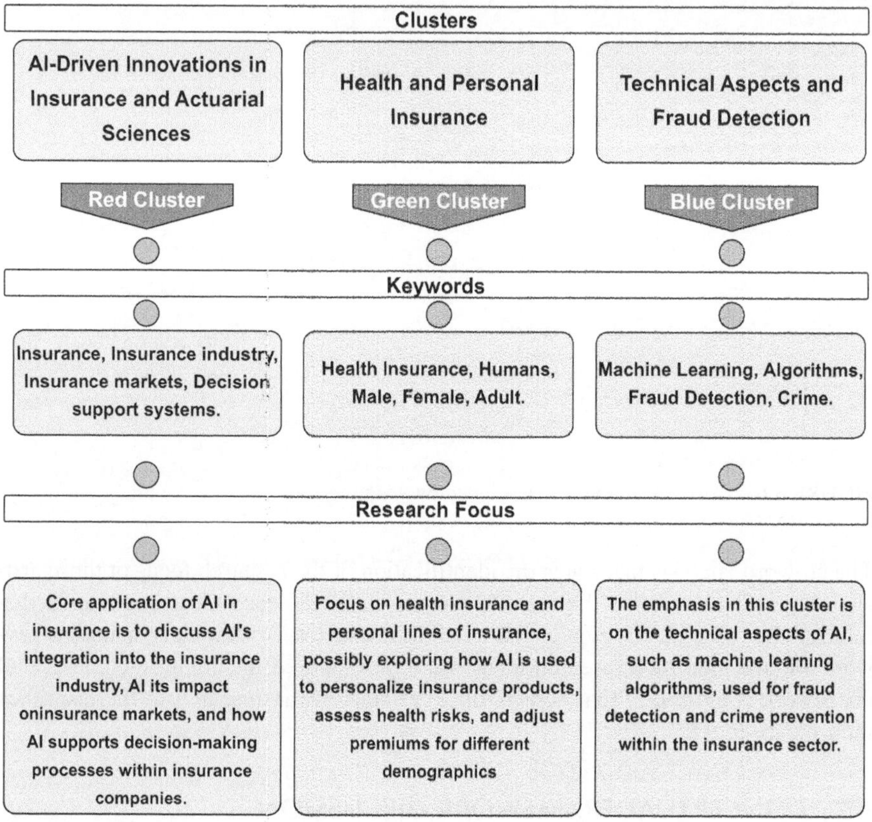

FIGURE 6.7 Conceptual framework. (Developed by Author.)

computing, fuzzy logic, and genetic computing can be used to classify medical, genomic data and also can be utilized for predicting the status of disease in the medical field and also in the education domain. Additionally, it can be employed for spotting the risk at students in the college or a school (Manne et al. 2020). Moreover, taking on AI models in healthcare delivery also brings new vulnerabilities, including ethical conflict, and data re-use consent (Banja 2020). The Holistic AI in Medicine (HAIM) framework using multiple inputs has been very successful in healthcare sector and it has great potential in performance and accuracy (Darwiesh et al. 2022, Sai et al. 2022), and this model can be used for the development of future multimodal predictive system for clinical or operational healthcare.

6.7.2 Health and Personal Insurance

AI and ML have significantly impacted the health and personal insurance industry. Insurers are using AI technologies to improve various processes such as sales, underwriting, and claims, as well as to evolve into wellness and lifestyle partners in life (Samiuddin et al., 2023). AI and DL techniques have been employed to predict and identify ailments, enabling insurers to provide accurate and efficient health insurance coverage (Jaiswal 2023). ML algorithms, such as multiple linear regression and random forest, have been used to predict the cost of health insurance, and XAI techniques like LIME and SHAP have been applied to provide explanations for the predicted results. The application of AI in the insurance industry, including healthcare companies, aims to enhance customer satisfaction and improve financial performance and market capitalization (Dutt 2020).

6.7.3 Technical Aspects and Fraud Detection in Insurance through AI

Insurance fraud detection is one of the important concerns that have to be addressed considering the repercussion it costs in terms of financial and reputational loss. Data analytics, ML, and AI have been suggested as techniques to work on this problem. In the healthcare sector, Sequential Forward Selection (SFS) and SMOTE oversampling have been used for fraudulent activities detection using K-Nearest Neighbors (KNN), Artificial Neural Network (ANN), and Gradient Boosting Machine (GBM) as classifiers (Malakar et al. 2023). A chaotic variational auto encoder (C-VAE) has been applied in certain situations to detect fake health and car insurance information. On top of that, fraud detection in auto insurance cases has been enhanced by combining NLP with computer vision techniques to analyze multi-modal datasets (Gangadhar et al. 2022). AI and analytics offer tools and techniques to facilitate the insurance fraud detection and safeguard the interests of the customers.

6.8 CONCLUSION AND FURTHER RESEARCH AGENDA

This study, being a bibliometric analysis of AI applications in insurance, has provided a very deep insight into the influence of AI over the various areas of the insurance sector. The present study highlights pace within which the insurance industry is capitalizing on AI technology and rapidly changing the insurance sector. We use bibliometric analysis approach to synthesize the present status of research on AI application in the insurance sector. The study has identified the important areas where AI technology is integrated in insurance operations. It mainly includes the integration of AI into claims processing, personalized policies, predictive analytics for risk assessment, and chatbots for improved customer service. These new steps more clearly signal the industry's direction toward leaner, much more consumer-responsive solutions.

Notably, the analysis highlights large obstacles to the use of AI in insurance. Such issues range from the moral dilemmas surrounding how data is used for the requirement of suites of cybersecurity measures to safeguard sensitive data to keep up with the many variations of regulations when operating in an increasingly digital environment. Second, attaining both domain expertise in insurance and also expertise in the appropriate advanced technological solutions used in both the practices; the absence of these elements would make a probable digital transformation a very daunting challenge, once again a case where the curriculum and practices of current and future workforce education and training play a key role on the agenda.

Looking ahead, the study outlines a number of directions for future research. There is a need to study the socio-economic impact of AI technology in the insurance industry. Further, there is a need to study how AI integration will affect the employment generation in the insurance sector. Furthermore, these should be more detailed exploration of the ethical frameworks and guidelines that need to be developed to regulate AI applications within insurance so that these innovations are implemented ethically and responsibly in the interests of all stakeholders. Lastly, given the rapidly changing nature of technology, continuous research will also be needed to track new AI technologies that may be coming around the corner, as well as the potential industry responses to them, in order to provide an insurer a competitive edge in a digital-first world.

This bibliometric analysis shows how AI technology is agile in altering the insurance industry that results in achieving improved operating effectiveness and better service delivery. Hence, AI integration in the insurance industry will not only provide a competitive edge but also will enable tackling of increased risk and environment challenges. Nevertheless, such potential can be realized only if its drawbacks are overcome by means of innovation, ethical implication, and regulation. When considering such an omnipresence of AI applications in the insurance industry, there are ample amount of further research into the possibilities for integrating AI in the insurance industry that benefits insurers, policyholders, and society at large.

REFERENCES

Ahanin, Elaheh, Abu Bakar Sade, and Huam Hon Tat. "Applications of artificial intelligence and voice assistant in healthcare." *International Journal of Academic Research in Business & Social Sciences* 12 (2022). https://doi.org/10.6007/ijarbss/v12-i12/16048

Alam, Ashrafe, and Victor R. Prybutok. "Use of responsible artificial intelligence to predict health insurance claims in the USA using machine learning algorithms." *Exploration of Digital Health Technologies* 2, no. 1 (2024): 30–45. https://doi.org/10.37349/edht.2024.00009

Alotaibi, Eid Mohammed. "Risk assessment using predictive analytics." *International Journal of Professional Business Review* 8, no. 5 (2023): e01723–e01723.

Banja, John. "How might artificial intelligence applications impact risk management?" *AMA Journal of Ethics* 22, no. 11 (2020): 945–951.

Christopoulos, Athanasios, Guido Coppo, Salvatore Andolina, Simone Lo Priore, Dario Antonelli, DimitriosSalmas, ChrysostomosStylios, and Mikko-Jussi Laakso. "Transformation of robotics education in the era of covid-19: challenges and opportunities." *IFAC-Papers Online* 55, no. 10 (2022): 2908–2913.

Darwiesh, Abdelaziz, A. H. El-Baz, Abedallah Zaid Abualkishik, and Mohamed Elhoseny. "Artificial intelligence model for risk management in healthcare institutions: towards sustainable development." *Sustainability* 15, no. 1 (2022): 420.

Dutt, Rajeev. "The impact of artificial intelligence on healthcare insurances." In Rajeev Dutt (Ed.), *Artificial intelligence in healthcare*, pp. 271–293. Academic Press, 2020.

Eling, Martin, Davide Nuessle, and Julian Staubli. "The impact of artificial intelligence along the insurance value chain and on the insurability of risks." *The Geneva Papers on Risk and Insurance-Issues and Practice* 47, no. 2 (2022): 205–241.

Gangadhar, K. S. N. V. K., B. Akhil Kumar, Yelleti Vivek, and Vadlamani Ravi. "Chaotic variational auto encoder based one class classifier for insurance fraud detection." arXiv preprint arXiv:2212.07802 (2022).

Han, Yi, Jinhao Chen, Meitao Dou, Jiahong Wang, and Kangxiao Feng. "The impact of artificial intelligence on the financial services industry." *Academic Journal of Management and Social Sciences* 2, no. 3 (2023): 83–85.

Jaiswal, Ravi. "Impact of AI in the general insurance underwriting factors." *CEMJP* 31, no. 2 (2023): 697–705.

Li, Chia-Ying, and Jin-Ting Zhang. "Chatbots or me? Consumers' switching between human agents and conversational agents." *Journal of Retailing and Consumer Services* 72 (2023): 103264.

Malakar, Madhuri, Bidisha Bhabani, and Judhistir Mahapatro. "NS3-based performance assessment of routing protocols AODV, OLSR and DSDV for VANETs." In *Advances in Distributed Computing and Machine Learning: Proceedings of ICADCML 2023*, National Institute of Technology, Rourkela, Odisha, India, 15–16 Jan 2023, pp. 1–14. Singapore: Springer Nature Singapore, 2023.

Manne, Ravi, Snigdha Kantheti, and Sneha Kantheti. "Classification of skin cancer using deep learning, convolutional neural networks-opportunities and vulnerabilities—A systematic review." *International Journal for Modern Trends in Science and Technology* 6 (2020): 2455–3778.

Mashrur, Akib, et al. "Machine learning for financial risk management: A survey." *IEEE Access* 8 (2020): 203203–203223. https://doi.org/10.1109/ACCESS.2020.3036322

Miranda, Oshin, Peihao Fan, Xiguang Qi, Haohan Wang, M. Daniel Brannock, Thomas R. Kosten, Neal David Ryan, Levent Kirisci, and Lirong Wang. "DeepBiomarker2: Prediction of alcohol and substance use disorder risk in post-traumatic stress disorder patients using electronic medical records and multiple social determinants of health." *Journal of Personalized Medicine* 14, no. 1 (2024): 94.

Richman, Ronald. "AI in actuarial science—A review of recent advances–part 1." *Annals of Actuarial Science* 15, no. 2 (2021): 207–229.

Rukhsar, Laiqa, Waqas Haider Bangyal, Kashif Nisar, and Sana Nisar. "Prediction of insurance fraud detection using machine learning algorithms." *Mehran University Research Journal of Engineering & Technology* 41, no. 1 (2022): 33–40

Sai, Siva, Vinay Chamola, Kim-Kwang Raymond Choo, Biplab Sikdar, and Joel J. P. C. Rodrigues. "Confluence of blockchain and artificial intelligence technologies for secure and scalable healthcare solutions: A review." *IEEE Internet of Things Journal* 10, no. 7 (2022): 5873–5897.

Samiuddin, Md., G. Rajender, K. Sai Abhiram Varma, A. Ravi Kumar, and Subhani Shaik. "Health insurance cost prediction using deep neural network." *Asian Journal of Research in Computer Science* 16, no. 2 (2023): 46–53.

Soori, Mohsen, BehroozArezoo, and RozaDastres. "Artificial intelligence, machine learning and deep learning in advanced robotics, a review." *Cognitive Robotics* 3 (2023): 54–70.

Sriram, V., Z. Fan, N. Liu, "ECLIPSE: Holistic AI system for preparing insurer policy data." *Risks* 11, 4, 2023. https://doi.org/10.3390/risks11010004.

Sriram, Varun, Zijie Fan, and Ni Liu. "Eclipse: Holistic ai system for preparing insurer policy data." *Risks* 11, no. 1 (2022): 4.

Wamba-Taguimdje, Serge-Lopez, Samuel Fosso Wamba, Jean Robert Kala Kamdjoug, and Chris Emmanuel Tchatchouang Wanko. "Influence of artificial intelligence (AI) on firm performance: The business value of AI-based transformation projects." *Business Process Management Journal* 26, no. 7 (2020): 1893–1924.

7 Examining the Factors Influencing AI Adoption in the Insurance Industry Specifically in Actuarial Process

Arwin Sandesh D'Souza, Daksha Malagatti, Ravi Prakash Bylappa, and Rama Moorthy Hejamdi

7.1 MEANING OF ACTUARIAL SCIENCE

Actuarial science is the study of the certainty or uncertainty of a natural event by using statistical and mathematical models as well as the assessment of the degree of risks in order to control the intensity of monetary losses to either client or the company by formulating different policies.

Actuarial science is mainly used to calculate the future financial impact of an uncertain event. Actuarial science is used to create models for real-world problems and to consider the events that are happening, can happen, or might happen, and it tries to analyze the risk associated with the aforesaid event. Actuarial science is useful in measuring, managing, and understanding the risks at present as well as the risks in future.

Complex problems related to risk management are solved, assessed, and predicted, and the monetary impact of these problems is evaluated using the concept of actuarial science.

Insurance companies predict the probability of the uncertain event and estimate the amount that needs to be provided as claims to their customers by using tools and techniques of actuarial science.

Usually, actuarial science is associated with insurance and finance, but it is not limited to one single field. The application of actuarial science is endless since most events in the world are part of a probabilistic and deterministic system.

Actuarial science derives its main concepts from the fields of statistics, economics, mathematics, finance, accounts, and computer science. Actuarial science also benefits from any advancements in the aforementioned fields as well.

DOI: 10.1201/9781003472551-9

Actuarial science rose to prominence in the 17th century. When it was introduced, it was a part of mathematics discipline. The 17th century saw a rise in the insurance sector, hence the process of calculation of risks associated with providing insurance also found its own significance.

Actuarial science has developed and grown in importance in the past few decades due to the improvements in technology of data storage and analysis, dynamic development of financial theories and models, as well as steady and massive increments of development in information technology.

Different kinds of risks are evaluated in actuarial science:

- **Financial risks**: Risks associated with finance.
  - **Credit risk:** Risk of defaulting of one of the parties to a contract in discharging or fulfilling financial obligations.
  - **Market risk:** Risk of losing money in an investment because of various events which take place in the external business environment. Most of the factors which are impactful in market risks are beyond the control of individuals and corporations. For example, economic policies, changes in interest rates, fluctuation in exchange rates, and uncertain events like terrorist attacks or a global pandemic.
- **Insurance risks:** Risks associated with insurance.
  - **Trade risk:** Risk of defaulting by the proposer of the insurance on premium payments.
  - **Technical life risk:** Risk of death or survival of the proposer of the insurance.
  - **Morbidity risk:** Risk of disability and health of the proposer of the insurance.
  - **Non-life risk:** Automobile, home, and casualty risks.

Far more important is the mean risk. This refers to the sum of all possible operating losses, each multiplied by their probabilities. This definition is well defined, permits no uncertainty, and can be used to compute the mean risk for a given insurance portfolio (Sherris 2006).

7.2 ARTIFICIAL INTELLIGENCE IN ACTUARIAL SCIENCE

Artificial intelligence (AI) has revolutionized numerous industries, which include actuarial technological know-how, with the aid of enhancing methods and enabling extra accurate danger evaluation strategies. Actuarial technology is often used to study economic risks and uncertainties using mathematical and statistical techniques. Machine learning, a subset of AI, has observed substantial software in this domain, imparting sophisticated algorithms that expect destiny occasions, determine risks, and optimize selection-making tactics.

One of the fundamental packages of AI in actuarial technological know-how is in risk assessment. Traditional actuarial methods rely heavily on ancient statistics and statistical fashions to estimate future dangers. However, device mastering strategies increase those strategies by studying enormous datasets more effectively and identifying complicated styles that won't be apparent via conventional analysis.

Machine gaining knowledge of algorithms, which include neural networks, selection bushes, and random forests, can process massive volumes of structured and unstructured statistics to identify correlations and trends. In risk evaluation, these algorithms can forecast historical claims facts, demographic statistical data, marketplace trends, and different relevant elements to expect the chance of future events, which include insurance claims, mortality charges, or funding returns. As an example, in insurance, system mastering fashions can anticipate policyholder statistics to examine the hazard of future claims primarily based on diverse hazard factors which include age, level of fitness, occupation, and lifestyle patterns. By using these predictions, insurers are able to alter their rates, ensure that they are competitive in the market, and sufficiently address resource issues.

In addition, tools acquire strategic knowledge to enhance risk categorization. Subgroups within a population are determined with identical risk profiles. This categorization allows insurers to customize their products and pricing techniques to better meet client's satisfaction. Furthermore, it responds to the demands of different categories of customers, ultimately increasing the profitability and pride of the clients. Additionally, enhanced AI-powered predictive analytics can benefit actuaries become more informed. Emerging risks like cybersecurity threats and weather-related business incidents are evaluated. Machine learning can be sued by analyzing enormous datasets and integrating real-time statistics. This approach can provide early risks about capacity risks and provide it to insurance firms and financial institutions, an organization that quickly counters and manages these types of hazards.

Another important use of AI in actuarial technology is fraud detection. Insurance fraud damages a massive economic burden on the enterprise, costing billions of greenbacks yearly. Algorithms for device monitoring can scan claim data for patterns that reveal anomalies or questionable activity, which could be signs of fraud. Those algorithms can flag possibly fraudulent claims for further investigation, assisting insurers reduce losses and hold the integrity of their operations. Moreover, AI can improve the performance of actuarial methods by automating repetitive tasks and reducing the reliance on manual calculations. As an example, machine learning algorithms can streamline underwriting strategies by evaluating applicant information and providing guidelines for hazard evaluation and pricing decisions. In addition, AI-powered tools can streamline actuaries in portfolio optimization, manage asset-liability and capital allocation, and allow extra informed and timely preference-making.

Despite the numerous advantages that AI offers to actuarial technology, many challenges need to be solved. One of the major challenges is this Interpretability of Machine Learning Capabilities. Although these models may provide precise data, the fundamental elements of using those predictions remain. Actuaries can make educational decisions and comply with regulatory requirements. Additionally, records satisfactory and privateness worries are important issues in leveraging AI for hazard evaluation. Actuaries ought to make sure the accuracy, reliability, and privacy of the information used to teach device getting to know fashions to avoid biased outcomes or unauthorized get right of entry to touchy statistics (Embrechts and Wüthrich 2022).

Basic principles and methods are very important for managing uncertainty and making informed decisions in these areas. This facility plays an important role in ensuring the financial stability of insurance companies, pension funds, and other organizations facing risk.

At the core of scientific analysis is the analysis of uncertain future events and their financial consequences.

The principle of risk sharing is a basic tenet of actuarial analysis. Insurance works by spreading risk over many insured individuals. Premiums are decided by actuaries, who do so based on the insured person's needs, such as age, gender, health status, and past risk experience. By risk pooling, insurance companies are both able to enhance their financial stability and enlarge their revenues, while also offering financial security for the policyholders in the case of unexpected events.

In addition to assessing risks, workers also help in managing debts and assets. ALM is making sure that an organization's assets match its debts to pay what it owes. In the insurance sectors, this means maintaining the equilibrium between resources and what they need to pay for insurance strategies and benefits to those who are insured. Actuaries use tools like financial plans and risk evaluations to make investment strategies. These strategies evaluate about things like how much money can be made from investments, income, and policy.

Financial liabilities and assets measurement are additional aspects of actuarial science. Estimating the fair value of insurance policies, pension liabilities, and other financial obligations falls under the responsibilities of actuaries. Predicting the upcoming financial circumstances, minimizing them to their current value, and taking into account a variety of risks, including inflation, mortality, and behavior, are all part of this procedure. For insurer and pension companies to comply with regulations and make wise decisions, precise measurement is crucial to their financial reporting.

Actuarial science is a combination of statistics, computer science, economics, and finance. Managing risk is an important task for employees. They assist businesses in identifying, assessing, and reducing the risks associated with the finances, daily activities, and business risks. Actuaries evaluate risk, generate plans to reduce the risk, and make informed choices to benefit the entire firm by employing mathematical models and statistics. Actuaries must have strong analytical skills, critical thinking skills, and a deep understanding of theory to be effective in assessing and managing risk in a complex and uncertain environment (Pathnaik et al. 2024).

7.3 APPLICATION AND CASE STUDIES FROM FINANCE AND INSURANCE

According to a broad understanding of actuarial science, some fields in finance and insurance have been identified, which can immensely benefit from the application of AI to it. They are:

7.3.1 Underwriting

The process of evaluating the risk profile of the proposer of the insurance as well as evaluating the risk profile of an asset is called underwriting. Underwriting is done at multiple levels; the first portion of underwriting and the most primary one is done on-site by the agent. Later on, the underwriting is approved by higher officers in the department.

Most types of life insurance require an estimate of expected lifetime of an individual at the time of application. This is referred to as mortality risk, and the process of collecting and analyzing data that describes such risk is known as underwriting (Maier et al. 2019).

Various information is collected during this process. Some of the information that are collected are listed below:

- Age group
- Gender
- Medical background
- Family illness history
- Lifestyle
- Geographical location

For finance sector, the information collected are

- Creditworthiness
- Financial stability
- Ability to repay
- Value of collateral asset

After proving the authenticity of the risk analysis, the terms and conditions associated with the contract are decided accordingly. In insurance, the terms generally refer to the premium payments and the duration of these payments as well as the type of payment.

If the underwriting process is accurate, it reduces the financial burden to the insurance companies or lenders. However, if the underwriting process is factually incorrect or flawed, then it can potentially create a lot of financial damage to the company (Figure 7.1).

AI can be useful in providing supplementary information as well as additional indicators to assist in estimation of the risk for the underwriter. AI also requires datasets to be precise, and pre-existing data sets based on previous underwritings can be used to analyze and create a system for providing suggestions, as well as create an early detection and warning system to flag high risk proposals.

AI can also help in providing precise plans based on the exact risk assessment of proposers of insurance. This can result in ultra-customization of plans that are specifically tailored with the variables of individual users.

AI can also be used to provide customer support and collect feedback as customer support in insurance holds a very high importance. An AI-assisted customer support

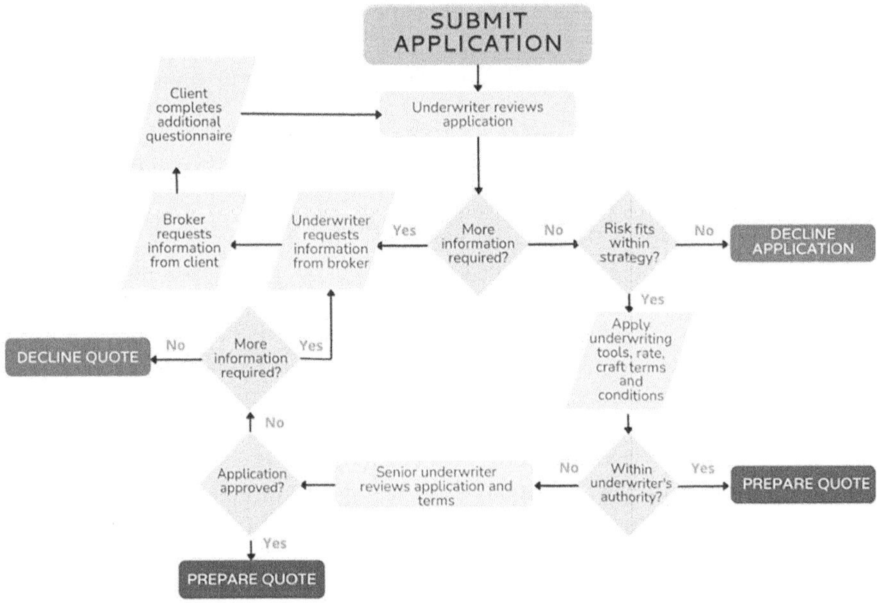

FIGURE 7.1 Flowchart for underwriting process. (Insurance training center.)

center will be more impactful in dealing with the doubts put forth by the customers and to deal with the feedback of the customers to bring in improvement to the system as well.

7.3.2 Case of Underwriting in India

In India, there are various parameters that need to be followed in order to efficiently proceed with the underwriting process. Different insurance companies have different processes, but the underlying essence still remains the same. The amount of information that needs to be collected from the proposer of the insurance is immense, whether the data is for life insurance, vehicle insurance, or health insurance.

The data that need to be collected by underwriters are then verified by their superior officers as the secondary underwriter. Only after this process can the insurance move ahead. There are various court cases regarding underwriting, which provide valuable insights into where AI can play a role.

7.3.3 Some Examples of These Cases

Case of Mr Hemanthkumar N Vasra v/s Reliance Nippon Life Insurance Co. Ltd. Ref no. AHD-L-036-1718-0086.

In this case, the customer had been insured for a sum of 742,500. The insured had failed to disclose the material facts during the underwriting process. The insured had taken treatment for diabetes as well as ischemic heart complications prior to taking the policy.

The court ruled in the favor of Reliance Nippon life insurance, and the insurance claim was repudiated.

Case of Reliance life insurance limited v/s Rekhaben Nareshbhai Rathod (2019) civil appeal 4261/2009.

In this case, the insured had taken policy by Max New York life insurance for a sum assured of 1,10,000 in the year 2009. During the same year, the insured had enquired with Reliance Life Insurance Limited for a sum insured of 1,00,000. During the underwriting process with Reliance Insurance Limited, the insured had not disclosed the fact about the previously held policy. The insured also agreed to cancel the contract and to forfeit the premium already paid in case the information provided was found to be untrue.

The insured died on 2010, and the dependent of insured filed an application for the insurance claim. On investigation, it was found that the claimant had an already existing policy with Max New York life insurance. The claim to insurance as well as the premium paid were repudiated, and the court ruled in favor of Reliance life insurance.

Case of Sushila Indravadan Gandhi and Anr. vs New India Assurance Co. Ltd. and others (2020).

In this case, a doctor died due to negligence of the ambulance driver. The issue was not with the claim, but rather with the interpretation of whether the doctor worked with the hospital or worked for the hospital. This distinction can make a difference on whether the insurance company is liable to paying the claim or not.

The judgment was in favor of the nominee of the deceased, and the claim was honored. As we can see with the above cases, the underwriting process is very complicated and needs meticulous focus and attention. An AI system that can act as supplementary information provider to the underwriter and help with risk analysis can be very useful in this scenario.

7.3.4 Classification of Risks

An actuary has to analyze multiple number of risks. Both insurance risks and market risks are considered by an actuary in his/her own capacities. However, while dealing with a specific problem, the point of failure has to be prioritized. Every risk can be categorized based on the likelihood of its occurrence as well as the impact of its occurrence. Identification of internal and external risks and being able to categorize risks on the basis of the likelihood of the risk impacting the investment is one of the functions of an actuary.

Classification of risks is done by actuaries on the basis of what they have been trained in and with the guidance of their superior officers, as well as some industry standards. Introduction of AI to this context would make the process of classification not only simpler but also more accurate. Risk classification on the basis of hard evidence by the AI models can also prove useful in the following circumstances.

In the future, actuaries may not be called on often to "predict" because the machines will have already done so. What will become more valuable is what is done with that prediction (Curtis 2020).

7.3.5 Fraud Detection

Fraud is one among the many possible sources of damage to the firm or a company, which lends or insures a property or life. But fraud is also one of the complicated issues for a company to resolve. The early detection of fraud can come off as doubting the customer, and this can cost heavily if the doubts are unfounded. These issues can cost the company as well as the trust of the consumer if not handled properly. On the other hand, being too lenient with the customer with a detection system might lead to an increase in the number of frauds happening. Deloitte's insurance fraud survey of 2023 revealed that insurance companies in India have experienced a rise in instances of fraud within the life and health insurance categories.

An AI system that could model behaviors and risks could be very helpful in this scenario to warn the company of an impending fraud or the likelihood of the consumer to be a part of a fraud.

By developing a data-based classification function that can be applied to existing and new claims, fraud examiners can continuously and automatically monitor fraud levels (which is useful because of the huge number of claims files daily) and signal suspicious claims as they come in (Ai et al. 2009).

There are a few cases in the Indian context that have been brought to the court where the presence of AI could make a difference. Some of these frauds include:

- Application fraud
- Claims fraud
- Forgery
- Phony policy fraud
- Identity theft

7.3.6 Case Studies for Fraud and Categorizing Risks

After interviewing an insurance officer from a reputed insurance company in India, we were able to gather some insights about the frauds that used to happen in the insurance system. One claimant had made 3 different policies for his father from different branches of the same company and claimed the insurance money. The insurance company had to visit and gain some information from the claimant about some other issue, where it was found out that the father was still alive and healthy.

While talking to an agent, it was the father himself who asked the agent to see how his other 3 insurance schemes were doing. Later, the agent while going through the system recognized that the claim has been collected and the presumed dead person was the one who spoke with the agent.

The company was able to catch hold of the fraudster. Due to improvements in technology and centralization of data, this fraud is not possible for anyone to do anymore, but it does provide a window into how loopholes can be found in a system with a huge repository of data.

7.3.7 Categorize Risk and Pricing Details of Premiums

To categorize risk and create a pricing of the premiums is also another function of the actuary. The majority of the time, this is done by using the company guidelines as a reference to categorize risk and have a pricing detail for the premium.

The system used for pricing is very similar to bundle pricing where an entire bundle is sold off at a pre-allotted price. The pricing model does not allow for variability in customization. AI can be used in this particular context to create tailor-made customization of pricing of premiums as well as to categorize risks with more accuracy and efficiency.

There have been various cases in India where the customer insures an asset and then intentionally damages it to claim the insurance. These kinds of instances are referred to as fabricated accidents. This usually occurs in circumstances involving business where the sum promised does not hold good anymore or the created product lacks in quality. Suppression of material facts regarding the type of damage to the asset that has occurred usually gets revealed later during the litigation or enquiry process.

There are also instances where hospitals are involved in reframing the cost of the procedure in order to claim more insurance amount from the companies. An AI system that could act as an early detection system to catch these discrepancies and warn the higher officials, as well as act as a support system for decision-making for field agents that could highlight the likelihood of occurrence of problems, would be very impactful in this area.

7.3.8 Asset and Investment Models

Insurance companies will collect premium from their customers from various types of plans. The plans might be for life, accident, vehicle, marine, general, health, etc. This will result in an accumulation of funds in the hands of the insurance companies. Now the responsibility of utilizing these funds, investing them, and diversifying the portfolio to maximize the returns in order to both make a profit margin as well as provide coverage to the claims lies in the hands of actuaries.

Without an actuary and without the knowledge possessed by an actuary, the insurance companies would not be able to efficiently handle the risks involved and fail to provide financial stability to both their customers as well as their assets. Actuaries use statistical models to summarize micro-level data, which subsequently need to be interpreted properly for financial decision-making (Frees et al. 2009).

Actuaries not only have to be well versed in the field of insurance and risk analysis for creation of pricing of premiums and claims, but they also have to be very knowledgeable in the field of finance. Most importantly with regard to investment avenues, their role is critical. Financial modeling, financial forecasting, capital budgeting decision-making, corporate restructuring, raising of funds through different sources or avenues, dividend policies and dividend decisions, and hedging techniques are all major functions of an actuary in the field of finance. They are also required to analyze the financial stability and performance of a business organization. These functions are completed by using statistical tools and complex models.

With the above list of functions associated with actuaries, it becomes quite apparent how important the role of an actuary is for an insurance company. A provision of an AI cannot replace an actuary, but it can help provide various parameters which help in decision-making for the actuary and provide relevant details and calculations so that the actuary can focus on the crucial matters that affect the company.

7.3.9 Insolvency and Projected Liabilities

Insolvency is the state of incapacity of the individual or a company to repay the debt taken. Insolvency can affect an insurance-based entity or a financial entity in a variety of ways.

The firm that the insurance company has invested in can become bankrupt which in turn makes it incapable of producing returns for the insurance company. Or the other scenario where an insurance company has to deal with insolvency is when a client, whether individual or a company, is unable or unwilling to pay the premiums which were decided as per the terms of the contract of insurance. This is when the projected liability becomes risky, increasing financial burden on the insurance company.

The period for payment of premiums is set by insurance companies. The insurance companies are also expected to provide a grace period in order to provide for payments in case of defaults in payments. If the premiums have not been paid at all in the span of 3 consecutive years since the beginning of the policy, then the insurance contract becomes void with immediate effect.

It is left to the discretion of insurance companies whether they want to provide a clause within the contract for reviving policies within specified periods with the payment of pending premiums.

If the customer is not able to pay the premiums even after 3 years and the period allotted for revival of the insurance, then the insurance contract is terminated and the policyholder is provided the surrender value.

The insurance companies can still provide opportunities for re-insurance by including penalties, new medical check-ups, applying charges and fines, etc.

The reason why insurance companies provide so many opportunities for non-payment of premiums is because it is much easier to maintain an older customer and onboard the older customer onto new plans and choices, while the same is difficult for new customers (Grosen and Jørgensen 2016) .

An AI system that could provide the associated risks based on history and personality of the customer or even a statistical model of a company to understand the acceptance the risks associated with investing into it can be very impactful in the field of actuarial science. As actuarial analysis and evaluation is a time-consuming, complex, and error-prone process, it can be improved or enhanced considerably by automated reasoning (Zhou & Ashby 2009).

7.3.10 Pension

The amount of money that is paid to an employee in the form of benefits at the time of retirement or after the time of retirement is called pension. There are two types of pensions:

- Defined contribution plan
- Defined benefit plan

7.3.10.1 Defined Contribution Plan

It is a plan where both the employer and the employee contribute a fixed amount of payment each month that is pooled and invested into the market by the use of various instruments based on risk tolerance of the employee. During the time of the retirement, the lumpsum amount is paid back to the employee.

Provident fund contribution is the best example for Defined contribution plan in India.

In this type of plan, the employer does not assume much amount of risk.

7.3.10.2 Defined Benefit Plan

A Defined Benefit Plan is however different from defined contribution plan in the sense that the employer promises or guarantees the employee a fixed amount of lumpsum at the end of the duration of the career regardless of the market fluctuations and company conditions.

In this type of pension, the employer shoulders the majority portion of the risk. Gratuity is the best example for Defined Benefit Plan in India.

In designing the defined benefit plan, the role of an actuary is very important. By considering different factors of the employee like age, gender salary, expected retirement date or time, and expected return on pension plan investments, the actuary is able to predict how much amount is to be contributed by the employer to a specific fund to fulfil the obligations guaranteed to the employee in the form of pensions.

The main considerations that are looked at by the actuary in order to create a model for prediction of the status of the fund are:

- Funding ratio
- Mortality tables
- Investment strategy
- Actuarial assumptions

Funding ratio refers to the ratio which determines the amount of assets to the amount of liabilities of a defined plan. This ratio is used by the actuary to understand whether contributions made to the fund are accurate. The fund can either found to be underpaid or overpaid. If the fund is underpaid, then the employer has to push more contribution to the fund. However, if the fund is overpaid, then the employer can take a contribution holiday and not pay the fund for a limited period of time as it is performing well on its own (England and Verrall 2006).

Different countries have different frequencies at which an actuary gets consulted for analyzing the direct benefit plan. In general, the standard time frequency for an actuarial consultation is 3 years to assess the funding ratio.

Mortality tables are tables used to predict life expectancy. By using statistical tools and historical data in the context of pensions, the life expectancy of a pensioner after retirement is taken into consideration. Mortality tables can help the actuary to predict the duration for which the company has to pay the pensioner after retirement and calculate the obligation of the company to the collection of fund during the present.

Investment strategies refer to the strategies used by the employer and their ability to handle risks in long-term duration. The actuary has to not only understand the risk tolerance or risk averseness in the strategies used by the employer but also predict the outcomes of these risks in the volatile market. After calculating the risks involved, the actuary then has to recommend whether to increase or decrease contributions to the fund in order to fulfil the expected obligation.

The amount of additional funding needed to supplement the specified future contributions is called the "unfunded liability". The unfunded liability can change in a funding method, not because of any reassessment of what has happened in the past, but because different methods promise different contributions in the future (Ezra, 1980).

An actuary makes a few assumptions to estimate the performance of the pension plan in the future, and these assumptions are called actuarial assumptions. These assumptions are based on certain factors like expected rate of return of the fund, economic conditions like inflation rates and interest rates, increment in salary component of an employee, trends in government regulations, etc.

The actuary has to be aware of the risks involved in the market as well as the variations in life expectancies. The statistical models for these purposes can get extremely complicated and here is where AI can lift the weight off the shoulders of an actuary.

7.3.10.2.1 Awareness

According to the "Pre launch survey report of insurance awareness campaign" sponsored by IRDAI and NCAER and conducted under the leadership of Anushree Sinha, even though a majority of Indian households are good savers, they do not undertake financial planning and are financially at risk. Households need to understand the risk of both "living too long" and "dying too young" (Sinha 2016).

The survey had a sample size of 15,000 plus families in India, and it accurately depicts the amount of awareness about insurance among the insured and uninsured families in India. Awareness about Insurance, the importance of insurance, and the paperwork involved as well as the general workings of scheme is extremely beneficial to the general audience. It increases financial literacy, makes way for good decision-making, and well-educated and informed audiences can make economic ripples in the society.

Due to the sheer number of policies, insurance companies, and products that are available in the catalog for the audience to choose from, good choices are possible only if there is proper awareness. Even with proper awareness about policies, it's also important that the audience has awareness about what policies suit their needs the best.

TABLE 7.1
Distribution of Households Based on Their Concept of Insurance in Percentage

Concept of Insurance	Insured Households Rural	Insured Households Urban	Insured Households Total	Uninsured Households Rural	Uninsured Households Urban	Uninsured Households Total
Prevent certain events	31.5	30.7	3.1	25.9	25.0	25.3
Prevent damage to assets from certain events	34.2	37.6	35.9	24.3	26.9	25.8
Compensate for losses from certain events	43.5	48.1	45.7	29.4	33.5	31.8
Rebuild the asset lost due to certain events	20.8	20.4	20.6	12.9	14.6	13.9
Compensate for loss of life	51.7	50.9	51.3	38.3	42.1	40.5
Any other	5.2	8.5	6.8	3.8	6.7	5.6
Can't say	2.1	1.8	2.0	19.7	15.9	17.5
All	100.0	100.0	100.0	100.0	100.0	100.0
Number of households	11,301	10,866	22,167	3,237	4,774	8,011

Source: "Pre launch survey report of insurance awareness campaign" sponsored by IRDAI and NCAER.

TABLE 7.2
Relevance of Insurance to Households and Reasons in Percentage

Perception of the Relevance of Insurance	Insured Households Rural	Insured Households Urban	Insured Households Total	Uninsured Households Rural	Uninsured Households Urban	Uninsured Households Total
Households who feel insurance is relevant	97.0	97.5	97.2	54.0	59.6	57.3
Reasons for relevance						
Natural calamity	22.4	21.4	21.9	22.2	20.0	20.9
Crop failure	18.1	7.8	13.0	14.4	9.7	11.4
Accidents	68.1	67.3	67.7	64.8	63.5	64.0
Theft/burglary	10.6	10.3	10.5	8.4	8.6	8.5
Physical disability	8.8	9.9	9.3	8.9	8.8	8.8
Chronic illnesses	3.5	5.3	4.4	3.6	4.2	4.0
Economic burden of higher education	7.5	10.2	8.8	4.9	6.8	6.1
Untimely death	60.7	60.7	60.7	55.0	56.1	55.7
Investment	21.7	29.9	25.7	17.0	22.5	20.4
Tax benefits	8.0	11.6	9.7	1.3	2.6	2.1
Others	1.3	1.5	1.4	1.7	1.8	1.8
All	100.0	100.0	100.0	100.0	100.0	100.0

(Continued)

TABLE 7.2 (*Continued*)
Relevance of Insurance to Households and Reasons in Percentage

	Insured Households			Uninsured Households		
Perception of the Relevance of Insurance	**Rural**	**Urban**	**Total**	**Rural**	**Urban**	**Total**
Households who feel insurance is not relevant	0.8	0.7	0.8	17.9	18.8	18.5
	Reasons for not being relevant					
Enjoy the present instead of securing the future	0.0	0.0	0.0	47.4	41.5	43.8
Companies swallow hard earned money	0.0	0.0	0.0	46.7	42.4	44.1
Don't feel the need	0.0	0.0	0.0	88.7	79.6	83.2
Others	0.0	0.0	0.0	21.4	19.9	20.5
Households who can't say/don't know whether insurance is relevant to them	2.3	1.8	2.0	28.1	21.6	24.2

Source: "Pre launch survey report of insurance awareness campaign" sponsored by IRDAI and NCAER.

The customers should also be aware of government institutions that listen to grievances about policies or insurance companies. This reduces the uncertainty that comes along while investing money into insurance schemes and provides a guarantee. The audience should also be made aware of clauses in the policy about revival of the insurance, surrender value, and other factors.

Overall, the amount of knowledge around insurance schemes and products is immense, and to make an informed decision, the awareness required by an average customer is way higher than the present levels. As of now, the majority of the effort is shouldered by the agents and government institutions like IRDA, but even this platform has its own disadvantages.

Awareness derived from agents depends heavily upon the knowledge and skill of the insurance agent himself/herself. And awareness from institutions is not personalized enough for the common man to gain insight that is required individually. AI-based chatbots that are fed with information can be of immense help in this area as they can provide personalized and unbiased information and can also provide so in multiple regional languages which increases the reach of the knowledge to both rural and urban areas.

7.4 CONCLUSION

In conclusion, the application of AI in the field of actuarial science is inevitable. The amount of convenience it provides in terms of efficiency, financial flexibility, and decision-making is nowhere comparable to raw human input. However, AI here can be used only as a supplementary mode of value addition, and hoping to replace actuaries altogether by AI systems might be far-fetched at the moment. It is true that the AI systems are vastly more capable and faster than the present systems, be it underwriters, agents, actuaries, etc., but the ground realities are most well understood by real people. The actual opportunity here is the combination of AI and its technical prowess, along with the foresight and inherent utility of people.

REFERENCES

Ai, Jing, Patrick L. Brockett, and Linda L. Golden. "Assessing consumer fraud risk in insurance claims: An unsupervised learning technique using discrete and continuous predictor variables." *North American Actuarial Journal* 13, no. 4 (2009): 438–458.

Curtis, Julie. "Technology and skill trends in the actuarial profession." *Predictive Analytics & Futurism, Society of Actuaries* 26 (2020): 1–2.

Embrechts, Paul, and Mario V. Wüthrich. "Recent challenges in actuarial science." *Annual Review of Statistics and Its Application* 9 (2022): 119–140.

England, Peter D., and Richard J. Verrall. "Predictive distributions of outstanding liabilities in general insurance." *Annals of Actuarial Science* 1, no. 2 (2006): 221–270.

Ezra, D. Don. "How actuaries determine the unfunded pension liability." *Financial Analysts Journal* 36, no. 4 (1980): 43–50.

Frees, Edward W., Peng Shi, and Emiliano A. Valdez. "Actuarial applications of a hierarchical insurance claims model." *ASTIN Bulletin: The Journal of the IAA* 39, no. 1 (2009): 165–197.

Grosen, Anders, and Peter Løchte Jørgensen. "Life insurance liabilities at market value: an analysis of insolvency risk, bonus policy, and regulatory intervention rules in a barrier option framework." *Journal of Risk and Insurance* 69, no. 1 (2002): 63–91.

Kulikova, L. I., N. B. Semenikhina, and E. Yu Vetoshkina. "Application of actuarial calculations when building a report on company's financial position." *Academy of Marketing Studies Journal* 20 (2016): 96.

Maier, Marc, Hayley Carlotto, Freddie Sanchez, Sherriff Balogun, and Sears Merritt. "Transforming underwriting in the life insurance industry." In *Proceedings of the AAAI Conference on Artificial Intelligence*, Honolulu, HI, USA, 27 January 2019–1 February 2019, vol. 33, no. 01, pp. 9373–9380. 2019.

Pattnaik, Debidutta, Sougata Ray, and Raghu Raman. "Applications of artificial intelligence and machine learning in the financial services industry: a bibliometric review." *Heliyon* 10 (2024): e23492.

Sherris, Michael. "Solvency, capital allocation, and fair rate of return in insurance." *Journal of Risk and Insurance* 73, no. 1 (2006): 71–96.

Sinha, Anushree. *Insurance Awareness Survey – Policy Holder – IRDAI.* Policy Holder. https://policyholder.gov.in/insurance-awareness-survey. (2016).

Zhou, Harry, and Tova Ashby. "An intelligent decision support model for actuarial profession." In *2009 10th ACIS International Conference on Software Engineering, Artificial Intelligences, Networking and Parallel/Distributed Computing*, Washington, DC, 27–29 May 2009. https://dl.acm.org/doi/proceedings/10.5555/1637864, pp. 140–143. IEEE, 2009.

8 Role of AI in Insurance Industry
Scope, Benefits, and Adoption Roadmap

Kumar Shalender and Rajesh Kumar Yadav

8.1 INTRODUCTION

The sweeping transformation that artificial intelligence (AI) is heralding across the industrial sectors is apparent today. Like other industries, the insurance sector is also experiencing transformative change thanks to using AI in its everyday operations. Specifically, the significance of AI in claim processing and management is nothing less than that of a miracle. AI has multiple capabilities of automated collection and analyses of data which can prove to be extremely beneficial for the insurance companies and associated functionaries and partners in the industry (Fathana and Fathana 2023). It is not an exaggeration to say that the role of AI is becoming central to the insurance industry. AI professionals can quickly take into consideration a large number of parameters of critical performance and map these dimensions against the current and emerging future scenarios to help companies make profitable business decisions. The stream of decision-making in insurance in the past was not very complex due to a limited number of variables and dimensions, but with time, the decisions related to the insurance claims, their processing, and analysis are becoming increasingly complex. AI can solve many complexities and challenges in the insurance industry. The technology uses algorithms to collect, analyse, and evaluate the data, which is very helpful for the insurance companies. In conjunction with ML, AI technology can also predict future scenarios and help stakeholders achieve better planning and operational capability (Shalender et al. 2023). By offering insights into the application potential of AI in the insurance industry, the study offers crucial implications for all the stakeholders in the business ecosystem. From research scholars and practitioners to regulatory agencies and policymakers, the chapter will help every stakeholder to integrate the application of AI in insurance and how this technology can bring numerous benefits to the doorsteps of the industry by enhancing the productivity and profitability of insurance companies' operations in the sector (Grover and Shalender 2023). Looking into the different prospective applications of AI, this study is expected to help the insurance industry develop an understanding and put in place the functional and operational mechanisms required for integrating AI into various aspects of doing their business (Gareiss 2023). Arguably, the

DOI: 10.1201/9781003472551-10

most important benefit of this integration will manifest in terms of increasing the accuracy and predictive analysis of insurance companies as these parameters are of utmost importance when it comes to ensuring the sustainability of the business going forward.

8.2 AI IN THE INSURANCE INDUSTRY: GAME CHANGING BENEFITS

8.2.1 Enhancing Productivity

By streamlining the entire cycle of raising the claim, assessing the claim, and settling claims by making the payment, AI can significantly enhance the productivity of insurance operations. As the number of insurance claims filed by claimants continues to reach a new high by the day, the application of AI can complement productivity by automating the process of assessing and evaluating a large number of standard claims that would have otherwise required human interventions (Kulshrestha et al. 2022). While it is important to understand that for resolving some specific discreet cases, human intervention is very much required. However, for other standardised scenarios, the majority of the claims can be processed with the help of AI, which not only helps organisations achieve a higher level of productivity and customer satisfaction, but also enhances customer satisfaction by crediting the money into the account for beneficiaries in a quick manner (Goyal 2023). AI can also be applied to fully digitise the entire mechanism of filing and processing claims while aiding underwriters to make superior business decisions by supplementing them with accurate predictive capabilities associated with their clientele. This increase in productivity can be turned into superior business results for insurance companies which will help them stay competitive in the long run (Aggarwal et al. 2023).

8.2.2 Predictive Analysis

AI can help insurance firms not only collect relevant data about current scenarios but also extrapolate to get important insights related to the future. Insurance companies need to make a comprehensive analysis of the business environment while taking into consideration the prospects of natural calamities, uncertain weather, and other uncontrollable variables associated with the business environment. The accuracy of the predictive analysis is very important for insurance firms as it helps them manage their operations effectively in the future (Shalender 2023). Take, for instance, the state of Florida in the US, where insurance companies are increasingly finding it difficult to offer policies because of the uncertain weather conditions. This is true for many other parts of the world including countries like Australia, New Zealand, and Canada. AI can help insurance companies address this challenge by offering accurate and precise features in Adios related to weather patterns, geological developments, and associated phenomena (Shalender and Sharma 2021). In conjunction with various IoT devices that can record weather data, AI can help insurance companies accurately predict future patterns and offer precise insurance quotes for prospective customers. The large and unprecedented quantity of data collected by drones, IoT, remote sensing, and other allied technologies can be easily analysed with the help of AI, and accordingly, insurance premiums can be decided realistically and accurately.

8.2.3 Exploring New Segments

AI can prove immensely beneficial for insurance firms to capitalise on new areas of business development that are allied with changing trends in customer and business space. Take, for instance, the growing prominence of cybersecurity. The wave of digitalisation is sweeping through the world, and with more people embracing the digital revolution with open arms, the threats related to cybersecurity are intensifying at an alarming speed (Shalender et al. 2023). AI can help insurance companies analyse the potential of cybersecurity space as a promising business category and help them develop this as an attractive business opportunity (Mittal et al. 2019). By offering actionable insights, AI can help insurance analyse their competencies and match them with various components of the external environment (Pangilinan 2023). The AI application in insurance will also equip category to analyse their current portfolio and then decide which categories they should expand the business or divest the services to run an overall profitable business. Similarly, emerging areas such as blockchain technology, non-fungible tokens (NFTs), and metaverse can be potentially analysed with the help of AI technology to understand their profit potential if insurance firms decide to make a foray into these categories.

8.2.4 Offering Flexible Options

AI can help insurance companies offer flexible insurance with a variety of premium payment options. Many insurance firms in the health category are now using smart apps, phones, and wearable devices to track the personal health of insured persons (Shalender and Yadav 2019). These habits, eating patterns, and associated activities of the insured persons are then analysed with the help of AI, and in line with the results, flexible options related to the insurance policies are being issued to customers (Shalender et al. 2023). The persons exhibiting safer and health-conscious behaviour might be offered lower premium payments, whereas others with high risky behaviour might be charged more as the likelihood of these people making the claim is greater than those of others. Rewarding those who are exhibiting safer and healthier options in their life is likely to inspire others to exhibit the same kind of behaviour and will help in the propagation of good practices among society members. This incentivisation can be adopted at a larger scale, and a push in this regard by the policymakers and regulators can help in motivating the society to stick to the good practices and also get rewarded in the process (Shalender and Shankar 2023). Specifically, in the development of the health insurance, the existing data related to customer attitudes and behaviour patterns can prove instrumental in enhancing the overall innovative capabilities of the segment.

8.2.5 Enhancing Customer Service

AI-enabled chatbots are increasingly replacing human intervention in customer service, and by speedily solving the complex issues associated with claims and processing, these can prove instrumental in enhancing customer satisfaction related to the insurance industry. No wonder, today we find an increasing number of insurance companies employing AI-powered chatbots for offering a complete constellation of services to the target market (Sharma et al. 2023). Unlike human resistance, AI can work around the clock, which is fantastic for companies that offer global insurance services in different parts of the world. The small and mundane issues related to the insurance sector such as difficulty in logging in, raising claims, processing requests, and asking for customer assistance can be easily solved with the help of automated chatbots. Having said that, insurance companies must realise that the use of chatbots should be assisted with human resources of the organisation. Especially when there is a query that is not standardised, the need to supplement the information manually by looking into different aspects of the problem has to be considered (Shalender et al. 2023). Therefore, insurance companies need to create a mix of automated chatbots and human resources that come together to offer better service experiences to the target market.

8.3 AI IN THE INSURANCE INDUSTRY: RECOMMENDED STRATEGIES AND ADOPTION ROADMAP

The following strategies (shown in Figure 8.1) will help insurance firms to adopt AI for their business ecosystem. By focusing on the specific steps, organisations will be able to leverage the immense potential associated with this new-age technology and achieve considerably superior results on multiple fronts such as business development, client acquisitions, and enhancing claims accuracy.

8.3.1 Start Internally

First and foremost, insurance companies should start by sensitising their employees about the immense potential of AI and the multiple benefits associated with its use cases. As insurers start integrating the practices of AI in their functional procedures and operational mechanisms, it will be important to involve the entire workforce so that the desirable results on efficiency and effectiveness can be achieved. The application of AI requires a considerable change in existing business processes, which means employees of the organisation have to bear with the change in their routine work. In the absence of motivation and encouragement, the employees might not be able to cope with the changes, and consequently, insurance firms won't be able to derive the desired benefits out of the adoption and integration of AI in their business processes. Also, it is important to make sure that employees are well-prepared to use AI in their operational procedures (Phansis 2023). To that end, organisations might be required to arrange various training sessions by industrial experts to enhance the current level of knowledge and information of their employees related to AI practices. It is very important to emphasise the technical skills related to the use of AI as without mastering the technicalities associated with the use of new technology, it might not be possible for employees to derive maximum benefit from the technology (Sharma et al. 2023).

8.3.2 Create Compliance

The regulatory norms related to the use of AI Technology are not standardised across the globe. In the insurance industry, no clear-cut rules and regulations have been framed when it comes to use of the AI by the industry firms. In such an environment, insurance companies might be required to come out with a clear AI compliance plan that will help organisations in the adoption of the technology without breaking the rules and regulations related to it (Shnaps 2023). This will not only clear the air when it comes to the adoption of AI within the organisation but also inspire other companies in the sector to follow the same strategy for encouraging the widespread adoption of AI in the industrial ecosystem (Snape 2023). While there are many dimensions associated with this adoption of AI, specific requirements to use AI for risk assessment and claim management processes need to be focused on, as these two critical areas can make or break the adoption prospects of AI in the industry. The development of such compliance by the players of the insurance industry will also encourage policymakers to deliberate on the matter and offer a framework that will help the integration of AI and other new-age technologies for the achievement of business results for participant stakeholders in the business ecosystem of the insurance industry.

8.3.3 Prioritise Areas

As shown in Figure 8.1, one of the practical and more realistic ways of adopting AI in the insurance industry is to start small and use the technology to experiment with less risky functions. For example, rather than outrightly using AI for processing of claims and clearance of payment, it is better to start with using the technology for collection of the data and analysis of the claims. Replacing human resources with AI technology in these less risky affairs will help the company to closely follow the integration of AI in the business and its impact on the profitability and operating efficiency of the company.

The use of AI in less risky areas also helps companies to become confident in the application of the technology in high-risk functions which are directly associated with claim processing and payment processing, among others. Remember, successful AI implementation should start small and use the insights derived from its applications in less-risk areas to make a robust system that will ultimately pave the way for its use in high-risk functions as well. Using AI in less-risk areas will make the employees of the company confident about the application prospects of the technology and will encourage them to learn the technicalities behind the application of AI in the sector (Sharma et al. 2020). Such moves, therefore, will prove conducive to the overall deployment of the technology in the insurance industry and will help the sector embrace the technology going forward.

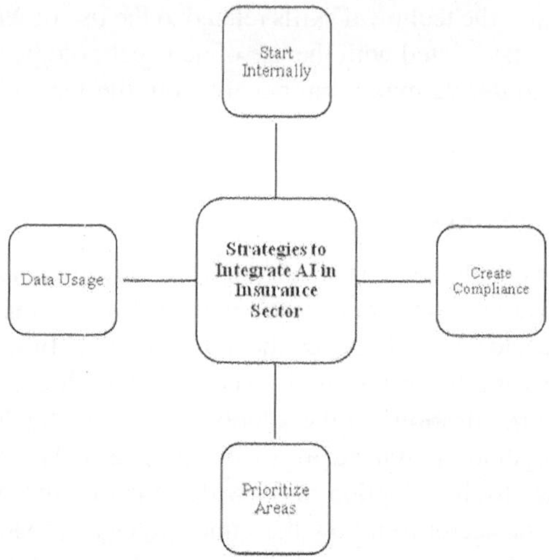

FIGURE 8.1 Strategies to help AI integration in the insurance industry. (Authors' own conceptualisation.)

8.3.4 Data Usage

The quality of data has important impact on the effectiveness of AI. The use of genuine data will offer accurate results while the fake data will yield wrong information. It is, therefore, essential for the insurance industry to use accurate data for right decision-making. The collection of the data needs to be done in a careful manner, and there must be quality checks for ensuring that only authentic data is used in decision-making. Safeguard measures should be taken and quality checks conducted for getting genuine data (Vyas et al. 2023). Data continuously remains at the centre of attention for policymakers and regulators, and any kind of discrepancy about the data might prove very harmful for the organisations. Hence, it becomes mandatory for organisations in the insurance sector to use AI to be very careful about the data structures and patterns and must work in collaboration with all the stakeholders in the ecosystem so that any leakage of sensitive data or information can be prevented right at its source.

8.4 DISCUSSION

AI in the insurance sector can bring many benefits to the table. Arguably, the most significant benefit associated with technology usage is the optimum utilisation of the available resources, which not only helps elevate efficiency but also reduces the wastages associated with business processes. Insurance firms should consider the adoption of AI in the insurance industry from a strategic viewpoint because this adoption is a long journey that will require commitment from all participating stakeholders for a long period. It is a process that involves the entire organisation, needs top management support, and takes time before offering visible improvements in various processes and procedures. Therefore, it is required for all the stakeholders in the insurance industry, especially the shareholders to commit to the integration process from a long-time perspective. The enormous growth prospects that organisations can easily reap by integrating AI into their business models, which is one of the sure-shot ways to convince shareholders about the adoption of AI. It is also important to understand that the implementation process will not be smooth, and organisations might also encounter some resistance from other stakeholders in the value chain while going ahead with the integration process. Production companies, supply chain intermediaries, and even consumers might oppose the idea of integrating AI in case they encounter any kind of inconvenience or time delay associated with the process. Hence, companies need to understand that before venturing out with the integration of AI in the customer segments, they must do their proper homework so that the integration and implementation can be achieved smoothly and seamlessly. This particular preparation will make sure that the adoption process related to AI will reach the customers as a novel measure that helps businesses achieve superior results. Given the fact that the regulatory environment is not very clear, the critical responsibility lies on the shoulders of policymakers to come up with clear regulations in this regard. By offering clarity about the rules related to AI and its use, governments worldwide can help the sector achieve higher growth and profitability while reaping more dividends in terms of the tax income generated by the sector. The support of the policymakers is also important in terms of making common citizens aware of the huge potential that AI offers to prospective insurance seekers.

8.5 CONCLUSION

The significance of AI as a technology in the field of insurance is lighting to gain momentum going forward. The adoption drive will be primarily felicitated by the fact that consumers are increasingly demanding more convenience from the insurance sector, especially when it comes to completing the processes associated with raising the claims, processing the applications, and releasing the claimed money to the account of the customers. The AI can fully automate the entire cycle, and by delivering enhanced comfort and convenience to companies and customers alike, it can strengthen the brand equity of insurance organisations while making the consumers more satisfied with the services of insurance companies. To summarise, AI in the insurance sector can do wonders, and by creating a mutually beneficial relationship throughout the value chain, this integration can help the insurance industry to offer more value-oriented and effective services to customers.

REFERENCES

Aggarwal, Arun, Ruchi Mittal, Sahil Gupta, and Amit Mittal. "Internet of things driven perceived value co-creation in smart cities of the future: a PLS-SEM based predictive model." *Journal of Computational and Theoretical Nanoscience* 16, no. 9 (2019): 4053–4058.

Choudhary, Vinita, Neha Kamboj, and SonalTrivedi. "Scoping Review of Literature on the Application of Blockchain in Finance." *Perspectives on Blockchain Technology and Responsible Investing* (2023): 1–28.

Choudhary, Vinita, and Sonal Trivedi. "The role of internal audit in risk management with a perspective of sustainability development." *The Impact of Climate Change and Sustainability Standards on the Insurance Market* (2023): 287–315.

Fathana, Rezka, and Rezka Fathana. "A Roadmap for Indonesia's AI-Driven Healthcare." *East Asia Forum*, December 7, 2023.

Gareiss, Robin. "Building a digital transformation team: 9 essential roles." *CIO*, October 19, 2023.

Goyal, Komal. "AI and Government: Transforming Public Services for the Digital Age." *Forbes*, July 17, 2023.

Grover, Atul, and Kumar Shalender. "Virtual world–Metaverse governance conceptual framework." In *Applied Data Science and Smart Systems, AIP Conference Proceedings*, vol. 2916, no. 1. AIP Publishing, 2023.

Kulshrestha, Dhiresh, Muklesh Kumar Tiwari, Kumar Shalender, and Sandhir Sharma. "Consumer acatalepsy towards buying behaviour for need-based goods for sustainability during the COVID-19 pandemic." *Indian Journal of Marketing* 52, no. 10 (2022): 50–63.

Malik, Reena, and Sonal Trivedi. "Blockchain Technology And Healthcare: Towards Combating COVID-19." *Blockchain Technology in Corporate Governance: Transforming Business and Industries* (2022): 57–74.

Mehta, Kiran Sharma, and Poshan Yu. (2023). "Revolutionizing Financial Services and Markets ThroughFinTech and Blockchain." Doi:10.4018/978-1-6684–8624–5.

Mittal, Amit, Rahul Dhiman, and ParmodLamba. "Skill mapping for blue-collar employees and organisational performance: A qualitative assessment." *Benchmarking: An International Journal* 26, no. 4 (2019): 1255–1274.

Pangilinan, Mika. "How Technology Is Shaping the Broker Landscape." *Insurance Business Canada*, August 31, 2023.

Phadnis, Shilpa. "IT Services Cos Strengthen genAI Offerings, Talent." *The Times of India*, August 1, 2023.

Shalender, Kumar. "Skill Development for Society 5.0: A Focus on the New-Age Skilling Process." *Business, Technology and Finance* (2023): 43.

Shalender, Kumar, and Naman Sharma. "Using extended theory of planned behaviour (TPB) to predict adoption intention of electric vehicles in India." *Environment, Development and Sustainability* 23, no. 1 (2021): 665–681.

Shalender, Kumar, Babita Singla, and Sandhir Sharma. "Adoption of ESG by the Insurance Industry: Conceptual Framework and Future Recommendations." *The Impact of Climate Change and Sustainability Standards on the Insurance Market* (2023): 349–358.

Shalender, Kumar, Babita Singla, and Sandhir Sharma. "Emerging Technologies and Their Game-Changing Potential: Lessons from Corporate World." *Contemporary Studies of Risks in Emerging Technology, Part A* (2023): 61–70.

Shalender, Kumar, and Shiv Shanker. "Building Innovation Culture for the Automobile Industry: Insights from the Indian Passenger Vehicle Market." In *Constructive Discontent in Execution*, pp. 131–148. Apple Academic Press, 2023.

Shalender, Kumar, Babita Singla, Sandhir Sharma, and Marina Oberemok. "COVID-19 and its impact on construction and transport construction economy: An integrated framework." In: Guda, A. (eds) *Networked Control Systems for Connected and Automated Vehicles. NN 2022. Lecture Notes in Networks and Systems*, vol. 510. pp. 747–753, Cham: Springer, 2022..

Shalender, Kumar, and Rajesh Kumar Yadav. "Strategic flexibility, manager personality, and firm performance: The case of Indian Automobile Industry." *Global Journal of Flexible Systems Management* 20 (2019): 77–90.

Sharma, Renuka, Kiran Mehta, and ArchanaGoel. "Non-linear relationship between board size and performance of Indian companies." *Journal of Management and Governance* 27, no. 4 (2023): 1277–1301.

Sharma, Naman, Ekta Sinha, and Kumar Shalender. "Espoused model of women entrepreneurship: antecedents to women entrepreneurial intention and moderating role of entrepreneurial self-efficacy." *Journal of Enterprising Communities: People and Places in the Global Economy* (2023), . ahead-of-print No. ahead-of-print..

Shnaps, Reuven. "AI, Personalization, and Telematics Will Redefine Insurance." *Unite.AI*, March 21, 2023.

Snape, Gia. "AI Roadmap – How Insurance Firms Can Prime Themselves for the Future." *Insurance Business Canada*, June 2, 2023.

Trivedi, Sonal."Blockchain Framework for Insurance industry." *International Journal of Innovation and Technology Management* 20, no. 06 (2023): 2350034.

Trivedi, Sonal. "Convention of blockchain in financial services: A state-of-the-art literature review." In Kiran Sood, Simon Grima, Ganga Sharma, and Balamurugan Balusamy (Eds.), *Revolutionizing Financial Services and Markets ThroughFinTech and Blockchain*, pp. 237–250. River Publishers.

Trivedi, Sonal. "Convention of blockchain in financial services: A state-of-the-art literature review." *Revolutionizing Financial Services and Markets ThroughFinTech and Blockchain* (2023): 237–250.

Trivedi, Sonal, Rashmi Aggarwal, and Sandhir. Sharma (Eds.), *Innovations and Sustainability in Society 5.0*. Nova Science Publisher, 2023.

Trivedi, Sonal, and Vinita Choudhary, Neha Kamboj, and Nirmaljeet Kaur Virk. "New avenues of opportunities and challenges for start-ups, MSMEs, the Indian Financial Sector, and the Indian Insurance Sector." *Business Drivers in Promoting Digital Detoxification* (2024): 226–250.

Trivedi, Sonal, and Reena Malik. "Blockchain technology as an emerging technology in the insurance market." In *Big Data: A Game Changer for Insurance Industry*, pp. 81–100. Emerald Publishing Limited, 2022.

Trivedi, Sonal, and Reena Malik. "Role and significance of data protection in risk management practices in the insurance market." In *Big Data Analytics in the Insurance Market*, pp. 263–273. Emerald Publishing Limited, 2022.

Trivedi, Sonal, Kiran Mehta, and Renuka Sharma. "Systematic literature review on application of blockchain technology in E-finance and financial services." *Journal of Technology Management & Innovation* 16, no. 3 (2021): 89–102.

Vyas, Vishal, Kiran Mehta, and Renuka Sharma. "The nexus between toxic-air pollution, health expenditure, and economic growth: An empirical study using ARDL." *International Review of Economics & Finance* 84 (2023): 154–166.

9 AI's Role in Improving the Quality of Insurance Actuarial Services

Gurpreet Kaur, Puneet Singh, and Anshull Bhalla

9.1 INTRODUCTION

In the present scenario wherein there is rapid technological development, the insurance industry is heading towards innovation by using AI for improvising the insurance services (Naim, 2022). With the development of AI technologies, there is vast transformation in the existing traditional insurance practices by bringing in opportunities that would ensure smooth processes for mitigating risks, streamlining operations, and better customer experiences (Holland and Kavuri, 2023).

The present study brings insights into the vital role of AI in bringing about revolutionizing change in the insurance industry, improving actuarial services covering the wide areas.

The application of AI enhances customer satisfaction and increases the efficiency and accuracy of insurance activities such as underwriting (Eling et al., 2022), fraud detection (Agarwal, 2023), and claims processing (Dhashanamoorthi, 2023).

Besides this, the subsets of AI such as machine learning, predictive analytics, and natural language processing provide additional benefits by giving better insights that enable better decision-making.

Furthermore, the integration of AI-powered solutions and chatbots has brought about revolution in customer interactions (Fong, 2023). This will further provide strategies to mitigate risk proactively (Gupta, 2020). The present paper aims to provide in-depth insight into the impact of AI in the insurance industry. By embracing AI-driven innovations, insurers can not only enhance operational efficiency and mitigate risks but also foster greater trust and loyalty (Bodemer, 2023) among customers in an increasingly competitive marketplace. The chapter is segregated on the following grounds. Section 9.1 provides the introduction to the study. Section 9.2 brings about justification from past studies. Section 9.3 presents an interpretation of past studies. Sections 9.4 and 9.5 deal with conclusion, recommendations, and future scope of the study. Section 9.6 provides references for the study.

9.2 REVIEW OF LITERATURE

Many studies in the past have been conducted, which provides in-depth analysis of how AI application has improvised the industry sector (Singh and Chivukula, 2020).

 DOI: 10.1201/9781003472551-11

The literature provides path for improvising the insurance industry by adopting new technologies such as blockchain and smart contracts. The studies from past enumerating the role of AI in providing better customer services are mentioned below.

Agrawal et al. (2024) explore how better AI predictions impact decision-making and risk management (focusing on risk, task connections, and existing uncertainty processes) using a model to analyse AI adoption. Khalisa (2024) explores how digitalisation and AI impact the insurance broker industry, using interviews to investigate if AI can replace brokers, but concludes that AI enhances efficiency while human expertise remains crucial. Ahmad et al. (2024) analyse secondary data to assess how InsurTech advancements improve efficiency in the insurance industry, examining the benefits for both insurers and consumers in a multi-perspective approach.

Srinivas and Gandra (2023) examine AI use in Andhra Pradesh insurance, assessing the use of AI for sustainability using surveys and data to recommend actions for policymakers. Amerirad et al. (2023) investigate how malicious actors can manipulate AI algorithms in the insurance industry, exploring specific vulnerabilities and potential solutions for fraud prevention. Fong (2023) explores AI for insurance agents, aiming to boost sales and efficiency for a stronger economy through increased insurance use in Malaysia. Bodemer (2023) combines blockchain and AI-enabled smart contracts to tackle insurance issues, finding that it improves transparency, reduces fraud, and optimizes risk assessment (mixed methods). Dhashanamoorthi (2023) investigates leveraging AI to streamline dispute resolution in road traffic accident insurance claims, proposing a method for cost estimation and negotiation to expedite the process. Komperla (2022) explores AI's applications and limitations, finding that it will likely assist doctors, not replace them, due to the importance of human interaction.

Khan and Khan (2023) explore the potential of AI in healthcare, examining its applications and limitations, and conclude that AI will likely augment doctors' capabilities rather than replace them entirely due to the importance of the human touch. Zhang et al. (2023) explores AI's potential to expedite RTA insurance claim resolution through real-case analysis and AI tools, aiming to benefit all parties.

Benedek and Nagy (2023) examine if AI is more cost-effective than traditional methods for car insurance fraud detection, using real data to show that traditional methods are currently better. Trivino (2023) examines AI's applications in insurance, including its impact on pricing, service, and technology use (analytics, geospatial), and he also highlights ethical considerations like fairness, privacy, and bias in AI use. Agarwal (2023) explores advanced machine learning to create a fraud detection system for medical claims, aiming to boost accuracy and efficiency in insurance and potentially improve healthcare systems.

Pradeep and Patil (2022) analyse the use of AI in insurance (including healthcare) across global firms, concluding that AI adoption is essential for financial institutions to compete globally despite challenges. Owens et al. (2022) investigate how explainable AI is used in insurance, focusing on methods like knowledge distillation, and find them common in claims, underwriting, and pricing. Aslam et al. (2022) build a system to spot auto insurance fraud using predictive models (like logistic regression) and show its promise for real-time detection.

Rukhsar et al. (2022; Dora et al., 2022) compare machine learning techniques to detect insurance fraud, aiming to benefit both insurance and healthcare industries. Lupačov and Stanković (2022) analyse AI's growing role in insurance, exploring its applications, tools, and implementation, concluding that it holds immense potential for the industry. Holland (2022) examines BGL Group (European insurance leader) use of AI to create a general AI customer lifecycle model applicable across the insurance industry, while also exploring future directions for AI in this field. Alli et al. (2021) examine Nigerian insurance's view of AI and its impact on claims, marketing, service, and underwriting. It finds that AI can significantly improve these areas using surveys and analysis. Eling et al. (2021) examine how AI impacts insurance using existing frameworks, analysing data from various sources, and concludes that AI offers cost savings, new revenue, and a shift from reacting to losses to predicting and preventing them.

Prajapati (2022) explores how AI, machine learning, and big data are used by insurers to enhance customer satisfaction, analytics, and trend identification. Lin et al. (2020) explore how applying AI algorithms' reasoning capabilities to analyse the link between AI and finance can significantly improve income generation within the financial field. Zarifis et al. (2023) investigate how the implementation of AI automation in insurance companies is leading to the emergence of four distinct business models within the sector.

AI-enabled technology has proved to be very effective in improvising the customer sector. All the above studies focused on the application of AI in insurance. AI has brought about more accuracy and transparency in customer services.

9.3 RESEARCH METHODOLOGY

The paper is based on secondary data which is collected from Journals, books, websites, etc. The paper describes the applications of AI in enhancing the actuarial services of the insurance industry.

9.4 INTERPRETATION OF PAST LITERATURE

Figure 9.1 depicts the year in which the maximum number of papers are published.

The above chart (Figure 9.1) shows that the maximum number of research on AI application in insurance is done in 2023.

The pie chart (Figure 9.2) shows papers with the maximum number of citations.

The above pie chart (Figure 9.2) depicts the paper titled "The impact of artificial intelligence along the insurance value chain and on the insurability of risks" published in 2021, which has the maximum number of citations.

Table 9.1 shows journals with the paper title and the country where this research was conducted.

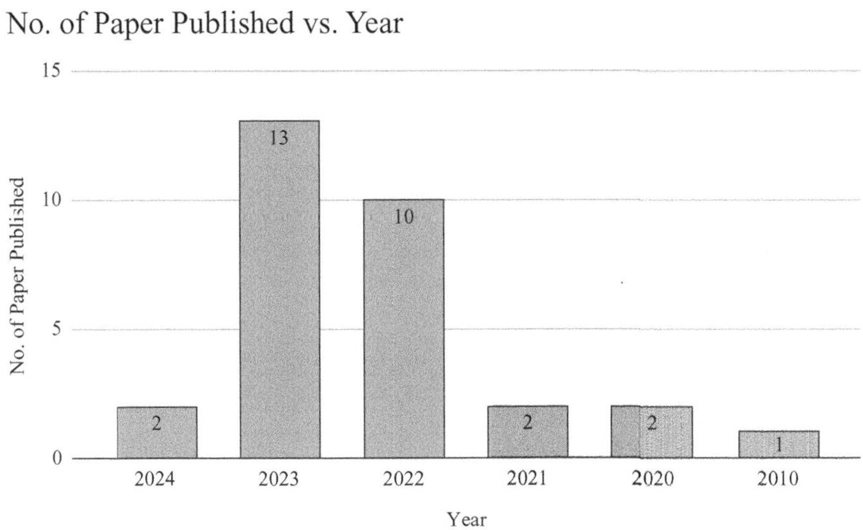

FIGURE 9.1 Number of papers published. (Author's Compilation.)

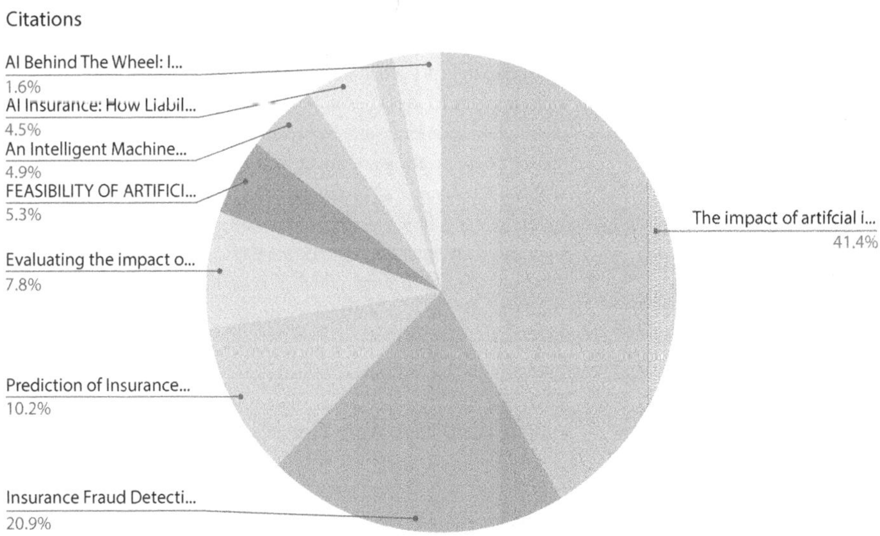

FIGURE 9.2 Impact of AI. (Author's Compilation.)

TABLE 9.1
List of Journals

Name of the Journal	Title of Paper	Country
Journal of the Japanese and International Economies	Prediction machines, insurance, and protection: an alternative perspective on AI's role in production	United States of America
Emerald Open Research	Evaluating the impact of AI on insurance: the four emerging AI- and data-driven business models	United Kingdom
SN Computer Science	Impact of Insurtech on the premium performance of insurance business	Singapore
International Conference on Social and Human Sciences	The Application of Artificial Intelligence in the Financial Field: Taking Insurance as an Example	China
Proceedings of the International Conference on Business Excellence	Process Optimization Models Using Artificial Intelligence and Digital Transformation of The Insurance Industry	Romania
Nigeria Journal of Risk and Insurance	Knowledge, attitude and perception of artificial intelligence and its application in the key operations of insurance in Nigeria	Nigeria
Journal of Informatics Education and Research	Role of artificial intelligence in Indian insurance industry: challenges and opportunities from sustainability perspectives	India
Ilomata International Journal of Management	The digitalization in insurance broker industry: how artificial intelligence affect their industry	Indonesia
Journal TTTP—Traffic and Transport Theory and Practice	Artificial intelligence in insurance companies	Bosnia and Herzegovina
European Actuarial Journal	Adversarial artificial intelligence in insurance: from an example to some potential remedies	Italy
Utar	Feasibility of artificial intelligence in improving sales and service of insurance agents in the life insurance industry of Malaysia	Malaysia
Shodh Drishti (an International Peer Reviewed Refereed Research Journal)	Artificial intelligence (AI) in insurance	India
International Journal of Science and Research Archive	Resolving insurance claims with artificial intelligence powered decision making	India
Journal of Management and Entrepreneurship	Role of artificial intelligence in life insurance organization: in respect of human resource functions	India
International Neurourology Journal	AI behind the wheel: innovations in auto insurance and healthcare	India
Cardiometry	Use of artificial intelligence in the Indian insurance sector, including healthcare companies	India

(Continued)

TABLE 9.1 (*Continued*)
List of Journals

Name of the Journal	Title of Paper	Country
The Geneva Papers on Risk and Insurance—Issues and Practice	The impact of artificial intelligence along the insurance value chain and on the insurability of risks	Switzerland
Scholars Journal of Engineering and Technology	An intelligent machine learning approach for fraud detection in medical claim insurance: a comprehensive study	India
Preprint from PsyArXiv	Influence of AI and machine learning in insurance sector	UK
Hawaii International Conference on System Sciences	Artificial intelligence (AI) and digital transformation in the insurance market: A case study analysis of BGL group	England
Scholarspace	Artificial intelligence (AI) and business innovation in insurance: a comparison of incumbent firms versus new entrants	England
Financial and Economic Review	Traditional versus AI-based fraud detection: cost efficiency in the field of automobile insurance*	Romania

Source: Author's Compilation.

9.5 CONCLUSION AND RECOMMENDATION

The technological development has given rise to numerous opportunities for the insurance to holistically develop and grow in its sphere. The studies have concluded that AI application has enabled coordinated decision-making (Agrawal et al., 2024) by forecasting the future. AI, by integrating with blockchain smart contracts, has a significant potential to build up more transparency, integrity, and safety to data stored. Further, it has led to speedy risk assessment, claim processing, underwriting, etc., which further enhances productivity and provides better customer services ensuring business growth and success (Sundari, 2024). Besides this, it is also observed that AI has led to better retention of clients and also attracted new client base which increased the premium level intensively (Ahmad et al., 2024). However, as the insurance landscape evolves with AI, it also presents new challenges and ethical considerations. From concerns surrounding data privacy and algorithmic bias to regulatory compliance (Bodemer, 2023) and cybersecurity risks, insurers must navigate a complex ecosystem to harness the full potential of AI while upholding trust and transparency (Bodemer, 2023). AI strategies have improvised decision-making, boosting the insurance efficiency and customer satisfaction (Komperla, 2022). The studies conclude that the insurance sector has great potential and opportunities for improving the market penetration by using AI (Fong, 2023) and so it is recommended that an awareness programme should be developed to educate clients on the adoption of AI technologies (Owens et al., 2022; Radu and Alexandru, 2022).

9.6 SCOPE FOR FUTURE RESEARCH

Despite so many potential benefits of AI, the adoption of AI is still in its infancy due to several challenges such as a lack of awareness and a lack of well-defined AI-enabled technology usage. Therefore, the study suggests that the future researchers should focus on estimating the influence of AI adoption on insurance protection on broader parameters. Owens et al. (2022) and Stern et al. (2022) explained factors that will help in overcoming the challenges in adoption of AI by the insurance industry.

REFERENCES

Agarwal, Shashank. "An intelligent machine learning approach for fraud detection in medical claim insurance: A comprehensive study." *Scholars Journal of Engineering and Technology* 11, no. 9 (2023): 191–200.

Agrawal, Ajay, Joshua S. Gans, and Avi Goldfarb. "Prediction machines, insurance, and protection: An alternative perspective on AI's role in production." *Journal of the Japanese and International Economies* 72 (2024): 101307.

Ahmad, Shakil, Charu Saxena, Saiful Islam, and Rejaul Karim. "Impact of insur-tech on the premium performance of insurance business." *SN Computer Science* 5, no. 1 (2024): 138.

Alli, Noah Gbenga, Kamal Ganiyu, and A. I. N. A. John. "Knowledge, attitude and perception of artificial intelligence and its application in the key operations of insurance in Nigeria." *Nigerian Journal of Risk and Insurance* 11, no. 1 (2021): 1–19.

Amerirad, Behnaz, Matteo Cattaneo, Ron S. Kenett, and Elisa Luciano. "Adversarial artificial intelligence in insurance: From an example to some potential remedies." *Risks* 11, no. 1 (2023): 20.

Aslam, Faheem, Ahmed Imran Hunjra, Zied Ftiti, Wael Louhichi, and Tahira Shams. "Insurance fraud detection: Evidence from artificial intelligence and machine learning." *Research in International Business and Finance* 62 (2022): 101744.

Benedek, Botond, and Bálint Zsolt Nagy. "Traditional versus AI-based fraud detection: Cost efficiency in the field of automobile insurance." *Financial and Economic Review* 22, no. 2 (2023): 77–98.

Bodemer, Oliver. "Blockchain with hyperledger and AI-driven smart contracts: Revolutionizing the insurance industry." *Authorea Preprints* (2023).

Choudhary, Vinita, Neha Kamboj, and Sonal Trivedi. "Scoping Review of Literature on the Application of Blockchain in Finance." In Kiran Sood, Simon Grima, Peter Young, Ercan Ozen, Balamurugan Balusamy (Eds.), *Perspectives on Blockchain Technology and Responsible Investing*, pp. 1–28. John Wiley & Sons, 2023.

Choudhary, Vinita, and Sonal Trivedi. "The role of internal audit in risk management with a perspective of sustainability development." *The Impact of Climate Change and Sustainability Standards on the Insurance Market* (2023): 287–315.

Dhashanamoorthi, Balaji. "Resolving insurance claims with Artificial Intelligence powered decision making." *International Journal of Science and Research Archive* 10, no. 2 (2023): 255–271.

Dora, Manoj, Ashwani Kumar, Sachin Kumar Mangla, Abhay Pant, and Muhammad Mustafa Kamal. "Critical success factors influencing artificial intelligence adoption in food supply chains." *International Journal of Production Research* 60, no. 14 (2022): 4621–4640

Eling, Martin, Davide Nuessle, and Julian Staubli. "The impact of artificial intelligence along the insurance value chain and on the insurability of risks." *The Geneva Papers on Risk and Insurance-Issues and Practice* 47, no. 2 (2022): 205–241.

Fong, Patrick Heng Yin. "Feasibility of artificial intelligence in improving sales and service of insurance agents in the life insurance industry of Malaysia." PhD diss., UTAR, 2023.

Gupta, Ruchi. "Artificial intelligence (AI) in insurance: A futuristic approach." *ShodhDrishti* 11, no. 8 (2020): 6–10.

Holland, Christopher. "Artificial intelligence (AI) and digital transformation in the insurance market: a case study analysis of BGL group." (2022).

Holland, Christopher, and Anil Kavuri. "Artificial intelligence (AI) and business innovation in insurance: A comparison of incumbent firms versus new entrants." *Journal of Management and Entrepreneurship*. ISSN 2229-5348. (2023).

Khalisa, Arvidhia. "The digitalization in insurance broker industry: How artificial intelligence affect this industry." *Ilomata International Journal of Management* 5, no. 1 (2024): 261–279.

Khan, Ausaf Ahmad, and Noor Alam Khan. "Role of artificial intelligence in life insurance organization: in respect of human resource functions." In *Proceedings of the 56th Hawaii International Conference on System Sciences,* 3–6 January, 2023, Maui, pp. 3807–3816, 2023.

Komperla, Ramesh Chandra Aditya. "Ai behind the wheel: Innovations in auto insurance and healthcare." *International Neurourology Journal* 26, no. 4 (2022): 30–36.

Komperla, Ramesh Chandra Aditya. "The auto health revolution Ai strategies for insurance and healthcare." *International Neurourology Journal* 27, no. 4 (2023): 1598–1605.

Lin, Liuxuan, Hengliang Qiu, and Jinfu Liu. "The application of artificial intelligence in the financial field: Taking insurance as an example." In *2020 International Conference on Social and Human Sciences (ICSHS2020), 10.38007/Proceedings*, vol. 29, Canberra, Australia, 7–8 March, 2020. 2020.

Lupačov, Jaroslav, and Željko Stanković. "Artificial intelligence in insurance companies." *Journal TTTP—Traffic and Transport Theory and Practice* 7, no. 2 (2022): 77–81.

Malik, Reena, and Sonal Trivedi. "Blockchain technology and healthcare: Towards combating COVID-19." *Blockchain Technology in Corporate Governance: Transforming Business and Industries* (2022): 57–74.

Naim, Arshi. "Market development and financial stability by the application of AI." *European Journal of Interdisciplinary Research and Development* 7 (2022): 28–39.

Owens, Emer, Barry Sheehan, Martin Mullins, Martin Cunneen, Juliane Ressel, and German Castignani. "Explainable artificial intelligence (xai) in insurance." *Risks* 10, no. 12 (2022): 230.

Pradeep, Akshat, and Kanchan Patil. "Use of artificial intelligence in the Indian insurance sector, including healthcare companies." *Cardiometry* 23 (2022): 499–508.

Prajapati, Nitin. "Influence of AI and machine learning in insurance sector." *Preprint from PsyArXiv* 13 (2022).

Radu, Nicoleta, and Felicia Alexandru. "Process optimization models using artificial intelligence and digital transformation of the insurance industry." In *Proceedings of the International Conference on Business Excellence*, Bucharest, Romania, 24–26 March, vol. 16, no. 1, pp. 1283–1294. 2022.

Rukhsar, Laiqa, Waqas Haider Bangyal, Kashif Nisar, and Sana Nisar. "Prediction of insurance fraud detection using machine learning algorithms." *Mehran University Research Journal of Engineering & Technology* 41, no. 1 (2022): 33–40.

Singh, Sushant K., and Muralidhar Chivukula. "A commentary on the application of Artificial Intelligence in the insurance industry." *Trends in Artificial Intelligence* 4, no. 1 (2020): 75–79.

Srinivas, Bijja, and Praveen Kumar Gandra. "Role of artificial intelligence in Indian insurance industry: Challenges and opportunities from sustainability perspectives." *Journal of Informatics Education and Research* 3, no. 2 (2023): 2724–2736.

Stern, Ariel Dora, Avi Goldfarb, Timo Minssen, and W. Nicholson Price II. "AI insurance: How liability insurance can drive the responsible adoption of artificial intelligence in health care." *NEJM Catalyst Innovations in Care Delivery* 3, no. 4 (2022): CAT–21.

Sundari, Deoh, Susi Melinasari, Ermi Suryani, and Hafid Fadilah. "Implementation of artificial intelligence at the insurance company." In *Proceeding of the International Conference on Multidisciplinary Research for Sustainable Innovation*, Virtual Conference, 13–14 March 2024, vol. 1, no. 1, pp. 249–255. 2024.

Trivedi, Sonal. "Blockchain framework for insurance industry." *International Journal of Innovation and Technology Management* 20, no. 06 (2023): 2350034.

Trivedi, Sonal. "Blockchain technology and structural change in financial services." In *The Application of Emerging Technology and Blockchain in the Insurance Industry*, pp. 249–263. River Publishers, 2024.

Trivedi, Sonal. "Convention of blockchain in financial services: A state-of-the-art literature review." In *Revolutionizing Financial Services and Markets Through FinTech and Blockchain* (2023): 237–250.

Trivedi, Sonal, Vinita Choudhary, Neha Kamboj, and Nirmaljeet Kaur Virk. "New avenues of opportunities and challenges for start-ups, MSMEs, the Indian financial sector, and the Indian insurance sector." *Business Drivers in Promoting Digital Detoxification* (2024): 226–250.

Trivedi, Sonal, and Reena Malik. "Blockchain technology as an emerging technology in the insurance market." In Kiran Sood, Rajesh Kumar Dhanaraj, Balamurugan Balusamy, Simon Grima, R. Uma Maheshwari (Eds.), *Big Data: A Game Changer for Insurance Industry*, pp. 81–100. UK: Emerald Publishing Limited, 2022a.

Trivedi, Sonal, and Reena Malik. "Role and significance of data protection in risk management practices in the insurance market." In Kiran Sood, Balamurugan Balusamy, Simon Grima, Pierpaolo Marano (Eds.), *Big Data Analytics in the Insurance Market*, pp. 263–273. UK: Emerald Publishing Limited, 2022b.

Trivedi, Sonal, Kiran Mehta, and Renuka Sharma. "Systematic literature review on application of blockchain technology in E-finance and financial services." *Journal of Technology Management & Innovation* 16, no. 3 (2021): 89–102.

Triviño, Jorge Luis. *Use and Application of Artificial Intelligence in Insurance*. EasyChair, 2023.

Zarifis, Alex, Christopher P. Holland, and Alistair Milne. "Evaluating the impact of AI on insurance: The four emerging AI-and data-driven business models." *Emerald Open Research* 1, no. 1 (2023): 15.

Zhang, Wen, Jingwen Shi, Xiaojun Wang, and Henry Wynn. "AI-powered decision-making in facilitating insurance claim dispute resolution." In Michael (Ed.), *Annals of Operations Research*. Springer, 2023: 1–30.

10 Fuzzy Artificial Intelligence as a Technique to Find Relative Desirability for Automated Insurance Premium Assignment

Firos A and Seema Khanum

10.1 INTRODUCTION

10.1.1 Generative Models for Assessing Relative Desirability for Automated Insurance Premium Assignment

Generative models, as explained by Pattnaik et al. (2021), is a paradigm shift in the field of artificial intelligence (AI), especially for automating insurance premium assignments that require subtle decision-making processes. These models, according to Adem and Dagdeviren (2016), are good at comprehending complex high-dimensional data distributions by design, making them well-suited for circumstances where understanding underlying patterns and producing new datapoints given such patterns is crucial. In the case of insurance, the generative models can be used to simulate different risk scenarios for premium assignment purposes by testing various risk scenarios and forecasting future events by taking into account historical information.

This characteristic is important in insurance settings because it helps understand how various risk factors relate to each other and contribute toward potential losses (Shapiro 2004). By simulating these relationships, insurers can classify policyholders into more accurate risk categories, thereby ensuring more aligned premiums.

Generative models have an added benefit of dealing with incomplete and unknown information for rating insurance premiums. This is one thing that Susanto and Utama (2022) found out. It is a feature that not only makes the risk assessment process more robust, but also allows insurers to cover policyholders who are traditionally excluded because they are too risky or difficult to classify.

In addition to these facts, Dhieb et al. (2020) maintain that generative models can be used to support personalized insurance premium pricing. Such models understand by taking into account abundant historical data which may contain patterns as well as

DOI: 10.1201/9781003472551-12

relationships that humans can fail to notice. It is this kind of know-how that enables underwriters in setting premiums according to each insured's specific risk profile instead of adopting the often flawed philosophy of "one size fits all," which ends up making some customer groups overcharged or others undercharged for their policies' coverage. Tatari et al. (2012) add on by saying personalized premiums do not only promote fairness but also improve customer satisfaction and loyalty, since then such policyholders will perceive that their unique circumstances were considered.

The other side of the coin is that, in premium assignment, the implementation of generative models also has wider implications on how insurers manage risk. According to Jia and Zheng (2024), this proactive orientation to risk management implies that insurance firms will be more financially stable and their policyholders will pay for premiums that are competitive with others hence contributing to a healthier insurance ecosystem as a whole.

However, Ivan et al. (2024) suggest several potential benefits of these models such as increased accuracy in risk identification, individualized pricing of premiums, and better assessment of policy risks that make them very attractive for the future insurance. Jong et al. (2024) observe that technology progresses and better generative models are invented; it is likely that they will play an increasingly significant role in reshaping the insurance arena, thereby signifying a new chapter on how insurers perceive risk and fix premiums.

10.1.2 Deep Neural Network for Giving Suggestions

Advent of Deep Neural Networks (DNNs) has brought a new dawn in the automated insurance premium assignment industry. Due to DNNs' multiple interconnected nodes, these systems have the capacity to go through and pick out subtle patterns in large datasets, as well as learn complex relationships between varying factors according to Li (2024). According to Zhang et al. (2024), this makes them extremely useful tools for insurance companies interested in refining their premium assignment functions such that they are fairer to policyholders and more financially prudent.

Their effectiveness in automated insurance premium assignment is derived from their ability to process and analyze the many variables impacting on risk assessment. Wang et al. (2023) argued that these include not only obvious factors such as age, driving history for auto insurance, or medical history for health insurance, but also less visible ones like lifestyle choices or behavior habits. Hu et al. (2021) asserted that DNNs could suggest better premium assignments by considering more variables which would better reflect an individual's risk profile.

In addition, DNNs can instantly learn from new data, improving and refining their predictions. Jia and Wang (2024) study believes that this negative learning process is important in risk adaptation, where new variables and changing environments can transfer policyholders' risk.

Another important benefit of using DNNs in this regard is the ability to detect fraud and anomalies in data. Bouramdane (2023) explains that DNNs help maintain the integrity of the cost allocation process by improving fraud detection and ensuring that honest employees are not penalized for the actions of a few. It also opens the door to personalization and collaboration opportunities with customers.

Osamy et al. (2022) study shows that DNN can analyze customer data to recommend the best health insurance products and premium plans that suit individual risks and preferences. Also, according to de la Torre-López et al. (2023), the "black box" nature of DNNs can make it difficult to explain how decisions are made, raising questions about transparency and accountability.

Despite these challenges, the potential of DNNs to transform the automated insurance premium assignment process is undeniable. By offering more accurate, fair, and personalized premium suggestions, DNNs not only benefit insurers by reducing risk and improving financial performance but also enhance the policyholder experience, marking a significant step forward in the evolution of insurance practices.

10.1.3 Fuzzy System AI for Automated Insurance Premium Assignment

According to Sircar et al. (2021), the integration of fuzzy system AI into the field of distribution of undistributed electricity is a significant change in the way insurance companies manage insurance. Tatari et al. (2012) explained that fuzzy methods, characterized by their ability to deal with bias and uncertainty, provide a flexible and effective way to model uncertainty in insurance risk assessment.

Central to the appeal of fuzzy systems for insurance applications are the principles of fuzzy logic, which, unlike traditional binary logic, allow for level of fact rather than importance. Jia et al. (2024) explain that in the context of insurance premiums, this means that beyond classifying risks as "high" or "low" risk, fuzzy systems can account for a wide range of risk factors. According to Chryssolouris et al. (2023), by transforming expert knowledge and understanding into fuzzy systems and property, insurance companies can directly interact with insurers in the healthcare delivery process. The combination of human perception and algorithmic precision improves the system's ability to make consistent and accurate decisions, especially in complex problems or extremes where traditional models may fail. Its main advantage is its adaptability and flexibility. Taylan et al. (2023) explain that this change not only increases the accuracy of risk assessment but also enables insurers to respond quickly to changes in market text or environmental management playing an important role. According to Hu et al. (2022), the perception of fairness is important in establishing and maintaining trust between insurance companies and their customers, as well as creating a relationship that benefits both parties. It cannot be used without competition. According to Mardani et al. (2020), as insurance companies continue to grapple with the complexity of risk assessment in an ever-changing world, fuzzy cognitive systems are emerging as powerful tools for more efficient, fair, and effective decision-making.

10.1.4 Fuzzy-Based Technique to Find Relative Desirability in Automated Insurance Premium Assignment

According to Zhang et al. (2024), fuzzy logic, a mathematical framework for dealing with uncertainty and ambiguity, has emerged as a good technique to improve the cost allocation process. This approach is rooted in the concept of fuzzy sets and allows for a more comprehensive consideration of many factors affecting risk assessment. According to Taboada et al. (2023), the adaptability of this approach and its ability to manage uncertainty make it suitable for determining the needs of insurance applicants because many of the effects cannot be analyzed in black and white. The application must first define the fuzzy set for each risk, such as age, driving history, or health. Each of these environments is associated with ownership, which gives some ownership to the strategy, thus measuring how much risk the patient is involved in. According to Hu et al. (2022), this process allows for continuous and overlapping decision-making in risky situations. These features contribute to the accuracy of risk assessment and ensure that the income distribution is closer to the actual risk of the insured. According to Taylan et al. (2023), insurance underwriters have a strong understanding of risk, which is difficult to regulate using quantitative methods. Hu et al. (2022) explained that fuzzy logic can transform this information into a fuzzy system that guides the assessment and classification of risk. By combining empirical data with expert judgment, insurers can gain a better and more accurate understanding of risk, leading to fairer and better personal values. Hu et al. (2021) explained that fuzzy-based methods can provide effective adaptation to changing situations. The insurance industry is constantly changing due to factors such as advances in technology, new standards, and the regulatory environment. The use of fuzzy logic in decision-making regarding insurance objectives also has an impact on customer satisfaction. Ecer et al. (2024) explained that insurance companies can offer more advantageous premiums to individual policyholders by providing accurate and fair evaluations. This personalization not only demonstrates the value of the insurance product, but also increases customer trust and confidence.

Although it has many advantages, the use of fuzzy logic in healthcare delivery is not without problems. These include the need to carefully design and maintain fuzzy logic and rules, the difficulty of integrating fuzzy logic into existing IT systems, and the need for ongoing training of employees to use the technology.

10.2 THE BACKGROUND

10.2.1 Automated Insurance Premium Assignment Systems

Automated premium allocation systems have become a widespread innovation within the cutting-edge insurance industry. Eling et al. (2022) explained that using superior technology which includes device mastering, AI, and fuzzy logic, these systems analyze clients' private traits and behavioral patterns as it should check for threat and calculate insurance charges.

One of the key benefits of automated premium allocation systems is the potential to more exactly examine individual danger via in-depth analysis of customer information. It is able to take into account a client's past coverage claims history, fitness information, way of life habits, or even social media pastime, creating a hazard profile that is a good deal more specific than traditional assessment strategies.

Meanwhile, the success implementation of an automatic premium allocation device relies heavily on the high quality and amount of records. For powerful risk evaluation and insurance premium calculation, correct and comprehensive information series is critical. Consequently, insurance corporations are actively investing in thoroughly dealing with and updating client data.

10.2.2 Advantages of Fuzzy ANN in Automated Insurance Premium Assignment Systems

Fuzzy artificial neural networks (Fuzzy ANNs) are becoming a very critical technology for computerized coverage premium allocation structures. Fuzzy ANN combines the learning capacity of artificial neural networks (ANNs) with the uncertainty dealing with capacity of fuzzy logic, demonstrating exceptional performance in fixing complex issues inside the insurance industry. Specially, this generation offers the potential to successfully deal with diverse uncertainties and ambiguities which can get up all through the coverage premium calculation process, permitting the proposal of more correct and personalized insurance products.

One of the largest benefits of Fuzzy ANN is its fantastic records processing potential. Moreover, Fuzzy ANN's overall performance improves over time through its learning potential. Any other critical benefit of Fuzzy ANN-based systems is their flexibility. This lets in insurers to reply quickly to market changes and consumer wishes, which is critical to stay competitive. Fuzzy ANN is likewise beneficial in handling complex insurance products and rules. The capacity to efficiently examine various coverage products and their threat elements and calculate customized insurance rates primarily based on this presents a widespread aggressive advantage to insurance groups. That is a way to offer better alternatives to customers and improve insurer profitability at the same time. There are various cases of applying ANNs in insurance premium allocation systems. Zhao et al. (2022) studied that ANNs have the capability to study complex styles and relationships from data, which can be used to calculate coverage charges and verify threat.

Inside the automobile coverage area, person risk is classified by way of thinking about diverse variables which includes the driver's driving conduct, accident history, and car type. ANNs can study critical styles from these big amounts of facts to determine the proper insurance premium for each driver.

As per Rahmani et al. (2021), ANNs can extract crucial information from this complicated health information, examine an individual's risk, and advise customized coverage rates. As an instance, by means of studying lifestyle facts including smoking or workout frequency, coverage premiums are allocated in line with health risk.

Home insurance considers a variety of factors, together with the region of the home, the year it was built, the substances it was made of, and the frequency of natural failures inside the area. ANNs can integrate this information to assess the chance of a home and calculate the right insurance premium. Thangavel et al. (2024) defined that this allows us to offer customized insurance products that take into account the characteristics of each domestic and nearby elements.

In this manner, ANNs play a key role in presenting more correct and personalized coverage products by means of analyzing and learning from diverse data within the coverage top rate allocation system.

10.2.3 Artificial Neural Networks for Automation

ANN is a technology that plays a crucial function in data evaluation and pattern recognition, and it is becoming a key thing of automatic systems. Chhipi-Shrestha et al. (2023) defined that due to these traits, ANNs can be used in an expansion of fields for automation, contributing to optimize decision-making procedure and increase efficiency.

10.2.4 Fuzzy Logic and ANN-Based Technique to Find Relative Desirability

Fuzzy logic and ANNs constitute two pivotal technologies within the realm of AI and computational models. Adem and Dagdeviren (2016) explained that once combined, they offer a robust technique for addressing complex problems which can be hard to resolve using conventional binary logic. This synergy is specially effective in tasks requiring the assessment of relative desirability among numerous options, making it valuable in fields including decision-making, manipulate systems, and optimization approaches.

Fuzzy logic, with its capability to address imprecision and uncertainty, presents a more human-like way of thinking, corresponding to how people process records and make decisions. It operates at the principle of the use of degrees of fact in preference to the usual "true or false" (1 or 0) binary logic. This permits for intermediate values to be described between traditional binaries, enabling a greater nuanced technique to reasoning and decision-making. While assessing relative desirability, fuzzy logic can manage the vagueness and ambiguity inherent in subjective assessments, translating these qualitative factors into quantitative analysis.

However, ANNs mimic the neural structure of the human brain, studying from examples and making predictions about new statistics based on learned patterns. ANNs are in particular adept at recognizing complicated patterns and relationships within massive datasets. While carried out to locating relative desirability, ANNs can analyze beyond choices and consequences to predict the most suited options based totally on a fixed of criteria, even inside the face of sizeable and apparently unstructured facts.

Integrating fuzzy logic with ANNs creates an effective tool for determining relative desirability. Fuzzy logic can be used to preprocess input records, converting subjective judgments into a format that can be processed by means of the ANN. The neural network, in turn, learns to associate these inputs with desired outcomes, successfully making decisions that reflect a nuanced knowledge of desirability underneath uncertainty. This combination leverages the strengths of both approaches: the intuitive, human-like reasoning of fuzzy logic and the sample reputation and getting to know abilities of ANNs.

In practical applications, this fusion of fuzzy logic and ANN is exceptionally useful.

The development and implementation of fuzzy logic and ANN-based techniques for locating relative desirability constitute an enormous development in choice aid structures. By accommodating the complexity and uncertainty inherent in many selection-making techniques, these techniques provide an extra flexible and correct method of comparing options and determining choicest outcomes. As research and technology continue to adapt, the combination of fuzzy logic and ANNs will certainly discover even broader programs, further improving our capacity to make informed and nuanced selections in an increasingly complex world.

10.3 PROPOSED MODEL

The integration of preference-leveled evaluation functions (PLEFs) with an ANNs in model design represents a groundbreaking method in the area of automatic insurance premium assignment. This revolutionary model goals to deal with the complexities and dynamic nature of risk evaluation in coverage, offering a more tailored and correct evaluation of policyholders' danger levels. By doing so, it enables insurance companies to assign premiums more efficaciously and fairly, reflecting the individual danger profiles of policyholders.

PLEFs are a complicated method for incorporating human-like reasoning into computational models. They permit the system to deal with numerous stages of preference or importance among distinct standards, mimicking the nuanced way humans assess more than one factors. Within the context of insurance premium assignment, PLEFs can be used to assess different threat elements along with age, driving records, fitness conditions, and lifestyle choices, assigning a level of importance or preference to each. This nuanced method ensures that the assessment of chance factors is not binary, but rather displays a spectrum of desirability or acceptability, similar to human judgment.

Integrating PLEFs with a synthetic Neural community (ANN) leverages the sample reputation and learning skills of ANNs, with the nuanced evaluation provided by means of PLEFs. The ANN aspect of the model is skilled on historic data, learning the complicated relationships among numerous risk elements and outcomes. it could become aware of styles and correlations that might not be immediately apparent, enhancing the model's potential to predict hazard with high accuracy. The mixing with PLEFs allows the ANN to weigh those elements in keeping with their assigned stages of desire, ensuring that the premium assignment reflects a complete and nuanced understanding of threat.

The proposed version operates in numerous tiers. Initially, the PLEFs preprocess input data, translating subjective judgments and choices into quantifiable values. This processed data is then fed into the ANN, which evaluates the complete risk profile of every policyholder. The ANN's output, a predictive risk degree, is then used to determine an appropriate insurance premium. This premium reflects not only the statistical chance of a claim being made, but also the relative significance of diverse danger factors as determined by using PLEFs.

One of the crucial blessings of this version is its flexibility and adaptability. The PLEFs can be adjusted to reflect changes in insurance policies or threat evaluation strategies, permitting the model to stay relevant over time. In addition, the ANN may be retrained on new facts, making sure that the model evolves in response to emerging traits and patterns in risk behavior.

The proposed model integrating PLEFs with an ANN offers a sophisticated and dynamic method to automated insurance premium undertaking. By combining the nuanced evaluation of threat elements supplied with the aid of PLEFs with the sample recognition and predictive capabilities of ANNs, this model guarantees to decorate the accuracy and equity of insurance premium assignments. As such, it represents a big development in the application of AI technology in the insurance industry, with the ability to enhance each operational efficiency and purchaser satisfaction.

The proposed model design involves several key components and steps:

1. Information collection and Preprocessing
    - **Collect historical facts:** Acquire complete information on policyholders, which include demographic facts, risk elements, past claims, and previously assigned rates.
    - **Clean and preprocess the data:** Ensure the records is easy, putting off any inconsistencies or errors. Normalize the statistics to make certain uniformity inside the input values for the ANN.
2. Outline PLEFs
    - **Discover key chance factors:** Determine which chance factors are relevant for assessing the insurance premium. These ought to encompass age, driving records, fitness situations, etc.
    - **Assign choice degrees:** For each chance aspect, outline ranges of desire or importance based totally on professional judgment or historic analysis. These degrees will guide how every factor influences the overall risk evaluation.
3. Design and train the ANN
    - **Design the ANN architecture:** Pick out an appropriate architecture for the ANN, such as the number of layers and nodes, considering the complexity of the threat evaluation task.
    - **Train the ANN:** Use the preprocessed historical records to train the ANN. The training method entails adjusting the weights of the neural network to reduce prediction errors, using algorithms which includes backpropagation.
4. Integration of PLEFs with ANN
    - **Integrate PLEFs into the ANN input:** Apply the PLEFs to the input records, remodeling the uncooked information right into a layout that reflects the assigned preference stages for every risk component.
    - **Feed processed information into the ANN:** Input the records processed by means of PLEFs into the ANN. This permits the ANN to assess the facts, thinking of the nuanced knowledge of risk provided by means of the PLEFs.
5. Top rate undertaking
    - **Generate risk assessments:** Use the ANN to generate a risk assessment for each policyholder, based totally on their individual risk factors and the possibilities assigned through the PLEFs.
    - **Determine premiums:** Primarily based on the danger tests, decide the insurance premiums for each policyholder. The premiums need to

replicate the assessed risk level, incorporating each the statistical chance of a claim and the relative importance of various chance elements.

6. Version evaluation and Adjustment
   - **Examine model performance:** Examine the accuracy and fairness of the charges assigned by the model. This will involve comparing expected threat ranges and assigned premiums against real outcomes.
   - **Regulate and refine the model:** Based totally on the assessment, refine the PLEFs and retrain the ANN as essential to enhance the model's performance. This step ensures that the version remains accurate and relevant through the years.

By following those steps, the proposed model aims to provide an advanced and dynamic approach to automatic insurance premium assignment. Through the mixing of PLEFs with an ANN, this model now not only enhances the accuracy of risk evaluation, but also guarantees that top rate assignments are nuanced and fair, reflecting a comprehensive information of each policyholder's risk profile.

This designed model synergizes PLEFs with synthetic Intelligence, particularly integrating Fuzzy logic, to refine the manner of automated insurance premium mission. By means of fusing dependent choice evaluations, fuzzy logic-based reasoning, and the dynamic learning abilities inherent in machine learning, the machine is crafted to be both sturdy and adaptable. Its number one purpose is to reinforce decision support mechanisms and heighten the precision in coverage premium calculations. A block diagram illustrating the proposed system, which utilizes PLEFs for the nuanced task of insurance premiums, is depicted in Figure 10.1, while the operational steps are outlined in Algorithm 10.1. The implementation leverages characteristic features from an insurance policyholder dataset, as illustrated in Table 10.1. The melding of preference-oriented assessments with the adaptive insights provided by machine learning enriches the model's capacity to discern complex value conditions. This, in turn, guides the execution of more informed and targeted insurance premium assignments, ultimately fostering a more efficient and satisfactory insurance procurement process.

Algorithm 10.1: PFMDMM Based on Preference Leveled Evaluation Functions to Assess the Relative Desirability of Premium

Input: Input x features of policyholder dataset

Output: Categorizes the premium for node and Alternate Choice.

Start

1. Input x features of data of policyholder dataset
2. PFMDMM to recognize accurate premium for the node; arranged in correct format to feed into the ANN for classification.
3. *Training stage*: Weights of the Feed Forward Neural Network were given by some arbitrary value as per Table 10.1 and is then tuned for optimal during the iterative learning procedure with the help of back propagation algorithm.

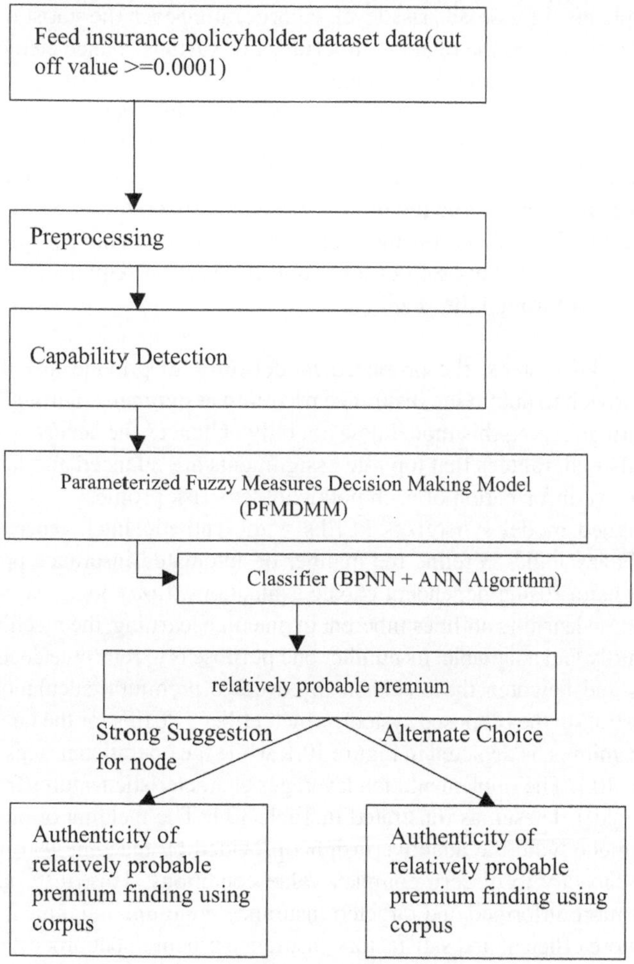

FIGURE 10.1 Block diagram of proposed PFMDMM based on preference leveled evaluation functions for finding relative desirability of premium. (Developed by Author.)

4. *Testing stage*: The neural network is tested against a variety of test samples to ensure whether the acquired system correctly categorizes the premium to best probable value and other valueparts.
5. Categorizes the value to best suggestion range and alternate opinion.

Stop

10.3 FINDINGS

AI might change the risk landscape significantly by transforming some risks from low-severity/high-frequency to high-severity/low-frequency. This requires insurance companies to rethink traditional insurance coverage and design adequate insurance products. Owens et al. (2022) suggested that it presents the potential to bring

TABLE 10.1
Examples Features of Policyholder Dataset

Time	Use x[0]	gen x[1]	Preference-1 x[2]	Preference-2 x[3]	Preference-3 x[4]	Preference-4 x[5]	Preference-5 x[6]	Preference-6 x[7]	Preference-7 x[8]
1.45E+09	0.932833	0.003483	0.932833	3.33E-05	0.0207	0.061917	0.442633	0.12415	0.006983
1.45E+09	0.934333	0.003467	0.934333	0	0.020717	0.063817	0.444067	0.124	0.006983
1.45E+09	0.931817	0.003467	0.931817	1.67E-05	0.0207	0.062317	0.446067	0.123533	0.006983
1.45E+09	1.02205	0.003483	1.02205	1.67E-05	0.1069	0.068517	0.446583	0.123133	0.006983
1.45E+09	1.1394	0.003467	1.1394	0.000133	0.236933	0.063983	0.446533	0.12285	0.00685
1.45E+09	1.391867	0.003433	1.391867	0.000283	0.50325	0.063667	0.447033	0.1223	0.006717
1.45E+09	1.366217	0.00345	1.366217	0.000283	0.4994	0.063717	0.443267	0.12205	0.006733
---	---	---	---	---	---	---	---	---	---

innovation in the insurance industry. Fuzzy Artificial Intelligence (FAI) is a technology that finds relative desirability in the automatic premium allocation process, especially through the integration of PLEFs and ANN. These integrated models can significantly improve the accuracy and fairness of premium allocation by combining the ability to recognize and predict patterns of complex risk factors with the ability to quantify subjective judgments and preferences. This fuzzy logic-primarily based technique plays a critical role in presenting a more designated interpretation of the complex interactions between various risk factors and a complete expertise of the hazard profile of individual policy owners.

The proposed version is an essential technology for efficiently handling uncertainty and ambiguity which can rise up during the insurance premium selection system. Through the application of FAI, the policy owner's danger assessment is not simply based on statistical probability, but develops into a customized evaluation that reflects the individual's danger elements and preferences. This allows coverage companies to calculate coverage charges that are more correctly tailor-made to every individual's actual threat stage, ultimately enhancing purchaser pleasure and operational efficiency.

Moreover, this version has the potential to enhance overall performance over time via continuous learning and adjustment. By continuously adjusting PLEFs and ANN to mirror changes in the insurance marketplace and policy owners' behavioral patterns, the machine can acquire extra specific and fairer premium allocation. This adaptive technique highlights the long-term benefits that the application of AI technology can provide inside the insurance enterprise and is anticipated to contribute to maximizing the efficiency of insurance procedures and customer satisfaction.

The primary findings can be summarized as follows:

- The proposed methodology is adept at facilitating premium allocation decisions within limited time.
- This examination proposes a revolutionary application of a parameterized fuzzy metric decision model primarily based on preference-based valuation functions for characteristic extraction technique within the context of insurance premium allocation.
- A dataset of policyholders was used for the empirical analysis, and a parametric version for premium allocation was developed by leveraging the robust measures of policyholder statistics contained on this dataset.
- Particularly, we constructed a new computerized system for insurance premium allocation with the aid of leveraging the decision-making strength of a parameterized fuzzy measurement decision model based on preference-based evaluation functions.

10.4 CONCLUSION

This study introduces an innovative technique to decide most fulfilling premium allocation to insurers by combining BPNN and FAI models using the PFMDMM data classification machine. Experimental results show that a parameterized fuzzy metric selection model optimized for insurance premium determination suggests promising effects in appropriately allocating insurance rates within a smart gadget.

The model is based totally on a preference-based evaluation function, and this study is the first to apply a parameterized fuzzy metric decision-making model using a preference-based evaluation function for data classification in the insurance sector.

REFERENCES

Adem, Aylın, and Metin Dagdeviren. "A life insurance policy selection via hesitant fuzzy linguistic decision making model." *Procedia Computer Science* 102 (2016): 398–405.

Ali, Abdualmtalab, Usama Heneash, Amgad Hussein, and Mohamed Eskebi. "Predicting pavement condition index using fuzzy logic technique." *Infrastructures* 7, no. 7 (2022): 91.

Bouramdane, Ayat-Allah. "Cyberattacks in Smart Grids: Challenges and solving the Multi-Criteria Decision-Making for cybersecurity options, including ones that incorporate artificial intelligence, using an analytical hierarchy process." *Journal of Cybersecurity and Privacy* 3, no. 4 (2023): 662–705.

Chhipi-Shrestha, Gyan, Haroon R. Mian, Saeed Mohammadiun, Manuel Rodriguez, KasunHewage, and Rehan Sadiq. "Digital water: artificial intelligence and soft computing applications for drinking water quality assessment." *Clean Technologies and Environmental Policy* 25, no. 5 (2023): 1409–1438.

Chryssolouris, George, Kosmas Alexopoulos, and ZoiArkouli. "Artificial intelligence in manufacturing equipment, automation, and robots." In *A Perspective on Artificial Intelligence in Manufacturing*, pp. 41–78. Cham: Springer International Publishing, 2023.

de la Torre-López, José, Aurora Ramírez, and José Raúl Romero. "Artificial intelligence to automate the systematic review of scientific literature." *Computing* 105, no. 10 (2023): 2171–2194.

Dhieb, Najmeddine, Hakim Ghazzai, Hichem Besbes, and Yehia Massoud. "A secure ai-driven architecture for automated insurance systems: Fraud detection and risk measurement." *IEEE Access* 8 (2020): 58546–58558.

Ecer, Fatih, İlkin Yaran Ögel, Raghunathan Krishankumar, and Erfan Babaee Tirkolaee. "The q-rung fuzzy LOPCOW-VIKOR model to assess the role of unmanned aerial vehicles for precision agriculture realization in the Agri-Food 4.0 era." *Artificial Intelligence Review* 56, no. 11 (2023): 13373–13406.

Eling, Martin, Davide Nuessle, and Julian Staubli. "The impact of artificial intelligence along the insurance value chain and on the insurability of risks." *The Geneva Papers on Risk and Insurance-Issues and Practice* 47, no. 2 (2022): 205–241.

Hu, Kuang-Hua, Fu-Hsiang Chen, Ming-Fu Hsu, and Gwo-Hshiung Tzeng. "Identifying key factors for adopting artificial intelligence-enabled auditing techniques by joint utilization of fuzzy-rough set theory and MRDM technique." *Technological and Economic Development of Economy* 27, no. 2 (2021): 459–492.

Hu, Chaofang, Ge Qu, and Yuting Zhang. "Pigeon-inspired fuzzy multi-objective task allocation of unmanned aerial vehicles for multi-target tracking." *Applied Soft Computing* 126 (2022): 109310.

Ivan, Bogdanov, Bogdanova Olga, Hlukhonets Oksana, Petryshyn Roman, Shkvarylyuk Marta, and Kirshak Khrystyna. "Application of Grey Relational Analysis for Utilizing Artificial Intelligence Methods in Aviation Management." In *AI in Business: Opportunities and Limitations*: Volume 1, pp. 113–123. Cham: Springer Nature Switzerland, 2024.

Jia, Yanhuai, and Zheng Wang. "Application of artificial intelligence based on the fuzzy control algorithm in enterprise innovation." *Heliyon* 10, no. 6 (2024): e28116.

Jong, Cha Yong, Akshay Mittal, Geordi Tristan, Vanessa Noller, Hui Ling Chan, Yongkai Goh, Eunice Wan Qi Yeap, Srinivas Reddy Dubbaka, Harsha Rao Nagesh, and Shin Yee Wong. "ANFIS-driven machine learning automated platform for cooling crystallization process development." *Organic Process Research & Development* 28, no. 4 (2024): 1129–1144.

Li, Fangyi. *Fuzzy Rule-based Inference: Advances and Applications in Reasoning with Approximate Knowledge Interpolation.* Springer Nature Singapore, (2024, Chapter 3, p. 49).

Mardani, Abbas, Mahyar Kamali Saraji, Arunodaya Raj Mishra, and Pratibha Rani. "A novel extended approach under hesitant fuzzy sets to design a framework for assessing the key challenges of digital health interventions adoption during the COVID-19 outbreak." *Applied Soft Computing* 96 (2020): 106613.

Osamy, Walid, Ahmed M. Khedr, Ahmed Salim, Amal Ibrahim Al Ali, and Ahmed A. El-Sawy. "Coverage, deployment and localization challenges in wireless sensor networks based on artificial intelligence techniques: a review." *IEEE Access* 10 (2022): 30232–30257.

Owens, Emer, Barry Sheehan, Martin Mullins, Martin Cunneen, Juliane Ressel, and German Castignani. "Explainable artificial intelligence (xai) in insurance." *Risks* 10, no. 12 (2022): 230.

Pattnaik, Chinmaya Ranjan, Sachi Nandan Mohanty, Sarita Mohanty, Jyotir Moy Chatterjee, Biswajit Jana, and Vicente Garcia Diaz. "A fuzzy multi-criteria decision-making method for purchasing life insurance in India." *Bulletin of Electrical Engineering and Informatics* 10, no. 1 (2021): 344–356.

Rahmani, Amir Masoud, Elham Azhir, Saqib Ali, Mokhtar Mohammadi, Omed Hassan Ahmed, Marwan Yassin Ghafour, Sarkar Hasan Ahmed, and Mehdi Hosseinzadeh. "Artificial intelligence approaches and mechanisms for big data analytics: A systematic study." *PeerJ Computer Science* 7 (2021): e488.

Shapiro, Arnold F. "Fuzzy logic in insurance." *Insurance: Mathematics and Economics* 35, no. 2 (2004): 399–424.

Sircar, Anirbid, Kriti Yadav, Kamakshi Rayavarapu, Namrata Bist, and Hemangi Oza. "Application of machine learning and artificial intelligence in oil and gas industry." *Petroleum Research* 6, no. 4 (2021): 379–391.

Susanto, Sumiatie, and Ditdit Nugeraha Utama. "Fuzzy based decision support model for health insurance claim." *Informatica* 46, no. 7 (2022): 119–130.

Taboada, Ianire, Abouzar Daneshpajouh, Nerea Toledo, and Tharaka de Vass. "Artificial intelligence enabled project management: A systematic literature review." *Applied Sciences* 13, no. 8 (2023): 5014.

Tatari, Farzaneh, Mohammad-R. Akbarzadeh -T, and Ahmad Sabahi. "Fuzzy-probabilistic multi agent system for breast cancer risk assessment and insurance premium assignment." *Journal of Biomedical Informatics* 45, no. 6 (2012): 1021–1034.

Taylan, Osman, Abdulaziz S. Alkabaa, Hanan S. Alqabbaa, Esra Pamukçu, and Víctor Leiva. "Early prediction in classification of cardiovascular diseases with machine learning, neuro-fuzzy and statistical methods." *Biology* 12, no. 1 (2023): 117.

Thangavel, Kathiravan, Roberto Sabatini, Alessandro Gardi, Kavindu Ranasinghe, Samuel Hilton, Pablo Servidia, and Dario Spiller. "Artificial intelligence for trusted autonomous satellite operations." *Progress in Aerospace Sciences* 144 (2024): 100960.

Wang, Ke, Ziyi Ying, Shankha Shubhra Goswami, Yongsheng Yin, and Yafei Zhao. "Investigating the role of artificial intelligence technologies in the construction industry using a Delphi-ANP-TOPSIS hybrid MCDM concept under a fuzzy environment." *Sustainability* 15, no. 15 (2023): 11848.

Zhang, Xuesong, Anping Fu, Changshu Zhan, Duc Truong Pham, Qiang Zhao, TiangangQiang, Mohammed Aljuaid, and Chenxi Fu. "Selective disassembly sequence planning under uncertainty using trapezoidal fuzzy numbers: A novel hybrid metaheuristic algorithm." *Engineering Applications of Artificial Intelligence* 128 (2024): 107459.

Zhao, Shuai, Frede Blaabjerg, and Huai Wang. "An overview of artificial intelligence applications for power electronics." *IEEE Transactions on Power Electronics* 36, no. 4 (2020): 4633–4658.

11 Opportunities and Challenges of Combining Artificial Intelligence Power with the Richness of Healthcare Claims Data

Chandrasekar Vijai and Sridevi Jayavelu

11.1 INTRODUCTION

Artificial intelligence (AI) is poised to revolutionize healthcare by leveraging superior algorithms and information analytics to enhance diagnosis, remedy, and patient care. AI technology provides extra-specific, customized, and proactive procedures for addressing medical challenges, transforming traditional healthcare practices. One key utility of AI in healthcare is clinical imaging evaluation. AI algorithms excel at interpreting complicated clinical photos like X-rays, MRIs, and CT scans, aiding radiologists in detecting abnormalities with excessive accuracy and performance. This capability expedites prognosis and treatment planning, in the long run enhancing affected person effects and reducing healthcare charges (Liu et al. 2019). Predictive analytics powered by AI is every other transformative location. By analysing widespread affected person datasets, AI can anticipate disorder development, become aware of at-danger populations, and optimize remedy techniques. Machine learning models can find diffuse patterns and developments that can elude human clinicians, enabling advanced interventions and more effective healthcare management (Rajkomar et al. 2019).

Furthermore, AI enables personalized remedies by leveraging character affected person information, consisting of genetic profiles and medical histories, to tailor treatment plans. This precision remedy method maximizes treatment efficacy while minimizing negative results, representing a shift in the direction of extra targeted and green healthcare delivery (Obermeyer and Emanuel 2016). In healthcare operations, AI streamlines administrative obligations, optimizes aid allocation, and enhances operational efficiency. From predicting patient admission charges to optimizing group worker schedules, AI-driven tools improve hospital workflows, ultimately enhancing patient care and experience (Kocaballi et al. 2019). While AI offers transformative capacity,

DOI: 10.1201/9781003472551-13

demanding situations together with information privacy, algorithmic bias, and clinician attractiveness should be addressed to comprehend its complete benefits. Nevertheless, AI's integration into healthcare guarantees to revolutionize affected person care and reshape the future of drugs.

11.2 APPLICATIONS OF AI IN HEALTHCARE CLAIMS ANALYSIS

AI's applications in healthcare claims evaluation are multifaceted, providing superior equipment to streamline methods, detect anomalies, and optimize resource allocation. These programmes leverage gadget mastering, herbal language processing (NLP), and predictive analytics to extract insights from large volumes of claim information. Here are some key programmes sponsored by using studies.

11.2.1 Fraud Detection and Prevention

AI-powered systems can analyse historical claims records to pick out patterns indicative of fraudulent sports, which include billing for useless strategies or upcoding. Machine getting to know algorithms can stumble on anomalies and flag suspicious claims, assisting in fraud prevention and reducing economic losses for healthcare payers and providers.

11.2.2 Claims Processing Automation

AI automates claims processing workflows by using relevant statistics from unstructured claims statistics. Natural language processing (NLP) strategies parse and interpret free-text fields in claims, allowing for faster adjudication and decreasing administrative burdens.

11.2.3 Predictive Analytics for Cost Management

By analysing claims information alongside different patient information, AI fashions can predict healthcare usage patterns, count on fees, and identify opportunities for price containment. This proactive technique allows players to optimize coverage strategies and allocate assets correctly.

11.2.4 Clinical Decision Support

AI-pushed analytics offer valuable insights to clinicians with the aid of analysing claims' facts along with medical facts. This supports evidence-based choice-making, improves care coordination, and complements patient consequences (Nguyen et al. 2019).

11.2.5 Optimizing Provider Networks

AI algorithms analyse claims statistics to assess company overall performance, assess network adequacy, and identify excellent, price-effective companies. This enables payers to build sturdy issuer networks and negotiate beneficial contracts

(Lee et al. 2018). These applications of AI in healthcare claims analysis reveal its capacity to force operational efficiencies, lessen expenses, and enhance the quality of care. However, demanding situations inclusive of records privacy, interpretability of AI-pushed insights, and regulatory compliance should be addressed to maximize the advantages of AI in healthcare claims control.

11.3 BENEFITS OF AI IN HEALTHCARE CLAIMS ANALYSIS

11.3.1 Fraud Detection and Prevention

AI algorithms play a crucial function in detecting and stopping healthcare fraud, which stays a good-sized task within the enterprise. This proactive method to fraud detection facilitates coverage organizations, and healthcare vendors reduce financial losses and preserve the integrity of the healthcare system. Research via Boland et al. (2017) demonstrates the effectiveness of AI-based fraud detection structures, highlighting their capacity to significantly lessen fraudulent claims and associated fees. Such systems constantly learn from historical statistics to decorate their detection abilities and adapt to evolving fraud schemes, offering a strong defence against fraudulent sports in healthcare claims.

11.3.2 Claims Processing Automation

The automation of claims processing through AI technologies streamlines administrative workflows, speeds up compensation cycles, and decreases manual mistakes. NLP algorithms extract pertinent records from unstructured claims records, which include diagnosis codes, method details, and patient demographics, facilitating quicker adjudication and selection-making. Studies through Obeidat et al. emphasize the efficiency profits done via AI-driven claims automation, leading to reduced processing instances and administrative charges. These structures beautify the overall responsiveness of healthcare payers and companies, ensuing in advanced customer pride and operational performance.

11.3.3 Predictive Analytics for Cost Management

AI-powered predictive analytics enable healthcare businesses to forecast healthcare usage styles, anticipate costs, and identify opportunities for price containment. By analysing ancient claims facts along demographic, medical, and socioeconomic elements, machine learning models can expect future healthcare costs and inform aid allocation strategies. Research by using Wang et al. (2019) highlights the fee of AI-pushed predictive analytics in optimizing healthcare spending and enhancing monetary performance. These insights empower healthcare selection-makers to put into effect focused interventions, which include preventive care packages or network optimization initiatives, to mitigate rising costs and beautify cost performance.

11.3.4 Clinical Decision Support

AI-based analytics offer treasured assistance to clinicians by integrating claims records with medical data to facilitate evidence primarily based choice-making and care coordination. By analysing patient histories, remedy styles, and outcomes, AI algorithms can pick out fine practices, propose appropriate interventions, and improve care quality (Nguyen et al. 2019). Studies by Obermeyer and Emanuel (2016) underscore the ability of AI-driven medical decision aid structures to enhance diagnostic accuracy and treatment results. These systems empower healthcare vendors with actionable insights, enabling personalized and effective affected person care while decreasing variability and mistakes in scientific practice.

11.3.5 Optimizing Provider Networks

AI analytics optimize company networks by evaluating provider performance, assessing community adequacy, and identifying high-fee, fee-powerful providers. By studying claims statistics and issuer attributes, device getting to know models enables healthcare companies to build robust networks, negotiate favourable contracts, and improve community efficiency (Lee et al. 2018). Research by Mehta et al. (2020) demonstrates the position of AI in improving issuer community control, which leads to improved affected person access, reduced network leakage, and better outcomes. These insights enable healthcare payers to optimize their provider networks and enhance collaboration with high-performing providers, ultimately benefiting both patients and stakeholders. The benefits of AI in healthcare claims analysis are extensive and multifaceted, encompassing fraud detection, claims processing automation, cost management, clinical decision support, and provider network optimization. The application of AI-driven technologies enables healthcare organizations to optimize operations, improve efficiency, and deliver higher-quality care while reducing costs and mitigating risks. As AI continues to evolve and integrate into healthcare systems, its transformative impact on claims analysis will drive innovation and efficiency across the healthcare ecosystem.

11.4 CHALLENGES OF UTILIZING AI WITH HEALTHCARE CLAIMS DATA

Integrating AI with healthcare claims statistics gives vast potential to improve operational efficiency, beautify decision-making, and optimize affected person care. However, this transformative integration additionally affords substantial demanding situations that must be addressed to maximize the blessings of AI in healthcare claims analysis. In this complete exploration, we delve into the key demanding situations associated with making use of AI with healthcare claims information, supported by means of relevant references and studies.

11.4.1 Data Quality and Integration

One of the number one demanding situation in leveraging AI for healthcare claims analysis is making sure the quality and integration of numerous facts sources. Healthcare claims information regularly come from disparate resources, together with digital fitness statistics (EHRs), billing systems, and coverage claims databases. Variations in information formats, coding requirements, and completeness can avoid the accuracy and reliability of AI models (Obermeyer and Emanuel 2016). Research by Kaggal et al. highlights the significance of records excellent assessment and normalization to beautify the usability of healthcare claims statistics for AI programs. Addressing record satisfactory troubles via information cleaning, standardization, and interoperability initiatives is critical to unlock the overall capability of AI in healthcare claims analysis.

11.4.2 Privacy and Security Concerns

Healthcare claims statistics include touchy and, in my view, identifiable data, making information privacy and protection paramount considerations in AI-driven healthcare analytics. Adhering to regulatory frameworks including the Health Insurance Portability and Accountability Act (HIPAA) is vital to shield affected person confidentiality and save you from unauthorized get right of entry to or information breaches (Fridsma 2018). Studies by Sweeney et al. (2013) emphasize the significance of privacy-maintaining AI techniques, inclusive of differential privacy and secure multiparty computation, to enable collaborative data analysis while safeguarding patient privacy. Building sturdy records governance frameworks and enforcing encryption and access controls are crucial strategies to mitigate privacy dangers associated with AI in healthcare claims evaluation.

11.4.3 Algorithmic Bias and Interpretability

AI algorithms educated on healthcare claims facts are at risk of biases inherent inside the statistics, leading to biased predictions or choices. Additionally, the complexity of AI fashions, inclusive of deep mastering neural networks, often results in "black box" consequences that lack transparency and interpretability (Rajkomar et al. 2019). Research by means of Price and Cohen (2019) underscores the want for bias detection and mitigation strategies to make certain equity and fairness in AI-pushed healthcare analytics. Exploring interpretable AI techniques, which includes explainable gadget mastering algorithms, can facilitate accept as true with and acceptance among healthcare stakeholders with the aid of imparting insights into how AI arrives at its decisions.

11.4.4 Regulatory Compliance and Ethical Considerations

Navigating regulatory requirements and ethical issues is a tremendous task when deploying AI in healthcare claims evaluation. Compliance with regulations governing facts privacy, patient consent, and algorithm transparency is crucial to make certain moral and responsible use of AI technologies (Obermeyer and Emanuel 2016). Research with the aid of Beam and Kohane (2018) highlights the moral dilemmas associated with AI in healthcare, along with troubles of bias, duty, and knowledgeable consent. Collaborative efforts between policymakers, healthcare companies, and AI developers are essential to establish pointers and frameworks that sell ethical AI deployment while also upholding patient rights and societal values.

11.4.5 Clinician Acceptance and Adoption

Achieving clinician recognition and adoption of AI-driven insights from healthcare claims information is some other significant tasks. Healthcare specialists can be sceptical of AI technology due to issues about activity displacement, perceived loss of medical relevance, or resistance to change (Beam and Kohane 2018). Studies by means of Cresswell et al. (2017) emphasize the importance of clinician engagement and schooling in fostering acceptance and popularity of AI gear in scientific exercise. Integrating AI seamlessly into existing workflows, offering schooling on AI packages, and demonstrating tangible blessings in affected person care are vital techniques to sell clinician adoption of AI-pushed healthcare analytics. While AI holds big promise for remodelling healthcare claims evaluation, numerous demanding situations must be addressed to realize its complete capacity. Overcoming data nice problems, making sure privacy and safety, mitigating algorithmic bias, navigating regulatory compliance, and fostering clinician recognition are vital steps in harnessing the blessings of AI in healthcare claims analysis. Collaborative efforts between stakeholders, together with policymakers, healthcare providers, statistics scientists, and sufferers, are important to address those demanding situations and pave the way for accountable and effective deployment of AI technologies in healthcare.

11.5 DATA PREPROCESSING AND CLEANING

Data preprocessing and cleansing are essential steps inside the data evaluation pipeline, critical for making sure the quality, reliability, and effectiveness of synthetic intelligence (AI) and gadget gaining knowledge of (ML) models. This technique includes transforming uncooked records into a format suitable for evaluation, addressing issues including lacking values, outliers, and inconsistencies. In this complete discussion, we are able to explore the importance of facts preprocessing and cleansing, common techniques hired, and pleasant practices inside the area, supported via applicable references and studies.

11.5.1 Importance of Data Preprocessing and Cleaning

Data preprocessing plays a pivotal role in records evaluation and modelling for numerous reasons:

11.5.1.1 Ensuring Data Quality

Real-international data is often noisy, incomplete, or inconsistent due to various factors which include human mistakes, dimension inaccuracies, or gadget screw-ups.

Data preprocessing involves identifying and addressing those problems to make certain the dataset's accuracy, completeness, and reliability (Dasu and Johnson 2003).

11.5.1.2 Improving Model Performance

Clean and preprocessed information results in higher version performance. By doing away with noise, irrelevant functions, and outliers, preprocessing allows AI and ML algorithms recognition on the most crucial styles and relationships inside the statistics, resulting in more correct and strong models (Brownlee 2016).

11.5.1.3 Facilitating Feature Engineering

Feature engineering involves creating new capabilities from present records to enhance the performance of ML fashions. Data preprocessing presents the inspiration for function engineering through reworking raw information into meaningful functions that seize applicable information for predictive modelling (Koehrsen 2018).

11.6 COMMON TECHNIQUES IN DATA PREPROCESSING AND CLEANING

Data preprocessing and cleaning are crucial steps in document education that make sure the first-rate, consistency, and suitability of data for evaluation and modelling responsibilities. These methods involve remodelling raw statistics right into a hooked-up layout that can be correctly utilized by device getting to know algorithms. Here are not unusual strategies utilized in statistics preprocessing and cleaning.

11.6.1 Handling Missing Values

Missing statistics is a not unusual challenge in real-international datasets. Several techniques can be used to handle lacking values:

Imputation: Replace missing values with statistical measures like the mean, median, or mode of the column.
Deletion: Remove rows or columns with lacking values, if they may be few or cannot be imputed accurately.
Prediction: Use device getting-to-realize algorithms (e.g., K-nearest pals, regression) to count on missing values based mostly on exceptional correlated capabilities.

11.6.2 Removing Duplicates

Duplicates can distort records for assessment and model training. Techniques to deal with duplicates encompass:

Identifying duplicate information primarily based on key attributes and getting rid of them to maintain instances.

Keeping the primary occurrence and casting off subsequent duplicates.

11.6.3 Standardization and Normalization

Standardization and normalization are techniques used to scale numerical features to a common range:

Standardization (Z-score normalization): Transform information to have an average of zero and a state-of-the-art deviation of 1.
Normalization (min-max scaling): Rescale records to a selection between zero and 1 while retaining the distribution's form.

11.6.4 Handling Outliers

Outliers can drastically influence the overall performance of a version. Techniques to manipulate outliers consist of:

Trimming: Disposing of excessive values beyond a selected threshold.
Winsorizing: Capping outliers with the aid of converting them with the closest non-outlier rate.
Robust statistical techniques: The usage of the median and interquartile range (IQR) to encounter and clean out outliers.

11.6.5 Encoding Categorical Variables

Machine getting to know algorithms require variables to be converted into numerical format:

One-warm encoding: Create binary columns for every magnificence, indicating the presence or absence of a class.
Label encoding: Replace lessons with numeric labels.
Target encoding: Encode instructions based on the advised target variable for each category.

11.6.6 Text Preprocessing

Textual records often require preprocessing earlier than evaluation:

Tokenization: Split text into words or tokens.
Removing stop phrases: Eliminate unusual words (e.g., "and," "the") that do not contribute to evaluation.
Stemming or lemmatization: Reduce words to their root form to address variations.
Vectorization: Convert textual content into numerical vectors for the usage of strategies like TF-IDF or phrase embeddings.

11.6.7 Handling Skewed Data

Skewed statistical distributions can affect model overall performance and interpretation. Techniques to address skewness encompass:

Log transformation: Apply a logarithmic feature to statistics to reduce skewness.
Square root transformation: Take the rectangular root of the facts to stabilize the variance.
Box-Cox transformation: A own family of strength changes that may normalize records distributions.

11.6.8 Data Scaling

Scaling numerical talents guarantees that no feature dominates others in algorithms like gradient descent:

Robust scaling: Scale data using the median and interquartile ranges to mitigate the impact of outliers.
Logarithmic scaling: Apply logarithmic transformation to statistics to compress huge values. Each of these techniques plays a crucial function in getting prepared information for evaluation and modelling. The choice of technique relies on the developments of the dataset, the requirements of the system learning algorithm, and the person of the evaluation venture. Proper statistics preprocessing and cleansing make sure that the ensuing dataset is accurate, steady, and geared up for effective evaluation and modelling, ultimately leading to more strong and reliable insights.

11.7 PRIVACY AND ETHICAL CONSIDERATIONS

Privacy and moral concerns are paramount in the context of records science, while managing sensitive statistics in fields like healthcare, finance, and social media. As improvements in technology permit the collection and analysis of widespread quantities of personal facts, it becomes vital to cope with privacy issues and ethical dilemmas associated with facts utilization. In this complete dialogue, we are able to explore the importance of privateness and ethical considerations in information science, key demanding situations, and best practices for making sure accountable statistics handling, all supported by relevant references and research.

11.7.1 Importance of Privacy and Ethical Considerations

11.7.1.1 Protection of Individual Rights

Privacy safeguards people's rights to manipulate their non-public records and ensures that information collected approximately about them is used responsibly and ethically (Solove 2006).

11.7.1.2 Trust and Transparency

Respecting privateness and moral principles fosters accept as true with between statistics collectors and individuals, selling transparency in facts practices and strengthening public self-belief in statistics-driven technology (Mittelstadt et al. 2016).

11.7.1.3 Prevention of Harm

Ethical considerations in information technology assist to mitigate capacity harms, which include discrimination, bias, and invasion of privateness that could arise from the misuse or mishandling of private facts.

11.8 MODEL DEVELOPMENT AND VALIDATION

Model improvement and validation are vital stages in the technique of building effective and reliable gadget learning (ML) and statistical models. These stages contain selecting suitable algorithms, training models on statistics, and comparing their overall performance to make certain generalizability and reliability. In this comprehensive discussion, we will discover the key principles of version development and validation, common techniques used, and pleasant practices for making sure robust and truthful fashions, supported by using applicable references and studies.

11.8.1 Accuracy and Generalizability

Model development and validation make certain that ML fashions appropriately capture underlying styles in the statistics and generalize well to unseen information, enabling dependable predictions and insights (Goodfellow et al. 2016).

11.8.2 Optimizing Performance

Through iterative development and validation, practitioners can best-tune model parameters, pick appropriate capabilities, and optimize performance metrics consisting of accuracy, precision, consideration, and F1-rating (Raschka and Mirjalili 2019).

11.8.3 Mitigating Overfitting and Underfitting

Validation allows become aware of and mitigate issues of overfitting (model memorizing schooling information) and underfitting (model failing to capture styles), making sure that fashions strike a top-rated balance among bias and variance (James et al. 2013).

11.9 KEY CONCEPTS IN MODEL DEVELOPMENT AND VALIDATION

11.9.1 Algorithm Selection

Choosing the proper algorithm based totally on the nature of the trouble (e.g., category, regression) and traits of the facts (e.g., established, unstructured) is crucial for model overall performance (Hastie et al. 2009).

11.9.2 Data Splitting

Splitting the dataset into training, validation, and test sets is essential to evaluate version overall performance. The schooling set is used to train the model, the validation set is used for hyperparameter tuning and version selection, and the take a look at set is used for final evaluation (Géron 2022).

11.9.3 Cross-Validation

Cross-validation techniques along with k-fold pass-validation assist in validating model overall performance by partitioning the records into a couple of subsets, schooling on specific combos of subsets, and averaging performance metrics throughout iterations (Kohavi 1995).

11.10 REGULATORY LANDSCAPE

The regulatory panorama governing statistics privateness and rising technologies is complicated and dynamic, with diverse regulations and necessities designed to defend individuals' rights and make sure moral practices in records-driven industries. Key rules, together with the General Data Protection Regulation (GDPR), Health Insurance Portability and Accountability Act (HIPAA), Payment Card Industry Data Security Standard (PCI DSS), and California Consumer Privacy Act (CCPA), set up guidelines for information safety, protection, and transparency. These policies intend to mitigate dangers associated with information breaches, unauthorized get right of entry to, and algorithmic biases, promoting perception and duty in records practices. However, compliance with those guidelines poses stressful conditions because of the evolving nature of the era, useful aid constraints, and the choice for worldwide harmonization of information safety necessities (Mayer-Schönberger and Cukier 2013). Despite the ones traumatic conditions, businesses that prioritize regulatory compliance can improve customer safety, foster innovation, and make sure superb contributions to society while also upholding ethical standards and responsible information and practices.

11.11 CASE STUDIES

Case studies and real global examples play a crucial role in illustrating the realistic implications and disturbing conditions of regulatory compliance, document privateness, and growing era. These examples highlight how businesses navigate complex regulatory environments, deal with compliance problems, and leverage era responsibly. For example, the implementation of the General Data Protection Regulation (GDPR) by using technology giants like Google showcases good sized efforts to enhance consumer consent mechanisms and statistics safety practices. Similarly, healthcare organizations facing HIPAA violations because of information breaches underscore the crucial significance of sturdy safety capabilities and compliance with healthcare policies. In the context of rising technology, blockchain startups striving to comply with GDPR hints display modern-day strategies to balancing statistics privateness with decentralized technology. E-trade structures adapting statistics safety practices exemplify how businesses combine compliance into their operations to preserve customer belief and adhere to policies just like the California Consumer Privacy Act (CCPA). These case research provide valuable insights into compliance demanding situations, moral problems, and the evolving regulatory panorama. They emphasize the need for continuous version, funding in cybersecurity, and alignment with moral concepts to navigate complexities and foster accountable innovation in a more and more digital international.

11.12 FUTURE TRENDS AND IMPLICATIONS

Looking in advance, numerous key future dispositions and implications are poised to form the landscape of regulatory compliance, record privacy, and rising technology. These inclinations reflect evolving regulatory frameworks, technological advancements, and societal expectancies, which will profoundly impact organizations, industries, and clients.

11.12.1 Rising Emphasis on Ethical AI and Responsible Technology Development

One notable destiny trend is an increasing emphasis on moral AI and accountable technology improvement. As AI systems become greater pervasive in diverse sectors, concerns around bias, equity, and transparency have garnered sizeable hobby. Future rules are likely to mandate moral guidelines for AI deployment, requiring businesses to prioritize fairness, accountability, and interpretability in their AI algorithms. Responsible AI frameworks turn into essential to deal with societal issues and build attractiveness of AI-driven applications.

11.12.2 Stricter Data Privacy Regulations and Cross-Border Data Flows

The regulatory landscape for facts privacy is anticipated to adapt similarly with the creation of stricter hints globally. Building on the inspiration laid by GDPR and CCPA, future guidelines may additionally impose greater stringent necessities on records management practices, along with advanced consent mechanisms, fact localization guidelines, and stricter enforcement measures. Simultaneously, facilitating cross-border data flows while ensuring compliance with several regulatory regimes will present a sizable task for multinational businesses.

11.12.3 Continued Focus on Cybersecurity and Data Protection

Cybersecurity will remain an important location of attention as corporations confront an increasing number of sophisticated cyber threats. Future tendencies factor towards proactive cybersecurity measures, together with non-prevent monitoring, threat intelligence sharing, and the adoption of superior encryption generation. Compliance with cybersecurity requirements and frameworks may be important to safeguarding touchy records and mitigating the dangers of facts breaches, which could have excessive regulatory and reputational results.

11.12.4 Integration of Privacy with the Aid of Design and Data Minimization

Privacy, using design and records minimization principles, will benefit prominence in future regulatory frameworks. Organizations can be required to embed privacy worries into the layout and development of products and services, ensuring that report series and processing are sensible, proportionate, and transparent. Implementing privateness-improving technology and strategies, in conjunction with differential privateness and federated information, becomes critical for minimizing privacy dangers at the equal time while allowing information-pushed innovation.

11.12.5 Regulatory Challenges Posed through Emerging Technologies

Emerging technology like blockchain, Internet of Things (IoT), and quantum computing will pose unique regulatory annoying conditions because of their disruptive nature. Regulators will need to evolve current frameworks to deal with privateness, protection, and moral implications associated with those generation. Collaborative efforts among policymakers, business enterprise stakeholders, and era professionals can be vital to develop agile regulatory processes that foster innovation while safeguarding privateness and security.

11.12.6 Heightened Consumer Awareness and Demands for Data Rights

Consumer awareness of information privateness troubles will maintain developing, driven through excessive-profile facts breaches and privateness scandals. This fashion will extend demands for stronger statistics rights, which consist of the right to get right of entry to, rectify, and delete private facts. Organizations will need to adopt obvious statistics practices, provide huge alternatives to customers, and empower human beings to exercise session manipulate over their statistics. Compliance with evolving purchaser privateness expectancies will be crucial for keeping trust and logo reputation.

11.12.7 Global Collaboration and Harmonization of Standards

Collaboration among regulatory authorities on the worldwide degree may be critical to harmonize statistics protection necessities and facilitate pass-border information transfers. Efforts to set up mutual recognition agreements and interoperability frameworks will streamline compliance for multinational agencies operating in multiple jurisdictions. Achieving worldwide consensus on statistics privateness standards and enforcement mechanisms can be pivotal within the interconnected virtual financial device. The destiny traits in regulatory compliance, facts privacy, and growing generation underscore the need for proactive version, ethical innovation, and collaborative governance. Organizations should count on and respond to evolving regulatory landscapes, prioritize moral concerns in era improvement, and put money into sturdy cybersecurity and privacy measures to navigate complexities and seize opportunities in a rapidly evolving digital atmosphere. Embracing these developments will permit companies to build trust, foster accountable innovation, and contribute to a greater secure and privacy-respecting destiny. Embracing these principles not only fosters compliance, but also cultivates lasting relationships with consumers and stakeholders. Looking in advance, the mixing of ethics into technological improvement can be crucial, shaping the responsible deployment of AI, blockchain, IoT, and other emerging technologies. By aligning innovation with moral issues and regulatory necessities, groups can navigate challenges and capture opportunities within the evolving digital panorama, in the long run contributing to a comfortable, obvious, and moral future.

11.13 CONCLUSION

In the end, the landscape of regulatory compliance, data privacy, and rising generation is coming into a transformative section marked by prolonged scrutiny, evolving regulations, and growing patron expectancies. The convergence of stringent facts protection standards, technological advancements, and ethical considerations underscores the need for groups to prioritize transparency, accountability, and responsible innovation. To attain this dynamic environment, agencies have to include moral facts practices, adapt to evolving rules via proactive compliance techniques, and invest in strong cybersecurity measures. Global collaboration and harmonization of requirements will facilitate pass-border data flows while also ensuring consistency in compliance requirements. Consumer empowerment and popularity are at the forefront of exchange techniques, with the use of companies prioritizing obvious information control and privateness-centric techniques.

REFERENCES

Beam, Andrew L., and Isaac S. Kohane. Big data and machine learning in health care. *JAMA* 319, no. 13 (2018): 1317–1318.

Boland, Mary Regina, Konrad J. Karczewski, and Nicholas P. Tatonetti. Ten simple rules to enable multi-site collaborations through data sharing. *PLoS Computational Biology* 13, no. 1 (2017): e1005278.

Brownlee, Jason. *Machine Learning Mastery with Python: Understand Your Data, Create Accurate Models, and Work Projects End-to-End*. Machine Learning Mastery, 2016.

Cresswell, Kathrin M., David W. Bates, and Aziz Sheikh. Ten key considerations for the successful optimization of large-scale health information technology. *Journal of the American Medical Informatics Association* 24, no. 1 (2017): 182–187.

Dasu, Tamraparni, and Theodore Johnson. *Exploratory Data Mining and Data Cleaning*. John Wiley & Sons, 2003.

Fridsma, Douglas B. Health informatics: a required skill for 21st century clinicians. *BMJ* 362 (2018).

Géron, Aurélien. *Hands-on Machine Learning with Scikit-Learn, Keras, and TensorFlow*. O'Reilly Media, Inc., 2022.

Goodfellow, Ian, Yoshua Bengio, and Aaron Courville. *Deep Learning*. MIT Press, 2016.

Hastie, Trevor, Robert Tibshirani, Jerome H. Friedman, and Jerome H. Friedman. *The Elements of Statistical Learning: Data Mining, Inference, and Prediction*. Vol. 2. New York: springer, 2009.

Hirschberg, D. The legal aspects of big data: Is privacy the only real issue? *International Data Privacy Law* 6, no. 2, (2016): 120–123.

James, Gareth, Daniela Witten, Trevor Hastie, and Robert Tibshirani. *An Introduction to Statistical Learning*. Vol. 112. New York: springer, 2013.

Kaggal, Vinod C., Ravikumar Komandur Elayavilli, Saeed Mehrabi, et al. Toward a learning health-care system–knowledge delivery at the point of care empowered by big data and NLP. *Biomedical Informatics Insights* 8 (2016): BII–S37977.

Kocaballi, Ahmet Baki, Shlomo Berkovsky, Juan C. Quiroz, Liliana Laranjo, Huong Ly Tong, Dana Rezazadegan, Agustina Briatore, and Enrico Coiera. The personalization of conversational agents in health care: systematic review. *Journal of Medical Internet Research* 21, no. 11 (2019): e15360.

Kohavi, Ron. A study of cross-validation and bootstrap for accuracy estimation and model selection. *Ijcai* 14, no. 2 (1995): 1137–1145.

Lee, J. L., Y. Jin, and A. Huang. Predictive modeling in urgent care settings: A case study with interventional machine learning. *JMIR Medical Informatics* 6, no. 4 (2018): e10744.

Liu, Xiaoxuan, Livia Faes, Aditya U. Kale, et al. A comparison of deep learning performance against health-care professionals in detecting diseases from medical imaging: A systematic review and meta-analysis. *The Lancet Digital Health* 1, no. 6 (2019): e271–e297.

Mayer-Schönberger, Viktor, and Kenneth Cukier. *Big Data: A Revolution That Will Transform How We Live, Work, and Think*. Houghton Mifflin Harcourt, 2013.

Mehta, N., A. Pandit, and V. Sarswat. Big data and artificial intelligence in healthcare: Current applications and future directions. *Journal of Pharmacy &Bioallied Sciences* 12, no. 1 (2020): S9–S14.

Mittelstadt, Brent Daniel, Patrick Allo, Mariarosaria Taddeo, Sandra Wachter, and Luciano Floridi. The ethics of algorithms: Mapping the debate. *Big Data & Society* 3, no. 2 (2016): 2053951716679679.

Nguyen, T., L. Van Nguyen, and H. Dang. Artificial intelligence in healthcare: Review and prediction case studies. *Studies in Computational Intelligence*819 (2019): 297–321.

Obermeyer, Ziad, and Ezekiel J. Emanuel. Predicting the future—big data, machine learning, and clinical medicine. *The New England Journal of Medicine* 375, no. 13 (2016): 1216.

Price, W. Nicholson, and I. Glenn Cohen. Privacy in the age of medical big data. *Nature Medicine* 25, no. 1 (2019): 37–43.

Rajkomar, Alvin, Jeffrey Dean, and Isaac Kohane. Machine learning in medicine. *New England Journal of Medicine* 380, no. 14 (2019): 1347–1358.

Raschka, Sebastian, and Vahid Mirjalili. *Python Machine Learning: Machine Learning and Deep Learning with Python, Scikit-Learn, and TensorFlow 2*. Packt Publishing Ltd, 2019.

Regulation Protection. Regulation (EU) 2016/679 of the European Parliament and of the Council. *Regulation (eu)* 679 (2016): 2016.

Solove, D. J. A taxonomy of privacy. *University of Pennsylvania Law Review* 154 no. 3 (2006): 477–560.

Sweeney, Latanya, Akua Abu, and Julia Winn. Identifying participants in the personal genome project by name (a re-identification experiment). arXiv preprint arXiv:1304.7605 (2013).

The Guardian. Facebook's response to data privacy concerns. (2018).

The Verge. Regulatory impact on AI and machine learning. (2021).

Wang, J., X. Liu, M. Yang, et al. Predictive modeling for healthcare cost and mortality using machine learning: A systematic review. *PLOS ONE*14 no. 7 (2019): e0219561.

Section C

Technological Advancement

12 Implementing Machine Learning in Actuarial Practice

Real-World Applications and Insight

Mamta and Gurpreet Singh

12.1 INTRODUCTION

The introductory section promotes a clear understanding of the demarcation between traditional analytics and machine learning (ML). This is supported with a revealing real-life scenario which can be related to by all practicing actuaries (Schwartz et al. 2017). An in-depth case study will describe a practical example of solvency monitoring by Lloyd's insurance syndicates. This case study spans across multiple chapters but is outlined in the introduction to give an overall understanding of ML in practice (Blier-Wong et al. 2020). A conceptual comparison of traditional actuarial analysis to a data analysis specification is used to convey the difference in how problems are approached. This comparison highlights the benefits of a more open-ended data analysis specification, in that it is more likely to provide the most effective solution to the problem, rather than solving an approximation of the problem (Balona and Richman 2020).

There is an increasing promotion of data science in the insurance industry. Actuaries are being urged not only to use data science tools, but also to think more broadly to be more innovative. Meanwhile, the world of ML is moving at a rapid pace (Kiermayer 2022). It is a discipline currently dominating discussion in the world of data analysis. It challenges traditional statistical methods by aiming to predict the future, not by modelling and testing, but by finding patterns in existing data. As a result, many are beginning to wonder what the uptake of ML across various industries will mean for the future of actuarial work (Manski et al. 2021). This chapter aims to give an introduction to ML methods and to investigate ways in which these methods may become useful to actuaries and influence actuarial work in the future. This is not a discussion around quickly replacing current methods of data analysis; rather, it is about understanding a possible future direction of actuarial work and how to best prepare for it. ML is a huge topic that is difficult to define. The broadest definition would say it is a field of study that gives computers the ability to learn without being explicitly programmed. It grew out of the quest for artificial intelligence and

DOI: 10.1201/9781003472551-15

has now taken on a life of its own with huge data availability from the internet and the need to organize it (Terzioğlu 2022). The general aim is to understand data, to make predictions or decisions, and to do so automatically. Any methods currently classified as ML are by no means a replacement to all current actuarial methods, but there are various tasks and areas of work that they may become useful for.

The introductory section is a concise definition of actuarial ML and the actuarial actuary's modern analytics toolkit. It is made clear what ML is and the type of data and problems for which it is suited. This is contrasted with traditional statistics and expert judgement, enabling the reader to appreciate the iterative and nonlinear nature of ML (Lee et al. 2015). The discussion on the use of ML is set out in the context of actuarial problem solving and decision-making, highlighting the difficulties and uncertainties in solving problems in a rapidly changing environment. The section concludes with an outline of the potential benefits and drawbacks of implementing ML in actuarial practice.

12.1.1 Overview of Machine Learning in Actuarial Practice

ML helps to generate idea about the nature of data under consideration. Different analytical observations can be possible with the help of ML tools. These algorithms worked over the part of extracting knowledge from the present data and try to utilize that information for prediction of the content under consideration. The overall impact of the input can be observed over the expected output by using these algorithms in advance. Often, the model used for prediction is of little interest, and the predictive algorithm may be treated as a black box. This is in contrast to traditional methods where the interest is often in the parameters and the model itself. An example will help to distinguish between the two methods. Random forest is an algorithm used for prediction (Levantesi and Pizzorusso 2019). This is in contrast to decision tree which is a model. Random forest utilizes decision trees to predict an outcome. This can be done in the form of traditional modelling using the trees to estimate a model. However, the strength of the algorithm is that it can predict very well even when a small amount of the data is supplied. The tree model can become overly complex if it uses the entire dataset. This can lead to poor prediction when new data is used. The interest in the model is lost if the trees are only estimated with a portion of the data. Often the decision tree is not the best method of prediction even though it is a model which is of interest to data analysts. By using random forest, there is no need to estimate trees and their models. The algorithm will learn from the data and predict using many trees (Nawar 2016). This has the potential to give a higher prediction power than a simple model such as a single decision tree.

ML is an area of artificial intelligence that is algorithm dependent and provides systems the capability to spontaneously gain knowledge and progress from experience without being unambiguously programmed (Senousy et al. 2020). ML is concerned with the development of computer programs that have the capability to access data and use it to learn for themselves. ML has progressed in leaps and bounds with research and development in different domains and has propelled its applicative extent in recent times. Actuaries have been using statistical techniques in prediction and modelling for decades (Castellani et al. 2021). With the rise of big data and better computing power, ML techniques have started to become a viable option for actuaries.

12.1.2 Importance of Real-World Applications

One of the biggest sectors where the ML algorithms can be effective is the prediction of insurance documents. This field requires extensive knowledge to go through from different ups and downs of the market. The different emerging fields where ML can prove to be effective have been defined as follows:

Predictive modelling: The concept of predictive modelling is used to ensure the making of different risk handling strategies in advance after the calculation of its different causes. This kind of prediction strategy must be required in the insurance sector. Different decision structures help in prediction of these risks and provide various ML algorithms to handle with the same (Barga et al. 2015). The major agenda of this phase is to avoid the unnecessary delays during the execution phase. The overall assessment of these models protected the efforts spend over different phases.

Fraud detection: Fraud detection, a critical element of actuarial science, has seen a fascinating transformation as a result of the incorporation of new methods (Trivedi 2023). Actuaries include procedures, developed parameters, and algorithms in the use of a multitude of advanced formulas, ML, and data analytics to identify related links and outliers in insurance data that indicate abnormal patterns of activity more effectively than ever before (Choudhary and Trivedi 2023). This technique is more common in exceptional instances by examining large datasets. These algorithms can search out modest differences in customer behaviour, policy operations, or insurance arrangements reimbursements that are indicative of deceit. The industry is safeguarded against criminal conduct by this proactive approach to both insurance companies. Due to the high level of creativity needed to detect attempts to conceal fraudulent conduct, which is growing more dynamic by the day, the fraud detection system must constantly change as insurers' first line of defence against fraudulent transactions, the function of an actuary.

Customer segmentation: Customer segmentation has transformed into a proactive approach enabled by sophisticated analytics and ML. Actuaries utilize advanced algorithms to classify policyholders according to their risk identities, behavioural trends, and demographic information. By adopting a tailored strategy, insurers are able to customize price, coverage, and marketing techniques to specific consumer segments, hence improving overall delight and customer continued employment (Meng et al. 2022). Actuarial specialists enhance risk assessment and underwriting procedures by understanding the specific demands of different customer groups. Customer segmentation enhances focused decision-making and guarantees that insurance products are tailored to the preferences and risk tolerances of distinct market segments. This ultimately strengthens the competitiveness and revenue of insurance establishments in a dynamic business environment.

Telematics: Telematics solutions are growing ever more widespread among drivers and insurers, yet only experience will reveal if they end up becoming the standard in the sector (Trivedi and Malik 2022). For the time being, an insurer seeking to expand the scope of their policy line (and therefore increase their loss proportion) or a driver seeking to reduce costs and perhaps even enhance their driving skills may find that a telemetry scheme is an ideal match. In order to identify the driving habits that are linked to insurance losses, insurers can develop models that link this driving pattern to actual expenses. As a result, an insurer can provide savings and rates that more accurately represent the real risk posed by a driver (Trivedi et al. 2021). By doing this, insurers can increase their profits by retaining fewer high-risk drivers. An insurer may also perceive a decrease in losses because many telematics programs also provide driver suggestions, such as urging a driver to brake less forcefully.

Loss reserving: There are several methods for projecting loss reserves, also referred to as technical provisions in various parts of the world. When estimating loss reserves, one might obtain a zone of trust, which is a range of potential outcomes, or an absolute estimation (Malik and Trivedi 2022). Loss Development (also known as Chain Ladder), Bornhuetter–Ferguson, Frequency/Severity, Backward Recursive, Berquist–Sherman, and Cape Cod are examples of conventional actuarial approaches. These techniques capture developments on referred to claims (case reserve development) in addition to the expected rise of late disclosed asserts (incurred but not reported, or IBNR). They can be applied to loss and loss adaptation expenditures as a distinct group or in combination (Trivedi et al. 2024a). These techniques can be used with received and case sustained data.

12.2 MACHINE LEARNING TECHNIQUES FOR ACTUARIAL ANALYSIS

In the field of actuarial science, there are various methodologies which used the concept of ML for performing different tasks of insurance sector, as shown in Figure 12.1. For example, ML algorithms are used for performing various predictions and clustering process. For implementing these, supervised learning and unsupervised learning are used for the modelling prediction and for clustering as well (Denuit et al. 2021). In large dataset, there are different abnormalities and patterns, which can be easily approachable by using unsupervised learning for their prior collection of history from past data and user experience methods to identify fraud detection, client classification using different patterns, and improvement of stock portfolio. The rate of mortality and claims of the insurance can be allowed to actuaries to forecast over the system by building the model from the information gathered prior or from past data.

12.2.1 Supervised Learning

Supervised learning is a method particularly used for modelling predictions, and this is crucial approach for the insurance sector in actuarial practice. It used techniques like regression method and classification process to perform these tasks from

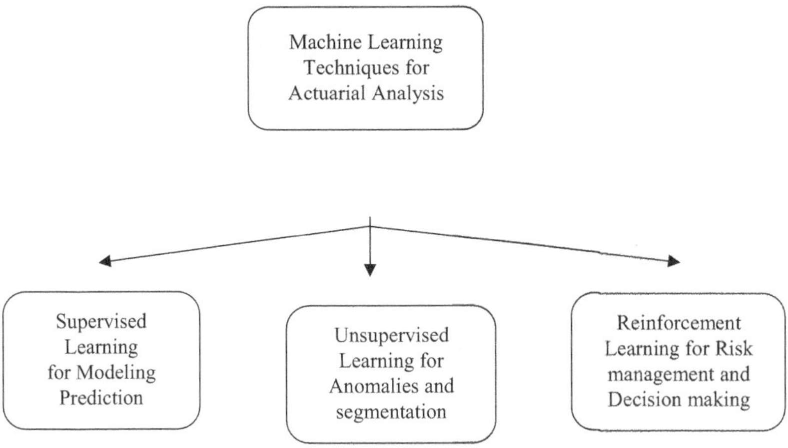

FIGURE 12.1 ML techniques for actuarial practice. (Compiled by Author.)

gathering information from data available from history. For mortality rates or claiming, the insurance estimation regression model is used for further consequences (Trivedi and Malik 2022). Risk evaluation and client segmentation are performed to divide the data into different clusters or separate groups of decision-making or logistic regression to maintain the records of different categories using different ML classification algorithms (Boodhun and Jayabalan 2018). Labelled datasets including historical data and significant values of the user can be used to train the model to produce the accurate estimation of commercial and economical situations, cost value, improvements methods, and the rate of mortality using prediction modelling.

12.2.2 Unsupervised Learning

The unsupervised learning method of ML is very effective approach used for anomaly detection and classification of unlabelled data. It is widely used to collect different unseen patterns and ambiguity of data by using different methodologies for detecting anomaly such as k-mean algorithm. Optimization of portfolio and client segmentation are executed by distinct grouping of comparable datapoints (Taha et al. 2022). In the actuarial method, there are the unstructured data, anomalies, risk plans, etc., all of which can be handled by these ML algorithms to detect anomalies, prevent fraud movement and forecast to make decisions, streamline insurance to enhance the effectiveness of feasibility of finance and insurance sector in the market (Trivedi et al. 2021).

12.2.3 Reinforcement Learning

With the usage of reinforcement learning methods, actuarial practitioners probably expand their decision-making approach and the evaluation of the risk through the ML algorithms like reinforcement learning algorithm together with deep Q-network including Q-learning. It can be further used for pricing campaigns in order to meet the instant response and fluctuate market circumstances, insure policies, and adjust the investment groups of insurance (Barabas et al. 2018). In the era of finance and insurance, actuaries allow innovations and the development for efficacy of the operational management (Trivedi et al. 2024).

12.3 APPLICATIONS OF MACHINE LEARNING IN ACTUARIAL PRACTICE

ML methods can be used to produce a variety of results by incorporating varying degrees of limitations. ML plays a crucial role for actuaries to perform various activities in different extent. By using prediction modelling, actuaries can estimate the risk by collecting the previous information provided by the user to exactly get ahead the incidence and the death rates contrary to claim insurance. Mathematical modelling is other significant model used by actuaries for the prediction and calculation of the exact estimation on prior basis for the prevention of loss (Wüthrich et al. 2023). In addition, ML also assists in medical facilities cost and enhances the enduring therapy by inspecting the usage of medical history. The behaviour modelling predicts customer behaviour to retain inventions and to facilitate marketing strategies.

12.3.1 Pricing and Underwriting

In the field of actuarial practice, pricing and underwriting is a critical part to define the profitability outcome of insurance evaluation of the risk factors. While evaluating these factors in the pricing, it is mandatory to find a stable outcome between the cost and retention (Trivedi et al. 2023). And then all these risk factors come across with the process of underwriting to find the insurability and the quality (Denuit et al. 2021). Actuaries often used the statistical models and data inquiring to measure the risk predictions such as its traits, health circumstances, and insurance claiming policies. With the usage of ML, significant information can be examined to get suitable risk signals and enhance the existing pricing models (Sadowski 2024). This combination of techniques with the actuaries assures the methods of underwriting and expands the correctness of pricing in order to reserve the stability of finance and give customer protection. This collaboration in the finance and technology offers consumer protection and fair premiums, which enhance the precision in this sector.

12.3.2 Claims Analysis and Fraud Detection

In actuarial science, for the detection of fraudulent movement and the duty assessment, many of the technology is used, but ML has changed the way of utilization for recognition of these activities. The misleading behaviour of the expressive identification activities and huge dataset can be enhanced with the usage of ML to decrease the financial loss (Lindholm et al. 2020). In the claim analysis, by setting the claims from previous collected data, ML is used to automate the further procedures. Through the investigation of transactions data, ML models use to provide defensive support to avoid the dishonest/wrong claims against medical insurance policies (Baudry and Robert 2019). Additionally, handling claims can be automated, faster settled, more accurately analysed with the application of ML. Aside from operational benefits, data-driven technological integrations provide an additional layer of defence to the portfolio with better risk management tools, ensuring affordable premium and long-term insurance policies amid evolving fraud landscapes.

12.3.3 Risk Assessment and Management

In actuarial execution, risk avoidance and evaluation become key in ensuring the longevity and financial stability of an insurance operation (Malik and Sonal 2022). Actuaries examine, estimate, and quantify all sorts of risk such as investment, operational, and underwriter risk, making use of statistics, methods to analyse data, and experience of business. Via historical information and current conditions of the market, examinations can surface anticipated risks and provide corrective mitigation strategies in place (Berk and Hyatt 2015). This involves establishing risk-control methodologies and rules, portfolio diversification of investment, adequate reserves, etc. Actuaries are also indispensable to compliance for the reason that they ensure that insurance business must retain enough loss reserves to satisfy reliability standards (Levantesi et al. 2020).

12.3.4 Customer Segmentation and Personalization

It can surface anticipated risks and provide corrective mitigation strategies in place (Berk and Hyatt 2015). Customer segmentation and tailoring are core to actuarial practice to adapt insurance products and service to reflect client's diverse goals and needs. Actuaries cluster their customers along a range of dimensions such as level of risk, behaviours, and statistics with ML algorithms and data analytics tools (Grize et al. 2020). The strategy to improve the interaction between clients while maintaining the retention and values has increased the effectiveness of profits in terms of categorization. By considering the necessities and preference of the clients, insurance companies bring offers on campaigns and goods (Ghasemi et al. 2021). Through the personalization access to the clients based on their needs and goal for satisfactory outcome, it enhances the user involvement and retention, which are highly impacted by segmentation and customization.

12.4 INSIGHTS AND CHALLENGES IN IMPLEMENTING MACHINE LEARNING

In the field of actuarial practice, ML has several advantages and drawbacks.

Advantages of ML in Actuarial Practice

Improved efficiency: For efficient outcomes and making accurate choices, ML algorithm improves the precision of risk evaluation in the presence of huge datasets.

Predictive modelling: In risk and planning approach, ML methodology assists in the risk prediction by evaluating the past history of insurance claims including risk factors (Barga et al. 2015).

Administrative effectiveness: Through the usage of ML algorithms, all the tasks of insurance sectors can be streamlined, which ensures the drop of physical labour assistance and increased the productivity in the terms of administration work by automation methods of repeated process which is required in the field (Denuit et al. 2021).

Customized offerings: Customer segmentation develops attentive decision-making and assurances that insurance products are personalized to the preferences and risk acceptances of dissimilar market sections. This ultimately supports the competitiveness and profits of insurance developments in a dynamic business for client retention (Richman 2021).

Fraud identification: ML algorithms are used to identify fraudulent activity to recognize the patterns from past information and assist on prior basis in the case of financial loss.

Limitations of ML in Actuarial Practice

Quality and accessibility of data: Accessing the relevant information that is exact to the current scenario is difficult in the field of actuarial science, which can have impact on insurance and pricing. It is limited to the underwriting process for retrieving the data. ML can only be used in this case of prediction due to limitation (Embrechts et al. 2022).

Interpretation: Due to the absence of convenience, it may be hard to find results and select predictions when it comes to interpretation along with ML algorithm.

Compliance with regulations: Implementation of ML has complications when it comes to meeting authorized ethics for defence information, impartiality, and honesty.

Overfitting: In actuarial science, when the ML algorithms train the dataset with the training model for making decisions, there is an occurrence of complexity while learning the model and generating data.

Prejudice and equality: Due to prejudgement of outcomes according to the availability of prior information, it probably falls in the biasness and required supervision.

12.4.1 Ethical Considerations and Data Privacy

Actuaries play an important role in the insurance industry. It uses mathematical and statistical techniques to assess and manage financial risk, including insurance premiums and estimating future financial liabilities, but like any other profession, actuarial science lacks ethical issues (Denuit et al. 2019). These issues range from the use of biased data to unclear pricing policies. It is important to consider ethical issues in actuarial science to ensure fairness, equity, and transparency in the insurance industry (Clemente et al. 2023). There are various ethical issues such as data biasness, transparency, fairness, privacy, and conflicts of interest. Actuaries have been under pressure to calculate all these factors to maintain customer retention by transparency in policies pricing in the insurance sector.

12.4.2 Integration with Traditional Actuarial Methods

In the technological environment, traditional research professions, including actuarial science, are experiencing a standard modification. The combination of data science, AI, ML, and deep learning provides a transformative lens through which actuaries can enhance their methods (Kunce and Chatterjee 2017). As more and more information become available, the integration of this technology provides actuaries with powerful tools to interpret complex models, optimize decision-making processes, and adjust risk analysis. What about rate formulation or funding analysis and loss reserve analysis, including statements of actuarial opinion (SAOs) or similar legal documents? Actuaries use ML algorithm to increase the efficiency and accuracy of conventional models (Hassani et al. 2020).

12.5 CONCLUSION

The insurance sector is being revolutionized by the use of ML in actuarial practice. In order to improve risk assessment, pricing, underwriting, and claims handling, actuaries are using advanced data analytics more often. For the purpose of producing precise forecasts, identifying fraud, and classifying clients according to risk profiles, ML models examine enormous volumes of historical data. The utilization of telematics data and IoT devices allows for the customization of price by assessing driving behaviour in real time. Predictive modelling facilitates the anticipation of forthcoming claims, while automation simplifies the processes of screening and asserts processing. Images are analysed to determine the state of health and damage, whereas natural language processing draws insightful conclusions from unstructured data. Optimization of reinsurance strategies and streamlining of regulatory compliance are achieved. Nevertheless, ethical considerations, data quality, and interpretability continue to be crucial. To fully utilize ML, actuaries must engage in multidisciplinary teamwork and continually acquire knowledge. This will guarantee the actuarial profession's competitive and ethical future.

REFERENCES

Balona, Caesar, and Ronald Richman. The actuary and ibnr techniques: A machine learning approach. Available at SSRN 3697256 (2020).

Barabas, Chelsea, Madars Virza, Karthik Dinakar, Joichi Ito, and Jonathan Zittrain. Interventions over predictions: Reframing the ethical debate for actuarial risk assessment. In Conference on fairness, accountability and transparency, pp. 62–76. PMLR, 2018.

Barga, Roger, Valentine Fontama, Wee Hyong Tok, and Luis Cabrera-Cordon. Predictive analytics with Microsoft Azure machine learning. Berkely, CA: Apress, 2015.

Baudry, Maximilien, and Christian Y. Robert. A machine learning approach for individual claims reserving in insurance. *Applied Stochastic Models in Business and Industry* 35, no. 5 (2019): 1127–1155.

Berk, Richard, and Jordan Hyatt. Machine learning forecasts of risk to inform sentencing decisions. *Federal Sentencing Reporter* 27, no. 4 (2015): 222–228.

Blier-Wong, Christopher, Hélène Cossette, Luc Lamontagne, and Etienne Marceau. Machine learning in P&C insurance: A review for pricing and reserving. *Risks* 9, no. 1 (2020): 4.

Boodhun, Noorhannah, and Manoj Jayabalan. Risk prediction in life insurance industry using supervised learning algorithms. *Complex & Intelligent Systems* 4, no. 2 (2018): 145–154.

Castellani, Gilberto, Ugo Fiore, Zelda Marino, Luca Passalacqua, Francesca Perla, Salvatore Scognamiglio, and Paolo Zanetti. Machine learning techniques in nested stochastic simulations for life insurance. *Applied Stochastic Models in Business and Industry* 37, no. 2 (2021): 159–181.

Choudhary, Vinita, and Sonal Trivedi. The role of internal audit in risk management with a perspective of sustainability development. *The Impact of Climate Change and Sustainability Standards on the Insurance Market* 1 (2023): 287–315.

Choudhary, Vinita, Neha Kamboj, and Sonal Trivedi. Scoping review of literature on the application of blockchain in finance. *Perspectives on Blockchain Technology and Responsible Investing* 1 (2023): 1–28.

Clemente, Gian Paolo, Francesco Della Corte, Nino Savelli, and Diego Zappa. Special issue "Data Science in Insurance". *Risks* 11, no. 5 (2023): 80.

Denuit, Michel, and Julien Trufin. Effective statistical learning methods for actuaries. Vol. 795. Berlin: Springer, 2019.

Denuit, Michel, Arthur Charpentier, and Julien Trufin. Autocalibration and Tweedie-dominance for insurance pricing with machine learning. *Insurance: Mathematics and Economics* 101 (2021): 485–497.

Embrechts, Paul, and Mario V. Wüthrich. Recent challenges in actuarial science. *Annual Review of Statistics and Its Application* 9 (2022): 119–140.

Ghasemi, Mehdi, Daniel Anvari, Mahshid Atapour, J. Stephen Wormith, Keira C. Stockdale, and Raymond J. Spiteri. The application of machine learning to a general risk–need assessment instrument in the prediction of criminal recidivism. *Criminal Justice and Behavior* 48, no. 4 (2021): 518–538.

Grize, Yves-Laurent, Wolfram Fischer, and Christian Lützelschwab. Machine learning applications in nonlife insurance. *Applied Stochastic Models in Business and Industry* 36, no. 4 (2020): 523–537.

Hassani, Hossein, Stephan Unger, and Christina Beneki. Big data and actuarial science. *Big Data and Cognitive Computing* 4, no. 4 (2020): 40.

Kiermayer, Mark Thomas. Machine and deep learning in present actuarial challenges. PhD diss., Universität Ulm, 2022.

Kunce, Jim, and Som Chatterjee. *A Machine-Learning Approach to Parameter Estimation.* Arlington, VA: CAS (2017).

Lee, Simon C. K., Sheldon Lin, and Katrien Antonio. *Delta Boosting Machine and Its Application in Actuarial Modeling.* Sydney: Institute of Actuaries of Australia (2015).

Levantesi, Susanna, and Virginia Pizzorusso. Application of machine learning to mortality modeling and forecasting. *Risks* 7, no. 1 (2019): 26.

Levantesi, Susanna, Andrea Nigri, and Gabriella Piscopo. Longevity risk management through machine learning: State of the art. *Insurance Markets and Companies* 1, no. 11 (2020): 11–20.

Lindholm, Mathias, Richard Verrall, Felix Wahl, and Henning Zakrisson. Machine learning, regression models, and prediction of claims reserves. In *Arlington: Casualty Actuarial Society E-Forum.* 2020.

Malik, Reena, and Sonal Trivedi. *Blockchain Technology and Healthcare: Towards Combating COVID-19. Blockchain Technology in Corporate Governance: Transforming Business and Industries* (2022): 57–74.

Manski, Scott, Kaixu Yang, Gee Y. Lee, and Tapabrata Maiti. Extracting information from textual descriptions for actuarial applications. *Annals of Actuarial Science* 15, no. 3 (2021): 605–622.

Meng, Shengwang, Yaqian Gao, and Yifan Huang. Actuarial intelligence in auto insurance: Claim frequency modeling with driving behavior features and improved boosted trees. *Insurance: Mathematics and Economics* 106 (2022): 115–127.

Nawar, Sandra Maria. Machine learning techniques for detecting hierarchical interactions in insurance claims models. PhD diss., Concordia University, 2016.

Richman, Ronald. AI in actuarial science–a review of recent advances–part 1. *Annals of Actuarial Science* 15, no. 2 (2021): 207–229.

Sadowski, Jathan. Total life insurance: Logics of anticipatory control and actuarial governance in insurance technology. *Social Studies of Science* 54, no. 2 (2024): 231–256.

Schwartz, Ira M., Peter York, Eva Nowakowski-Sims, and Ana Ramos-Hernandez. Predictive and prescriptive analytics, machine learning and child welfare risk assessment: The Broward County experience. *Children and Youth Services Review* 81 (2017): 309–320.

Senousy, Youssef, Abdulaziz Shehab, Wael K. Hanna, Alaa M. Riad, Hazem A. El-bakry, and Nashaat Elkhamisy. RETRACTED: A smart social insurance big data analytics framework based on machine learning algorithms. *Cybernetics and Information Technologies* 20, no. 1 (2020): 95–111.

Taha, Ayman, Bernard Cosgrave, and Susan Mckeever. Using feature selection with machine learning for generation of insurance insights. *Applied Sciences* 12, no. 6 (2022): 3209.

Terzioğlu, M. Kenan, ed. *Advances in Econometrics, Operational Research, Data Science and Actuarial Studies: Techniques and Theories*. Springer Nature, 2022.

Trivedi, Sonal, and Reena Malik. Blockchain technology as an emerging technology in the insurance market. In *Big Data: A Game Changer for Insurance Industry*, pp. 81–100. Emerald Publishing Limited, 2022.

Trivedi, Sonal, and Reena Malik. Role and significance of data protection in risk management practices in the insurance market. In *Big Data Analytics in the Insurance Market*, pp. 263–273. Emerald Publishing Limited, 2022.

Trivedi, Sonal, Kiran Mehta, and Renuka Sharma. Systematic literature review on application of blockchain technology in E-finance and financial services. *Journal of Technology Management & Innovation* 16, no. 3 (2021): 89–102.

Trivedi, Sonal, Vinita Choudhary, Neha Kamboj, and Nirmaljeet Kaur Virk. New avenues of opportunities and challenges for start-ups, MSMEs, the Indian Financial Sector, and the Indian insurance sector. *Business Drivers in Promoting Digital Detoxification* (2024): 226–250.

Trivedi, Sonal. Blockchain framework for insurance industry. *International Journal of Innovation and Technology Management* 20, no. 06 (2023): 2350034.

Trivedi, Sonal. Blockchain technology and structural change in financial services. In *The Application of Emerging Technology and Blockchain in the Insurance Industry*, pp. 249–263. River Publishers, 2024.

Trivedi, Sonal. Convention of blockchain in financial services: A state-of-the-art literature review. *Revolutionizing Financial Services and Markets Through FinTech and Blockchain* (2023): 237–250.

Wüthrich, Mario V., and Michael Merz. *Statistical Foundations of Actuarial Learning and Its Applications*. Cham: Springer Nature, 2023.

13 Telematics System in Usage-Based Motor Insurance

Vinita Choudhary, Neha Kamboj, and Sonal Trivedi

13.1 INTRODUCTION

13.1.1 Importance of Telematics in Vehicle Insurance

The insurance sector has reached a mature lifecycle stage, at least in the case of car insurance. Most of the market's established and incumbent insurance businesses are seeing a considerable decline in revenue due to intense competition and a lack of product uniqueness (Pierce 2009). This creates a considerable risk to the viability of the firm, particularly in less developed areas where vehicle insurance is the most essential portion of the product line (Pandiangan et al. 2022).

There are two main reasons why insurance businesses could see a decline in income. First, there's a good chance that prices will drop on these exchanges (Nuti 2023). Second, prices do not reflect individual risk. People who drive 45,000 km year, for instance, pay the same amount as those who travel fewer than 15,000 km annually (Hassan et al. 2023). By providing new usage-based insurance (UBI) policies, this has caused a radical change in old-style insurance policies.

UBI is based on a wide range of information derived from telematics devices, including mileage, speed, location, time, total trip duration, and G-force. Businesses may obtain a competitive edge by monitoring the conduct of drivers, as this data has the potential to be predictive (Chaba 2021; McDonnell et al. 2021). Since UBI products are still relatively new in some regions, insurance firms will need to work hard to improve UBI acceptance in such markets. Emerging markets, such as those in Eastern and South Eastern Europe, are restricted to modest UBI activity but growing interest, in contrast to developed markets (Che et al. 2022; Soleymanian et al. 2019).

In 2022, the automotive telematics market was valued at USD 72.85 billion globally. The market is expected to expand at a compound annual growth rate (CAGR) of 18.5% from USD 85.36 billion in 2023 to USD 280.78 billion by 2030 (Report by Astute Analytica, 26, May, 2023). The goal of vehicle telematics technology is to enhance driving pleasure and driver safety by gathering, storing, and analyzing data. The system integrates wireless telematics devices, GPS systems, onboard vehicular diagnostics, and more devices to capture and send vehicle information, including location speed and vehicle maintenance (Che et al. 2022; Ziakopoulos et al. 2022).

 DOI: 10.1201/9781003472551-16

These benefits of car telematics are contributing to market expansion. This data comes from a research called "Vehicle Telematics Market, 2023–2030" by Fortune Business Insights. According to the data, insurance companies stand to gain from these developing markets.

Thus, in addition to developed markets, emerging markets such as Asia Pacific need to be included in the current discussions and viewpoints surrounding the implementation of User-Based Insurance.

13.1.2 Importance of Abundant Amount of Telematics Data

The policyholder's car insurance premium is established using telematics information. More valuable data is needed by insurance firms to better comprehend driving behavior and estimate risk (Monkiewicz & Śliwiński 2023). Insurance firms must recognize between these information and guarantee that the suitable telematics parameters are collected by their UBI frameworks. Besides, this might make it conceivable for insurance firms to appropriately correlate individual pricing and risk, hence progressing their charging strategies (Umut 2020).

Insurance telematics is driven by the accuracy of the GPS data, which is being collected through the telematics devices. On the other hand, there are abundant environmental factors available (including air influences and sky blocking, introducing noise into GPS data) which can make GPS data inaccurate or less accurate or reliable (Li et al. 2023). This might put the insurance firm at relevant risk of income loss.

Furthermore, contextualizing the telematics data that was received is an important step in guaranteeing accurate and trustworthy data for offering personalized insurance. The term "context" describes the surrounding circumstances, including the place where specific incidents took place, the state of the roads, the weather, and how much of an overall risk they provide (Pandya et al. 2023). The most recent generation of UBIs and improved comprehension of driver behavior have been shown to be mostly dependent on the environmental aspect.

For example, it would be simple to explain why breaking incidents on busy highways have a higher risk of accident than those on rural roads. However, other kinds of incidents that have distinct environmental features could be harder to explain. To decide between these kinds of occasions and give insurance companies more exact information for billing reasons, a universal benefit index (UBI) system must be put in place (Verma et al. 2021).

Therefore, it is essential to provide insurance firms with extensive data in order to expand their understanding of driving behavior. Insurance firms may therefore use contextualized data to analyze driver behavior more precisely, in addition to measuring typical telematics characteristics (mileage, speed, acceleration, breaking incidents, etc.). An enhanced approach to estimating insurance costs that minimizes rating mistakes resulting from the classification of drivers into broad actuarial classes is achieved by the utilization of more precise data (Quintero et al. 2020).

13.1.3 The Next-Generation Solution for Telematics-Based Insurance

Around the world, a number of UBI solutions have been put into practice, including AIOI, AVIVA, Winterthur, AXA, MAPFRE, and RSA Insurance Group, which compares the 24 primary UBI alternatives.

The primary drawback of these systems is their propensity to evaluate the driver's behavior solely based on standard telemetry information. A summary of different UBI options and their salient characteristics may be seen in Table 13.1.

TABLE 13.1
Summarized List of Some of the UBI Solutions Implemented World Wide Telematics

Insurance Company	Country	Name of the UBI Program	Insurance Concept	Technology Platform	Data Transmission
AIOI	Japan	Pay as you drive	Distance-based vehicle insurance	G-book (Telematics subscription service provided by Toyota Motor Corporation)	Mobile data service
Aviva	Canada	Autograph	Insurance is based on telematics parameters with several levels of risk within 24-hour period	Device connected to vehicle diagnostic port	Universal serial bus
AXA Winterthur	Switzerland	Crash Recorder	Recording events	Event-data recorder	Data retrieved from event-data recorder
AXA	Italy	Autometrica	Distance-based vehicle insurance	GPS-based	Mobile data service
Generali	Italy	Protezione Satellitare	Insurance is based on traditional telematics parameters	GPS-based	Mobile data service
MAPFRE	Spain	YCAR	Insurance is based on telematics parameters with several levels of risk within 24-hour period	GPS-based	Mobile data service
RSA Insurance Group	United Kingdom	More than Green Wheels Insurance	Insurance is based on telematics parameters with several levels of risk within 24-hour period	Device connected to vehicle diagnostic port	Mobile data service

Source: Compiled by Author.

There are 648 companies in Usage-Based Insurance which include Zego, Root, BitSight, Security Scorecard, and Getsafe (www.tracxn.com accessed on December 21, 2023). Furthermore, UBI solutions such as in India (Verma et al. 2021) are taking into consideration several levels of risk. There might be several problems with this strategy, which would lead to bias in the way price and risk are matched for each individual. Consequently, it is imperative to examine other circumstances in which certain occurrences transpire.

A lot of the UBI options available now can lead to inconsistent pricing and individual risk. Furthermore, the majority of these earlier systems were unable to accurately contextualize telemetry data by including the ambient component. An essential component of the next-generation UBI is the environment.

Thus, this chapter aims to investigate the use of telematics in auto insurance and consumers' attitudes about it. It also discusses this technology's future directions. The advantages and disadvantages of telematics have been examined for this study.

13.2 OBJECTIVES OF THE STUDY

- To study the role of telematics in Motor Insurance.
- To study the benefits of telematics in Motor insurance.
- To study the challenges faced in implementing telematics.

13.3 REVIEW OF LITERATURE

Navneet (2020) explained in an article published by The Economic Times that the implementation of telematics in motor insurance could lead to customized premiums based on driving habits, rather than the traditional approach of pricing premiums solely based on the make and model of the vehicle. This means that individuals who demonstrate safer driving behaviors may qualify for lower premiums. Siniša Husnjak et al. (2014) highlighted in their study on "Telematics System in Usage Based Motor Insurance" that current billing models often overlook crucial factors like driving behavior, mileage, and road types when calculating premiums, leading to a lack of customization for end-users.

Furthermore, Friedman and Canaan (2014) discussed in Canaan's report titled "Overcoming speed bumps on the road to telematics" how insurers, as telematics programs mature, will utilize gathered data to more accurately price risks. This could result in safer drivers benefiting from usage-based insurance (UBI) at lower rates, while riskier drivers may face increased premiums. Yao (2018) suggested in his research on "Evolution of Insurance: A Telematics-Based Personal Auto Insurance Study" that despite minor drawbacks, telematics insurance offers a fairer premium payment method and enables insurers to accurately calculate expected costs, potentially becoming the dominant pricing method for personal auto insurance.

Boucher, Côté, and Guillen (2017) proposed in their research paper "Exposure as Duration and Distance in Telematics Motor Insurance Using Generalized Additive Models" a rating system considering both exposure time and distance traveled for premium calculation, acknowledging that risk exposure depends on both factors. Guillen et al. (2019) demonstrated in their research on "Improving automobile insurance ratemaking using telematics" how GPS-collected data can inform insurance ratemaking, considering factors such as distance traveled, driver habits, and accidents to determine risk exposure and insurance costs.

Martin Eling and Mirko Kraft (2020) analyzed in their study "The impact of telematics on the insurability of risks" the implications of telematics on insurance, including changes in loss frequency and severity, legal constraints, and ethical implications. Constantinescu, Stancu, and Panait (2018) found in their research on the "Impact study of telematics auto insurance" that telematics-based auto insurance contracts could potentially offer up to 25% savings for careful drivers. Narwani et al. (2020) proposed in their research on "Categorizing Driving Patterns based on Telematics Data Using Supervised and Unsupervised Learning" a method to categorize driving patterns using telematics data and insurance claim history, ensuring fair assessment and rewarding of driving quality.

Additionally, Pareek, Pandey, and Priyadarshi (2020) highlighted in their study on "Emerging technologies enabling the digital transformation of motor insurance in India" the importance of data-driven decision-making in insurance, with technologies like telematics, machine learning, and artificial intelligence enabling faster and more efficient decision-making processes. Kumar (2019) developed a scoring system for rating variables in his research on "Insurance Telematics: Risk Assessment of Connected Vehicles" to assist actuaries in calculating risk exposure for each vehicle accurately.

13.3.1 Usage-Based Car Insurance in India

India has more than 1.4 billion people living there in 2024, making it the first most populous nation on Earth. The World Bank reports that there are over 450,000 accidents on Indian roads annually, with 150,000 people dying as a result. This indicates that deaths on Indian roads account for 11% of all deaths worldwide, although accounting for just 1% of the world's automobile parc. Furthermore, the uninsured rate in India's auto insurance market is quite high; based on our calculations, it will approach 60% 2020 (UBI Global Study 4th Edition: Connected Auto Insurance (2023) PTOLEMUS Consulting Group. Available at: https://www.ptolemus.com/ (Accessed January 6, 2024)).

Therefore, in an effort to decrease the number of fatalities on Indian roads, Indian authorities are searching for ways to promote innovation in the insurance sector and boost insurance penetration. They are also trying to raise awareness about safe driving practices.

In India, usage-based auto insurance has been the subject of many news stories implying that the Insurance Regulatory and Development Authority of India (IRDAI) supports usage-based auto insurance. Major auto insurance providers will probably begin to provide these kinds of plans in the future, as the nation's top insurance authority encourages insurers. Although some insurers have started implementing such policies, the obstacles – such as the widespread usage of tracking/telematics devices in cars – mean that it will take some time before all parties engaged in the auto insurance sector fully embrace the idea.

The IRDAI published a circular on July 5, 2022, to formally impose usage-based insurance products in India. Concretely, Indian motor insurers can now provide UBI products as supplements to the fundamental own-damage coverage, such as Pay-As-You-Drive and Pay-How-You-Drive programs. Customers can now own several automobiles with a single policy thanks to this circular.

On July 21, Bajaj Allianz General Insurance introduced its Pay As You Consume scheme. A second iteration of Edelweiss General Insurance's Switch PHYD initiative, which is smartphone-based, was also just introduced. Drivers receive a driving score that determines their monthly insurance cost based on many factors such as speeding, braking, and distracted driving. The better the person drive, the lower the premium.

In July 2022, ICICI Lombard introduced innovative motor insurance policies designed to revolutionize the industry. These policies leverage cutting-edge telematics technology to track driving behavior and kilometers traveled, paving the way for personalized premiums. Termed as "pay-as-you-use" and "pay-how-you-use" plans, these offerings break away from traditional models by tailoring costs to individual driving habits. Additionally, the introduction of "kilometer plans" marks a significant shift, where customers are charged based on their actual usage, promising fairer and more flexible insurance options.

13.3.2 Understanding Pay As You Drive (PAYD) Insurance

Pay As You Drive (PAYD) represents a modern and cost-effective approach to car insurance, where premiums are determined by the number of kilometers driven by the insured. This model's premiums are reduced because they reflect how the car is really used. In India, where it is required to have auto insurance, PAYD becomes a desirable choice for people who drive seldom or never. With PAYD, an insurance solution that is more affordable and customized is possible instead of paying full rates for vehicles that are not used.

For instance, drivers can save a significant 25% on insurance premiums if they drive up to 3,500 km a year. The annual kilometer slabs and the odometer reading are used to compute this discount.

PAYD policies cover both own damage (OD) and third-party insurance components, much like comprehensive auto insurance. But the real difference is how smart technology is used to track driving patterns, which allows insurers to provide much lower rates based on actual miles driven.

To put it simply, PAYD insurance makes insurance more accessible and cheaper for those with different driving habits by providing a flexible and equitable substitute for standard comprehensive policies.

13.3.3 Decoding Telematics in Insurance

The term "telematics" emerges from the fusion of "telecommunications" and "informatics," embodying the integration of communication and information technologies. Within the insurance industry, the application of telematics results in "Telematics Insurance," which is also referred to by a number of other names, including Black Box Insurance, GPS Car Insurance, Smart Box Insurance, Pay-as-you-Drive Insurance, and Usage-Based Insurance (UBI). Primarily prevalent in the motor insurance sector, Telematics Insurance harnesses telecommunications and information technology to enhance services tailored to vehicles. These services encompass real-time navigation, roadside assistance, and vehicle tracking, among others. In the context of insurance, telematics serves a pivotal role in the Motor segment, facilitating insurers in achieving refined customer segmentation and adopting pricing methodologies that accurately reflect the risk exposure of individual customers and their vehicles. As a result, insurance telematics represents a flexible approach to risk assessment and pricing, enabling insurers to provide their clients with more individualized and equitable insurance options.

13.3.4 Harnessing Telematics for Risk Assessment and Pricing

With the use of tools like the Black Box, telematics technology plays a major part in contemporary insurance procedures by giving insurers access to a multitude of data for risk assessment and quotation. This information, which was sent to the insurance provider, includes a wide range of driving habits and trends. Many elements are carefully documented and examined, including the distance covered, speed, braking and acceleration patterns, trip durations, frequency of stops, kinds of routes followed, and general driving competence. The abundance of data enables insurers to precisely evaluate the risk associated with certain drivers and automobiles. In terms of cost, insurers usually impose an annual premium after an initial charge for the device installation. This premium is variable; it changes on a regular basis in response to the driver's competence as well as other pertinent information extracted from the telemetry data. Crucially, the monitoring system is active throughout the duration of the program, allowing for the ongoing assessment of driving behaviors and rate adjustments as needed. By ensuring that insurance pricing takes into account actual driving behavior, this dynamic method helps customers receive more equitable and individualized insurance solutions.

13.4 ADVANTAGES OF TELEMATICS

Refer Figure 13.1.

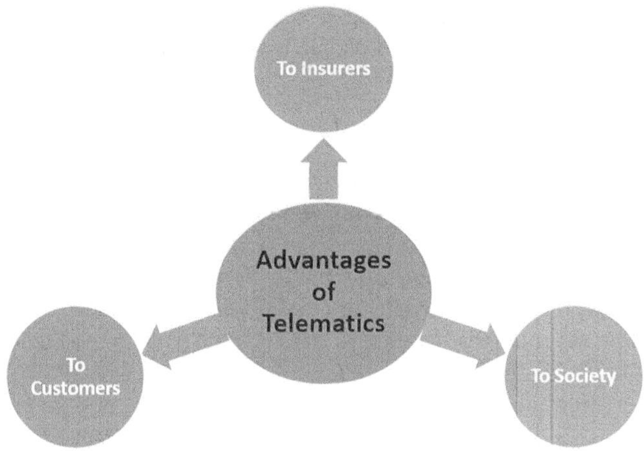

FIGURE 13.1 Advantages of telematics. (Author Compilation.)

13.4.1 To Customers

Customized charges: For the drivers who drives safely, follow all safety rules, having low mileage and off-peak driving patterns may be eligible for lower rates to promote fairness in pricing.

Transparency in tariffs: Using telematics, insurance companies can guarantee equity and transparency benefits to Customers as premiums are directly associated with performance and usage of vehicles.

Better vehicle safety: The black box functions as a tracking device, making it possible for emergency services to find automobiles in the event of an accident or emergency and assisting in the quick recovery of stolen vehicles.

Simplified fleet management: Telematics can be a useful tool in choosing the efficient route as manpower, fuel, and service costs are being reduced by Fleets.

The use of geofencing for safety: This advances safety of the vehicles, predominantly while transferring data to the owner, by updating the owner if the vehicle deviates outside of predetermined borders.

Better vehicle safety and service: The use of telematics devices is very helpful in monitoring the vehicle's service time and safety because this device comes with few extra features such as speedometer messages, tracking the condition of engine, and breakdown possibilities; it also provides improved connectivity with vehicle as well as able to monitor results for better vehicle security and longevity.

Effective notifications and alerts: Telematics devices provide services like a range of alerts and notifications, such as crash alarms, emergency calls, and breakdown assistance, which improve overall vehicle safety.

GPS-based support: Drivers are getting continuous support during their trips, from the insurers who can assist them proactively by alerting them to high-risk regions for theft or accidents and providing information about local garages. All thanks to cloud competences installations in these devices.

Using telematics Fleet operators as well as drivers can gain from insurers' facility to make available more customized and secure insurance options.

13.4.2 To Insurers

Improved customer segmentation: By helping insurers precisely classify clients according to risk profiles, telematics enables them to provide more specialized insurance products.

Better settlements evaluation and fraud detection: Insurers may process claims more accurately by detecting fraudulent claims and estimating damages more accurately by evaluating driving data, such as speed and braking patterns, during collisions.

Next-generation analytics: By using predictive analysis to analyze the collected data, insurers can leverage next-generation analytical insights that facilitate aggressive risk mitigation and strategic decision-making.

Improved customer relationships and profitability: Telematics-driven risk segmentation boosts customer retention rates, fosters better relationship management, and provides insurers with deeper consumer insights.

Simplified accident response: Telematics makes it possible for data to be automatically transmitted to insurers after an accident. This speeds up the claims process by allowing for a prompt assessment of the accident's severity and the start of the necessary steps, such as calling emergency services or renting a car.

Effective claims handling: By streamlining the claims handling procedure, the telematics data generated reduces loss adjustment costs and enhances the overall effectiveness of claims management.

13.4.3 To Society

Attentive and expert drivers: By giving feedback on methods of driving, telematics encourages and provides awareness to the drivers, which successively develop safer driving habits and an overall development for competence.

Promotion of roads safety: Telematics-encouraged harmless and more considerate driving behaviors, which will ultimately help in making roads safer for everyone. The community benefits because of less pollution and traffic congestion.

13.5 CHALLENGES POSED BY TELEMATICS

There are few challenges as well which are associated with Telematics, they are:

Experienced installation requirement: Installing the telematics device in the car requires the knowledge and skills of an experienced installation, which presents a first logistical challenge.

Mileage effect on premiums: Even with excellent driving, people who drive a lot may still pay more for their insurance, which could be annoying.

Issues with data portability: The transferability of telematics data may become problematic when insurance carriers change, as newer firms might not accept older data, making the transfer procedure more difficult.

Privacy considerations: Questions concerning data protection and the parameters of information sharing are raised by privacy concerns around the exchange and use of telematics data.

Cost integration: Integrating telematics requires upfront expenses that must be considered when determining insurance policy prices, thereby affecting affordability.

13.6 FUTURE SCOPE

Usage-based insurance (UBI) and telematics have an excellent future in India, as evidenced by recent data that points to substantial room for growth and technological advancement in the insurance industry. The sector for telematics-based insurance is anticipated to grow quickly as connection and technology use increase nationwide. Insurers now have access to an abundance of data from the growing number of IoT devices that are linked to cars, which they can use to create more dynamic and individualized insurance products. More client satisfaction results from insurers being able to provide highly customized solutions based on unique driving habits and risk profiles thanks to telematics and UBI. Additionally, by using these technologies, insurers may better understand and control risks, which results in enhanced tactics for mitigating losses. In order to foster innovation in telematics and UBI, regulatory measures like the sandbox laws put in place by IRDAI allow insurers to test out innovative products and services while maintaining regulatory compliance. Future telematics systems should be able to perform more sophisticated risk assessment, fraud detection, and claims processing thanks to the integration of telematics with cutting-edge technologies like blockchain, artificial intelligence, and machine learning. To spur innovation and broaden their market reach, insurers are expected to collaborate and cooperate with digital companies, automakers, and other players. All things considered, telematics and UBI could completely transform the Indian insurance market by providing more individualized, data-driven, and effective insurance options that cater to clients' changing demands.

13.7 CONCLUSION

In summary, by informing customers about UBI's advantages and highlighting how it may assist them save money, brokers, agents, and intermediaries can support and enhance the market's adoption of the program. An important step toward individualized and data-driven insurance solutions has been made in India with the addition of telematics into usage-based insurance. Thanks to their increased access to data, insurers are now able to analyze and price risks more accurately. Nevertheless, there are advantages and disadvantages to using this data wisely. Profitability and customer happiness can be increased by data-driven decision-making, but data privacy and regulatory compliance issues must be addressed. To innovate and maintain their competitiveness in the digital marketplace, insurers need to manage these difficulties while utilizing cutting-edge technologies. Adoption of sandbox legislation and cooperation with Insurtech companies can promote innovation and advancement of products in the insurance industry. In the end, an approach that is customer-centric – in which insurers modify their organizational structures and business models to accommodate new technology and satisfy changing client demands – is what will ultimately determine their performance in the digital age. In order to stand out in the market and achieve long-term success, insurers must embrace digital transformation and make intelligent use of emerging technology.

REFERENCES

Boucher, Jean-Philippe, Steven Côté, and Montserrat Guillen. "Exposure as duration and distance in telematics motor insurance using generalized additive models." *Risks* 5, no. 4 (2017): 54.

Chaba, Rafał. "Influence of telematics of UBI insurance on the management of the fleet of company vehicles." *Archiwum Motoryzacji* 92, no. 2 (2021): 69–82.

Che, Xin, Andre Liebenberg, and Jianren Xu. "Usage-based insurance—Impact on insurers and potential implications for InsurTech." *North American Actuarial Journal* 26, no. 3 (2022): 428–455.

Constantinescu, Cornel Coca, Ion Stancu, and Iulian Panait. "Impact study of telematics auto insurance." *The Review of Financial Studies* 3 (2018): 17–35.

Eling, Martin, and Mirko Kraft. "The impact of telematics on the insurability of risks." *The Journal of Risk Finance* 21, no. 2 (2020): 77–109.

Friedman, Sam, and Michelle Canaan. "Overcoming speed bumps on the road to telematics: Challenges and opportunities facing auto insurers with and without usage-based programs." *Deloitte Insights*. https://www2.deloitte.com/us/en/insights/industry/insurance/telematics-in-autoinsurance.html (2014).

Guillen, Montserrat, Jens Perch Nielsen, Mercedes Ayuso, and Ana M. Pérez-Marín. "The use of telematics devices to improve automobile insurance rates." *Risk Analysis* 39, no. 3 (2019): 662–672.

Hassan, Md Kamrul, Nazra Hameed, Md Delwar Hossain, Md Rayhan Hasnat, Grahame Douglas, Sameera Pathirana, Payam Rahnamayiezekavat, and Swapan Saha. "Fire incidents, trends, and risk mitigation framework of electrical vehicle cars in Australia." *Fire* 6, no. 8 (2023): 325.

https://www.astuteanalytica.com/industry-report/usage-based-insurance-market

https://www.policyboss.com/news/Tejuja_June_1_2023.pdf

https://www.ptolemus.com/insight/motor-insurance-is-being-disrupted-as-usage-based-insurance-in-india-is-officially-approved/

Husnjak, Sinisa, Dragan Perakovic, and Ivan Jovovic. "Possibilities of using speech recognition systems of smart terminal devices in traffic environment." *Procedia Engineering* 69 (2014): 778–787.

Kumar, Ranjan. "Insurance telematics: Risk assessment of connected vehicles." In *2019 IEEE Transportation Electrification Conference (ITEC-India) 17–19 December 2019, Bengaluru, India* (2019), pp. 1–4. IEEE.

Li, Hong-Jie, Xing-Gang Luo, Zhong-Liang Zhang, Wei Jiang, and Shen-Wei Huang. "Driving risk prevention in usage-based insurance services based on interpretable machine learning and telematics data." *Decision Support Systems* 172 (2023): 113985.

McDonnell, K., B. Sheehan, F. Murphy, and M. Guillen. "Are electric vehicles riskier? A comparative study of driving behaviour and insurance claims for internal combustion engine, hybrid and electric vehicles." *Accident Analysis & Prevention* 207 (2024): 107761.

Monkiewicz, Marek, and Adam Śliwiński. "Telematics in motor insurance: New opportunities and challenges for insureds 1." In Lech Gąsiorkiewicz, and Monkiewicz Jan (Eds.) *The Digital Revolution in Banking, Insurance and Capital Markets* (2023): 164–189. Abingdon: Routledge.

Narwani, Bhumika, Yash Muchhala, Jatin Nawani, and Renuka Pawar. "Categorizing driving patterns based on telematics data using supervised and unsupervised learning." In *2020 4th International Conference on Intelligent Computing and Control Systems (ICICCS), 13–15 May 2020, Madurai, India* (2020), pp. 302–306. IEEE.

Navneet, D. "Driving habits could determine your motor insurance premium: IRDAI proposal." *ET Online. The Economic Times*, 4th June, 2020.

Nuti, Domenico Mario. "Feasible financial innovation under market socialism." In Domenico Mario Nuti, Estrin Saul, and Uvalić Milica (Eds.) *Collected Works of Domenico Mario Nuti, Volume I: Socialist Economic Systems and Transition* (2023), pp. 189–221. Cham: Palgrave Macmillan.

Pandiangan, Saut Maruli Tua, Fida Oktafiana, Santi Rohdearni Panjaitan, and Mutiara Shifa. "Analysis of public ownership and management ownership on the implementation of the triple bottom line in the plantation sector listed on the Indonesia Stock Exchange." *Budapest International Research and Critics Institute-Journal (BIRCI-Journal)* 5, no. 1 (2022): 349–3497.

Pandya, Sohil, Nilay M. Vaidya, Jaimin N. Undavia, Atul M. Patel, Krishna Kant, and Abhilash Shukla. "Model for mobile app-based premium calculation for usage-based insurance (UBI) of vehicles." In Jagannath Singh, Das Debasish, Kumar Lov, and Krishna Aneesh (Eds.) *Mobile Application Development: Practice and Experience: 12th Industry Symposium in Conjunction with 18th ICDCIT 2022* (2023), pp. 141–152. Singapore: Springer Nature Singapore.

Pareek, Manoj, Manoj Kumar Pandey, and Pratik Priyadarshi. "Emerging technologies enabling the digital transformation of motor insurance in India." *Indian Journal of Science and Technology* 13, no. 45 (2020): 4532–4540.

Pierce, Lamar. "Big losses in ecosystem niches: How core firm decisions drive complementary product shakeouts." *Strategic Management Journal* 30, no. 3 (2009): 323–347.

Quintero, Juan, Alexandr Railean, and Zinaida Benenson. "Acceptance factors of car insurance innovations: The case of usage-based insurance." *Journal of Traffic and Logistics Engineering* 8, no. 2 (2020).

Soleymanian, Miremad, Charles B. Weinberg, and Ting Zhu. "Sensor data and behavioral tracking: Does usage-based auto insurance benefit drivers?" *Marketing Science* 38, no. 1 (2019): 21–43.

Umut, Muharrem. "Towards digitalization in insurance market: Telematic insurance." *Mugla Journal of Science and Technology* 6, no. 2 (2020): 1–10.

Verma, Rajesh, Stuti Gupta, Ajay Kumar Sharma, Vernika Sahni, and Kunal Goyal. "Role of telematics in motor insurance: A way forward." *Academy of Marketing Studies Journal* suppl. Special 3 (2021): 25.

Yao, Yuanjing. "Evolution of insurance: A telematics-based personal auto insurance study." Honors Scholar Theses. 590 (2018).

Ziakopoulos, Apostolos, Virginia Petraki, Armira Kontaxi, and George Yannis. "The transformation of the insurance industry and road safety by driver safety behaviour telematics." *Case Studies on Transport Policy* 10, no. 4 (2022): 2271–2279.

14 Secured and Scalable
Integrating Blockchain Solutions for Health Insurance Claim Using Client Support Chatbot Automation

Vijayakumar T, Revathi A, Janarthanan S, and Vanitha A

14.1 INTRODUCTION: BACKGROUND AND DRIVING FORCES

In light of the COVID-19 pandemic, it has become important for all businesses, including the insurance industry, to use digital technology. As a consequence of this, digitalisation has evolved, particularly in the medical field. It was necessary for the healthcare industry, which included Medicare facilities, to make a quick shift to processes that were networked and conducted remotely. It was necessary for them to improve their digital capabilities in order to meet the increase in business that occurred across the whole healthcare organisation. In addition to this, they were required to work together with hospitals, diagnostic centres, pathological labs, corporations that manufacture medical equipment, and other organisations in order to make sure the timely payment of client claims. Aleksieva et al. (2020) explained that the advent of advanced technologies such as AI and blockchain has caused a significant upheaval in the healthcare industry, revolutionising the way health insurance companies operate. RPA, or Robotic Process Automation, is a technology that may significantly decrease expenses in several sectors by automating jobs that include repetitive, consistent, and well-defined data and procedures. During e-health era, these systems along with Electronic Medical Records (EMR), Electronic Document Interchange (EDI), Patient Management (PM), Order Communication System (OCS), Hospital Information System (HIS), etc. have been implemented in a medical business that has evolved. Asquarepartners (2019) studied a hospital information system with a hospital administrative department (PM, EDI) and a clinical information department (EMR, OCS).

A Chatbot is an Artificial Intelligence (AI)-based software that provides text interaction with users that helps users to access information and service, and the user can communicate with the software service without human interaction. Brill (1995) explained there are also quite a few industries that have already started to use chatbots in place of human customer service agents, mainly for those low-end of the funnel

 DOI: 10.1201/9781003472551-17

questions. Buterin (2014) suggested that a majority of customers (74%) want automation to deliver fast answers to their questions, and they usually prefer chatbots as a tool to do that. Zaboj (2020) explained that Chatbot market is expected to reach 2.6 billion USD in 2020 and 9.4 billion USD by 2024. This expansion is most likely due to the rise in chatbot usage. Abdul-Kader and Woods (2015) explained that to address this phenomenon the service industry is eyeing at financial chatbots that might serve as an instrument for quicker and seamless financial transactions. Chowdhury et al. (2019) suggested that over the past decade, a new term on the radar that has made waves in the world of technology is "blockchain" or blockchain technology. In traditional insurance systems, residents must go through many different transaction steps with different departments by hand, and payment settlement through the system takes a longer period of time. Also, Ferdous et al. (2019) explained that the insurance industry spends tens of millions of dollars every year on claims handling and loses up to millions of dollars every year because of fake claims. Gatteschi et al. (2018) described that a number of researchers have looked into how blockchain technology could be used in the insurance industry to get around these problems. Insurance plans could be turned into smart contracts, which could be used to handle the steps needed to process claims, make sure they are valid, and pay out. The result will be many benefits, such as saving time and money, and maybe even stopping scams. Certainly, it is possible to set up a smart contract in order to keep track of the details of individuals who express interest in purchasing insurance policies from the firm, to make it simpler for them to monitor the progression of their claims, and to automatically pay them back. Smart contracts are used in current blockchain-based methods to improve asset exchanges, stop scams, and lower operating costs. However, these methods don't put joint insurance at the top of their list of priorities. Jiang et al. (2020) described that this type of insurance lets people with similar traits form small groups and cover themselves in a more helpful, fair, and open way.

Collaboration has several benefits for insurers and insureds. Some of these are cutting health insurance rates, making the customer experience better, and letting standard insurers invest in new ideas to stay competitive in the insurance business. Present joint insurance systems aim to provide a platform where customers may communicate directly with one another, but none of them use blockchain technology to build an immutable, open, and secure network. Collective health insurance, AI, and blockchain technology have not been looked into together before, as far as we know.

The strategy that has been suggested not only makes it possible for many organisations within the insurance system to engage in manual contacts with one another, but also cuts down on the expenses of operations and administration and saves time. It is possible that individuals, financial institutions, and insurance firms might all profit from the potential of smart contracts to encourage cooperation in the insurance industry, the pooling of resources, and mutual protection. The smart contract that is being discussed here contains a collection of insurance policies that function as contracts between insurance firms and the policyholders of those businesses. A smart contract that encodes the insurance policy connects with external oracles in order to initiate a new claim and transfer the amount that is being claimed to the insured, who also happens to be the owner of the smart contract. The advantages of the use of blockchain in the insurance industry include the following: ensuring that all participants adhere to the collaborative insurance model; improving the transparency of insurance transactions; automating and speeding up operations from insured enrollment to claim handling; reducing administrative and operational expenses by eliminating manual interactions across insurance system entities; and guaranteeing adherence of the non-repudiation principle between several insecure collaborative entities.

1. Provide an overview of the benefits of using smart contracts and blockchain technology into a new programme that provides PPS (Public Private Sidechain) collaborative insurance. There is no longer a need for a governing body under this paradigm since patients rely on one another to meet their healthcare needs. All the digital insurance options that we've looked at so far don't seem to cover every base, from managing relationships with carriers to handling claims.
2. Introduce the core concepts of the proposed blockchain-based insurance system and its automated enforcement using AI processes and external oracles, including machine-readable insurance policies and claims.
3. It is important to evaluate the scalability and performance of PSC whenever there is an increase in the number of insurance claims and insurers. It is possible to gauge the suggested system's efficacy by measuring its execution time, scalability overhead, and gas consumption.

14.2 THE BLOCKCHAIN IN HEALTH INSURANCE: AN ANALYSIS

Blockchain innovation has revolutionised several domains, including finance, governance, commerce, and control, among numerous others. Reduced costs, more transparency, and simplified tokenisation are all possible outcomes of blockchain technology. An investigation was carried out by Fallucchi et al. in order to substantiate the accuracy of the data without relying on a centralised authority. Blockchain technology was used to record data hashes in transactions in order to guarantee the capability of tracking the data. However, Internet Protocol File System (IPFS) was applied in order to supply ongoing accessibility to the data. Jiang et al. (2018) suggested that a number of nations are now in the process of putting pilot projects into action in order to evaluate blockchain technology and get familiar with emerging technologies. According to the authors, their architecture is particularly accessible for the open data portal programme that is being implemented by the Valls council. Joshua (2018) suggested that this programme makes use of blockchain and IPFS technologies in order to publish datasets on the website of the municipal administration. In addition, Khan et al. (2021) described that it has the potential to be used for the blockchain project that is centered on the protection of digital identity management and has been awarded funding by the Department of Homeland Security (DHS).

Kunde et al. (2017) described that the insurance industry has used blockchain technology, which has the potential to transform the way claims are processed, automatic payments are made, asset transfers are made, and fraud prevention is carried out. According to this paradigm, we are able to classify insurances into three separate groups: insurances that have automated claim processing, insurances that are pay-per-use, and insurances that are peer-to-peer.

Lamberti et al. (2018) described that Oracles have the capability of getting data from the actual world and immediately activating the smart contract that is appropriate to the situation. In the case of travel insurance, for instance, an expert might check on a flight's condition on a regular basis. Lepoint et al. (2018) described that after that, a smart contract can access this outside data and start a payment to repay the covered tourists if there is a delay in their flight. Moon and Kim's (2020) insure chain is a strong idea that depends on a smart contract that includes rules for setting the fee and making sure the payment is real. The conditions for repayment are checked using the services of an oracle, which verifies the weather data and makes sure it is correct. Using oracles could speed up the process of handling claims and cut down on mistakes made by people doing administrative work. It is important to keep in mind, though, that relying on outside oracles is only practical in a few situations. Most cases are taken care of by insurance companies, and they need to be looked at by a professional before they can be settled.

Payments made possible by smart contracts have made it easier for new ways to make money to appear, such as pay-per-use insurance plans. Lamberti et al. offered a car insurance system that works when it's needed, utilising smart contracts and Internet of Things (IoT) technology to lower the costs of policy changes and lower the number of cases of insurance theft. It was created by Vo et al. (2017) and is a pay-as-you-go auto insurance app that works on a blockchain. People who don't drive very often but still want insurance coverage for certain trips can use this programme's "pay-per-trip" option. If pay-per-use insurances use blockchain technology, customers may be able to save money compared to standard insurances. This strategy can also give insurance companies an edge over their competitors by speaking to young people and tech-savvy people. However, in order to stop insurance scams, these pay-per-use systems need up-to-date information about the covered person. So, these methods need to put privacy protection for the covered at the top of their list of priorities, even though it's not necessary for the applications to work.

Peer-to-peer insurance plans make it possible to send an object to someone else without going through a broker. Friendsurance is a digital tool for bank guarantee that can be expanded and changed as needed. It's made for banks, insurance companies, and other partners who want to keep clients and make money from them by giving them useful services. Okuda and Shoda (2018) described that dynamics is a blockchain-based system that helps a group of self-managed people get jobless insurance. Its main job is to underwrite this insurance and handle cases. However, as explained in Pang and Lee (2008) study, the modern peer-to-peer insurance systems are not really peer-to-peer models because most of the insurance work is done by a traditional insurance model or risk provider.

The term "permissionless blockchain" refers to a decentralised system in which everybody may actively participate. Blockchains like Bitcoin and Ethereum are permissionless examples. Hyperledger Fabric and other permissioned blockchains limit which users may do specified tasks on the network. Recently, McGrath (2018) described that the insurance business has begun to employ distributed ledger technologies such as Ethereum, Hyperledger Fabric, and IOTA. The goal of creating

BlockCIS, a cyber insurance system, was to create an automated, real-time, and immutable feedback loop among all parties involved so that cyber risks could be assessed. For the purpose of keeping business transactions private, the system was built using permissioned Hyperledger blockchain technology. In contrast to permissionless blockchains, which suffer from poor performance and limited data confidentiality, permissioned blockchains address these issues. Nevertheless, by doing so, they undermine the concept of genuine decentralisation.

The existing insurance solutions that use blockchain technology do just that use it to streamline payment processes and do away with middlemen. This is something that should be remembered. However, they continue to operate within the confines of a traditional insurance mechanism. The automation component of the smart contract is included into our solution, which functions as a peer-to-peer insurance system that is permanent. The conventional insurance model is not meant to be replaced by collaborative insurance, even if it may be built expressly for electric autos, pet care, and other objectives that are comparable to those of traditional insurance. Consequently, our purpose is to develop a unique cooperative insurance framework that allows people with similar traits to establish local communities in order to insure themselves in a way that is more compassionate, egalitarian, and transparent inside a network that is safe and tamper-proof. Neither automated claim processing nor peer-to-peer insurance scenarios need the use of expert views on claim verification. This is a crucial point to bring up since the solutions that are now available do not contain this requirement. Consequently, the purpose of this study is to circumvent this limitation by resorting only to the use of oracles in order to automate the process of claim production. After that, authorisations from both the insurer and the insured are required in order to recognise the claim that has been created.

14.3 SMART CONTRACT-BASED HEALTH INSURANCE ENHANCEMENT

Blockchain is a record of events that is not controlled and is organised by time. The transactions are stored in blocks. Blockchains are incredibly difficult to alter, making them a trustworthy approach. There is no need for a single authority since blockchain develops confidence via separate agreement procedures. Any physical or digital asset may be stored on a distributed ledger and then shared over a global network. It is essential that all participants in this network own a precise replica of the ledger. Singh and Urolagin (2017) described that the year 2019. Although blockchain technology was initially developed for use in the financial sector, it has subsequently found numerous other applications, including healthcare information exchange, smart packaging of industrial IoT data, supply chain management for food tracking, and insurance solutions based on blockchain. On a blockchain network, programmes called "smart contracts" are installed and executed.

The execution of their predetermined tasks is conditional on the satisfaction of certain requirements. Suciu et al. (2018) defined that there is no ability to filter or change smart contracts after they have been deployed, and their functionality is always responsive when invoked. Smart contracts allowed for the automation of networks

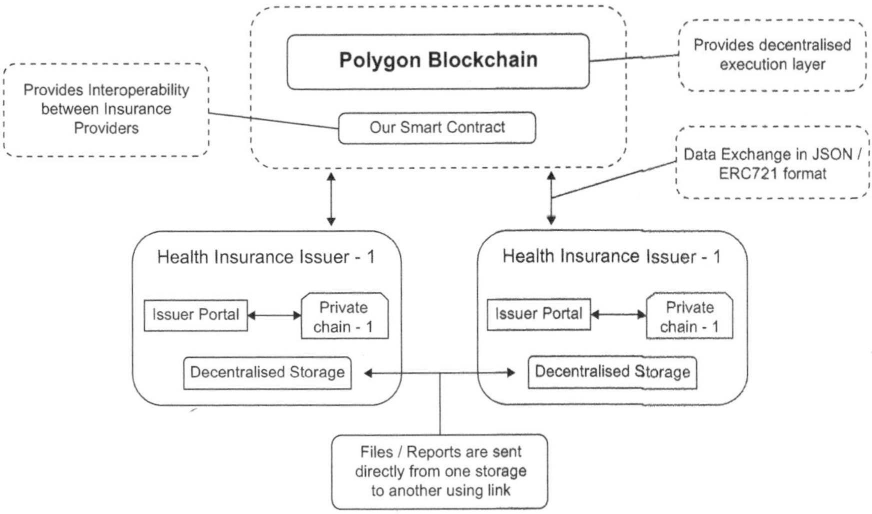

FIGURE 14.1 Blockchain's function in expediting the claim lifecycle. (Developed by Author.)

and the transition from physical to electronic contracts. Vo et al. (2017) suggested that smart contracts allow users to formalise their agreements and trust relationships by automating automated transactions without the need for a central authority.

Smart contracts also allow users to maintain their confidence in one another. Wu et al. (2019) described the fact that smart contracts are unable to establish direct connections with other systems is an essential point to keep in mind. Oracles are the means by which this communication is made possible as a consequence. Oracles are external sources of information that provide data to smart contracts on blockchains via the use of Application Programming Interfaces (APIs). Oracles are also known as cloud databases.

The Provable Ethereum API is the most popular service on the Polygon blockchain for development of blockchain apps and smart contracts (Figure 14.1).

14.4 CLAIMS AUTOMATION PROCESS FOR CLIENT SUPPORT CHATBOT

An application programme that can have real-time audio or written interactions with users is called a chatbot. Aleksieva et al. (2020) described that this AI technology offers a sophisticated user experience by enabling conversations across several channels in a user-friendly manner. It is the emerging forefront technology with immense promise for boosting sales, enhancing customer service, and improving marketing strategies. In the next part, we will examine many facets of a chatbot.

The use cases: The usage of chatbots as personal assistants is becoming more common. This enables users to have conversations with chatbots, ask questions, and do duties such as making phone calls, paying bills, organising meetings, and performing a wide variety of other chores that are traditionally performed by a personal assistant.

Siri is an artificial intelligence chatbot that was built by Apple. On March 24, 2017, a youngster called Roman, who was just four years old at the time, was able to successfully rescue his mother by utilising Siri. Additional, as per Zaboj (2020), chatbots that are commonly used include the Google Assistant and Alexa, which is offered by Amazon. Chatbots are often used in contact centres to provide customers with the ability to ask about their products and get instant replies at any time of the day or night.

Category: Bots may mostly be categorised into two groups:

Text-based: A text-based chatbot exclusively uses text to communicate with its users. Users will input text queries and get text-based replies. There are two sorts of chatbots. The bot operates by offering predetermined choices, and users must choose one option in order to engage with it. The second option is a dynamic chatbot that generates dynamic responses to random user requests.

Voice-activated: Chatbots that employ voice interaction are the most advanced kind of chatbots.

Mechanisms: The basic operation of a chatbot is laid forth here. A chatbot has many components. The User Interface (UI) is the front-facing component of a text chatbot that allows users to interact and submit inquiries or pick alternatives. A voice-activated chatbot uses the microphone of the related devices to accept instructions or inputs from the user. A text chatbot that is based on alternatives is the most straightforward to create, since it just requires the capability to handle a restricted set of predetermined choices. Dynamic chatbots that include both textual and speech capabilities need the integration of several supplementary elements and sophisticated algorithms, such as voice translation and Speech To Text Reporter (STTR), in order to operate well.

In addition, Abdul-Kader and Woods (2015) described that these chatbots must use additional Natural Language Processing techniques, such as Part-Of-Speech Tagging and Sentiment Analysis, in order to comprehend the inquiry and provide an appropriate response.

As per Ferdous et al. (2019), Bitcoin is thought to be the first widely used decentralised digital currency because it is not controlled by a governing bank or other body. An important technology development in this system is its main idea, which is called blockchain. Blockchain is a type of distributed record that is shared among a network of Peer-to-Peer (P2P) nodes. The ledger is an organised list of blocks that are tied together using complicated maths. There are several transactions in each block. Each transaction lets a user send a certain amount of bitcoin to one or more other users. A digital hash connects each block in a blockchain to the block before it, making a chain of blocks that are read in order.

Algorithm 14.1

1. Begin
2. User login
   //Credential validation
3. Login details ← valid
4. Home page login
5. Search for amount in user account

6. Return to home page
7. Search Premium payment schedule
8. If (premium due date = true)
9. Pay the due through gateway
10. Else
11. Return to home page
12. Search Claim settlement details
13. If (claim settlement needed)
14. Proceed
15. Else
16. Return to Home Page
17. End

With AI and blockchain, the insurance claim process will be transformed. AI can help you fill out forms and pre-screen claims for speedier approvals. It saves insurers money by detecting false claims. Blockchain stores insurance data, claims history, and insurer communication securely and transparently. Smart contracts, self-executing agreements that trigger rewards depending on pre-defined criteria, are possible without tampering (Figure 14.2). AI for efficiency and blockchain for security will make insurance claims quicker, more transparent, and better for policyholders and insurers.

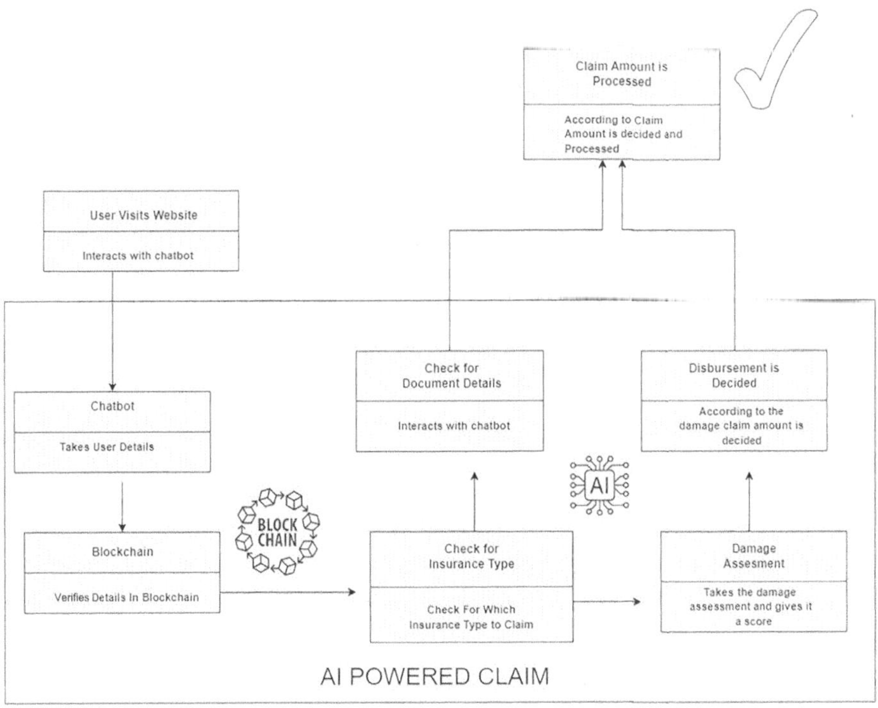

FIGURE 14.2 Blockchain-chatbot integration for real-time information retrieval. (Developed by Author.)

As a result of the Bitcoin blockchain, a new blockchain system has emerged that lets computer software, called "smart contracts," be put into action and run independently on the related ledger as described by Gatteschi et al. (2018). By taking part in the ledger, you make sure that smart contracts and their actions can't be changed or undone. This is a very useful property that has many uses in many fields. A blockchain system that allows smart contracts also has many other benefits, such as autonomous data control, data longevity, tracking data origins, accountability, and openness. Jiang et al. (2018) described that there are two main types of blockchain systems, which are based on how much access each person has to a record. Anyone can access a public blockchain, which is an open digital log that can be used to record and check activities. If someone is in a public blockchain, which is also sometimes called a permissionless blockchain, anyone can join and interact with the network at any time for the purposes of managing the blockchain and making transactions. As examples, Bitcoin, Ethereum, Litecoin, Monero, and other public blockchains can be used. A private blockchain, which is also sometimes called a permissioned blockchain, only lets trusted institutions join and gives users different levels of privacy and access. Private blockchain platforms are shown by Hyperledger Platforms.

14.5 ETHEREUM MAINCHAIN DATA TRANSPORT BASED ON TECHNICAL IMPLEMENTATION

The Ethereum mainchain is shown at the very top of Figure 14.3. Because it is an open blockchain, everyone may join and participate. Coexisting with Ethereum's mainchain is a secondary blockchain known as a Polygon sidechain. A sidechain is a separate blockchain that is interconnected with the mainchain. By processing transactions that do not take place on the mainchain, they let the latter to handle more transactions.

The main text of the graphic highlights the benefits of using a sidechain:

Permissioned sidechains, made possible by the Consortium Smart Contract, limit involvement to permitted participants alone. For businesses that value data privacy, this may be a good thing. Cooperation between different manufacturers: Interoperability between different blockchains is made possible by sidechains. Assets pertaining to non-fungible tokens (NFTs) may be transferred between the mainchain and the sidechain via policy transfer.

Choosing the right blockchain platform and consensus mechanism. Ethereum mainchain processing time is 15 minutes for Consortium smart contract and 15 minutes for interoperability using polygon sidechain. Data transfer is based on decentralised storage and transferred between two vendors. The current insurance market is struggling with issues including policy transfer facilitation and provider interoperability. Conventional systems are plagued by a lack of communication among insurers, which makes it more difficult to maintain a seamless transition when moving providers or transferring coverage. In addition, the process of filing a claim is hampered by an excessive amount of administrative formalities and a lack of transparency.

Making use of blockchain technology, a solution may be achieved via the combination of smart contracts and the Polygon sidechain. Polygon, which is a layer-2

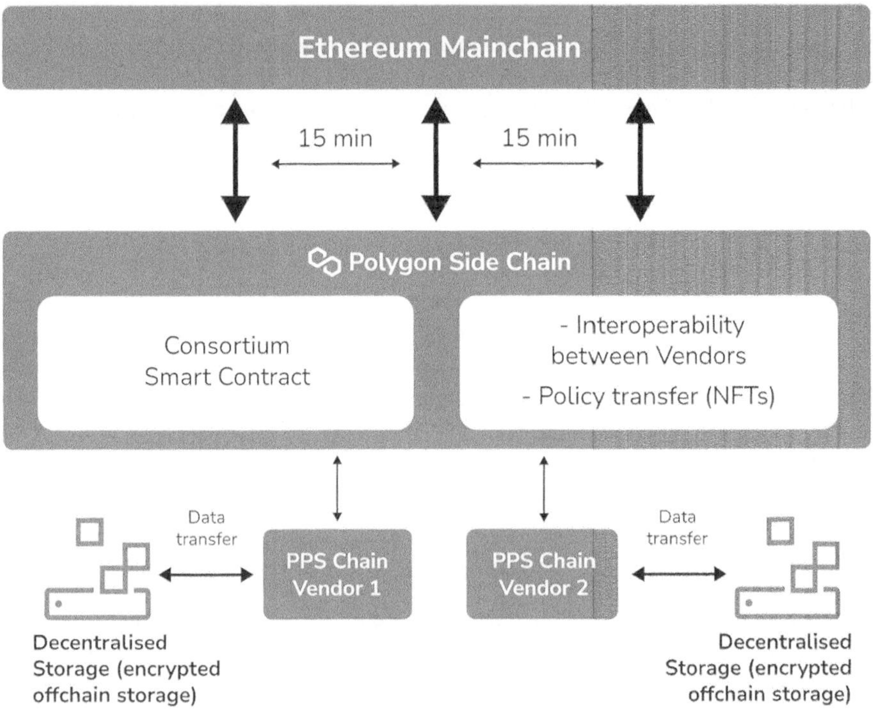

FIGURE 14.3 Overall structure of PSC. (Developed by Author.)

solution for Ethereum, provides a framework that is both dependable and flexible for insurance and financial applications. It is particularly suitable for insurance task that involves an enormous number of transactions due to the problem tackled with high costs and slower transaction speeds over the main Ethereum network. Smart contracts, or contracts comprising automatic execution of terms and simplifying significant elements of policy transmission, have been rendered feasible through blockchain technology. While the policy is transmitted, the appropriate vendors – such as healthcare providers – can receive an immediate update. The policy's data are securely stored on the blockchain. Moreover, conditional repayments that correspond with policy terms might be programmed into smart contracts, simplifying the claim submission process.

This method has a great contract of reimbursements. By controlling the transmission of data and updates from vendors, smart contracts make the policy transmissions easy and quick. By employing the blockchain to make use of specific information about their insurance coverage details and the present status of their claims, policyholders may enhance the transparency. Moreover, the inherent tamper-proof characteristics of blockchain technology significantly reduce the danger of fraud. Ultimately, the use of smart contracts enhances efficiency by minimising the need for human labour. Polygon sidechain and smart contracts have the potential to fundamentally transform the transfer of policies and the capacity for different insurance systems to work together seamlessly. This establishes the foundation for a robust, open, and effective system that advantages both individuals with insurance policies and insurance providers, eventually resulting in a quicker, more efficient, and customer-focused insurance process (Figure 14.3). Insurance portability using NFTs (ERC-721 Tokens): Public blockchains enable insurance portability. We created ERC-721-compliant NFTs for insurance coverage. Our proof of concept (PoC) includes the following data:

- Basic customer and vendor data.
- NFT metadata, including policy and portability details such as porting time, originating and destination vendors.
- Secure and reliable claims are conveyed by hashed data.

Formula: Total NFT Metadata Size = Number of Policies × Size of Metadata per Policy

Example: If each policy's metadata is 2 kB and there are 5,000 policies, then the total metadata size would be: 5,000 × 2 kB = 10 MB

14.6 SCALABILITY AND PERFORMANCE OPTIMISATION

Analysis of the computational cost associated with time, scalability, fuel consumption, and claim authorisation is used to evaluate the performance of our proposed approach.

$$\text{Gas Cost} = \text{Gas Price} \times \text{Gas Used} \quad (14.1)$$

Example: If the gas price is 20 Gwei (0.00000002 ETH) and the gas used for a transaction is 500,000 units, then the gas cost would be: 20 Gwei × 500,000 units = 0.01 ETH

14.6.1 Blockchain Network Throughput

$$\text{Transactions Per Second (TPS)} = \frac{\text{Block Size}}{\text{Average Transaction Size}} \times \text{Block Time} \quad (14.2)$$

Example: If the block size is 8 MB, the average transaction size is 200 bytes, and the block time is 15 seconds, then the TPS would be:

$$\frac{8\text{ MB}}{(200\text{ bytes} \times 15\text{ seconds})} = 26.67\text{ TPS} \quad (14.3)$$

14.6.2 Computation Time Cost

The amount of time needed to handle and confirm a monthly payment activity is found. The PayPremium function is part of this transaction, as well as an API link update transaction that calls the updateClaimDetectionURL function, a claim creation transaction that calls the claimCreation function, and a policy cancellation transaction that calls the cancelPolicy function. Therefore, calculate the time required to complete Insurance Policy smart contract jobs. Figure 14.3 displays the cost of called jobs for one covered organisation. Covered people may initiate a new Claim smart contract instance in 222 ms, compared to minutes or hours with traditional insurance policies. Other called processes execute in 100–160 ms (Figure 14.4). Our response achieves all of our goals: speeding up insurance business procedures, cutting operational and managerial expenses by eliminating human interactions, and securely storing insurance transaction data.

14.6.3 Cost for Scaling

The Insurance Policy smart contracts were deployed to 1,000 insured accounts. It shows the Insurance Policy smart contract call time. Processing time increases proportionately with covered accounts, from 0 to 240 seconds. Figure 14.5 shows that the number of insured accounts closely correlates with the smart contract engagement length.

14.6.4 Cost of Overhead

Gas use in the Insurance Policies smart contract after blockchain implementation. Claim creation, premium payment, URL change for claim detection, and insurance cancellation are these dutics. Figure 14.5 illustrates petrol prices for "called" Insurance Policy smart contract functions. Gas use may be adjusted by modifying the called code. This may be because functions that employ greater computer resources consume more gas. Deploying a new Insurance Policy smart contract and using the

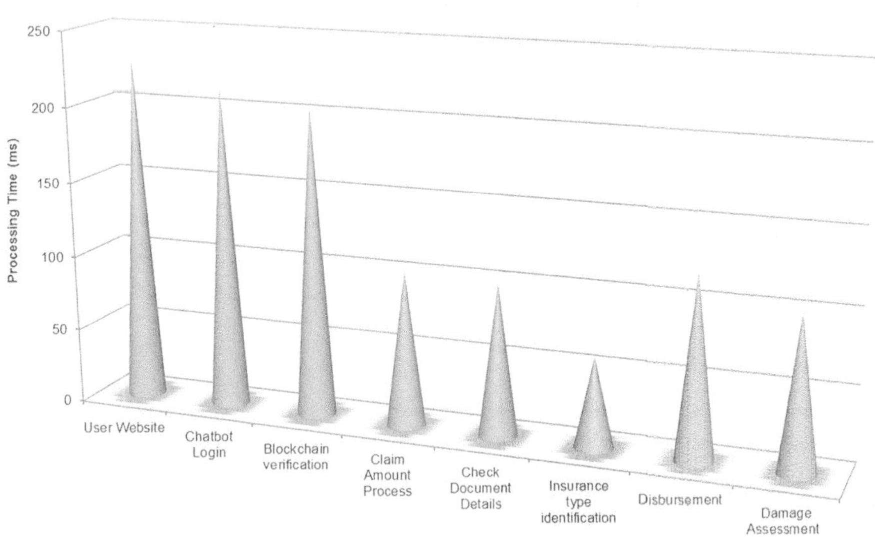

FIGURE 14.4 Analysis of process control. (Developed by Author.)

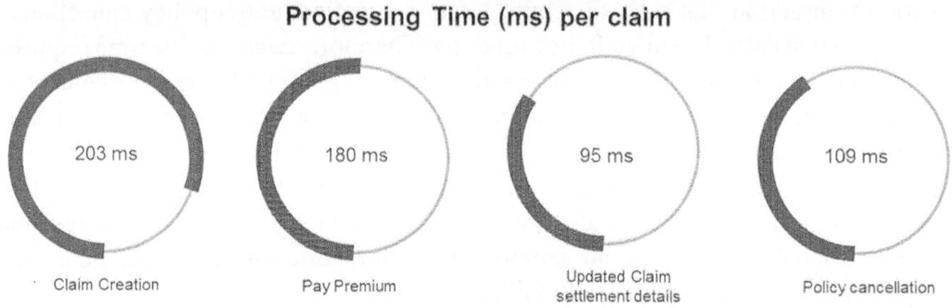

FIGURE 14.5 Processing time per claim. (Developed by Author.)

claimCreation function, which instantaneously installs a new Claim smart contract, were projected to require more gas than executing the other actions (Table 14.1).

$$\text{Cost per Transaction} = \text{Gas Cost} + \text{Transaction Fee} \quad (14.4)$$

Example: If the gas cost for a transaction is 0.01 ETH and the transaction fee is 0.001 ETH, then the total cost per transaction would be: 0.01 ETH + 0.001 ETH = 0.011 ETH (Table 14.2).

14.7 SECURITY MEASURES

There are two levels of protection in the idea that was offered. The person who is in charge of the ChainSure system is called the "Manager." The boss is in charge

TABLE 14.1
Analysis of Different Insurance Companies

Insurance Company Name	Premium	Celling Value	Polygon Usage Cost
A	0.1868	0.0698	0.050
B	0.1660	0.1396	0.043
C	0.2075	0.1326	0.031
D	0.1868	0.1047	0.030

TABLE 14.2
Overview of Gas Cost

Entities	Function Execution Cost (Gas)	Cost ($) Using Polygon
User	1,50,000	0.30
Insurance company	6,00,000	1.00

of keeping the system's privacy safe. Outsiders who aren't supposed to be there are watched and can't get in without permission. There are hostile nodes in the system that try to damage the data's security and dependability. A good consensus procedure protects against threats and looks out for the interests of the users. In a few words, Table 14.1 shows what ChainSure's security features are. It carefully looks at the suggested blockchain-based solution's security, focusing on how well it can handle important security problems like data consistency, privacy, data hacking, identification, and access control. It also look at how a blockchain based method might help protect against hacking.

Claim Verification Efficiency:

$$\text{Verification Time per Claim} = \text{Time to Retrieve} + \text{Time to Validate} \quad (14.5)$$

Example: If it takes 0.5 seconds to retrieve a claim hash from the blockchain and 0.3 seconds to validate it, then the verification time per claim would be:

$$0.5 \text{ seconds} + 0.3 \text{ seconds} = 0.8 \text{ seconds}$$

14.7.1 Data Integrity

Traditionally, third parties are responsible for managing legacy health insurance systems (Figure 14.6).

This not only increases the expenses associated with processing transactions, but also presents opportunities for the manipulation and improvement of data. Using a blockchain platform to automate insurance processes and keep insurance data is beneficial. The data stored on the blockchain is resistant to tampering since it utilises tamper-proof encryption to connect the transactions.

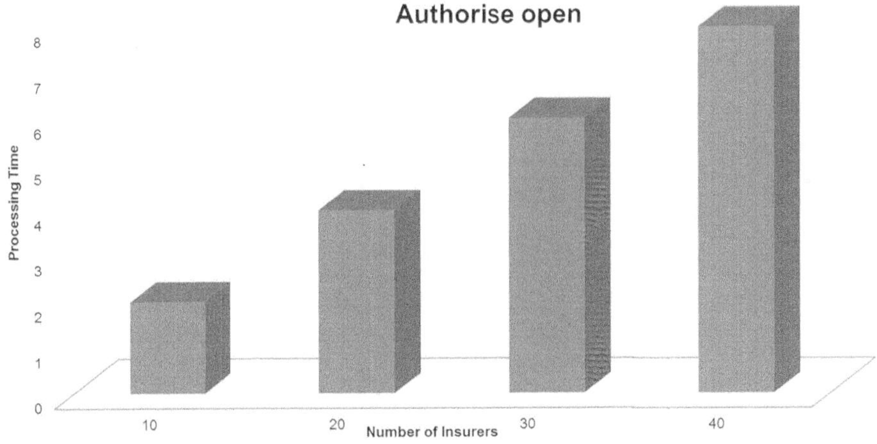

FIGURE 14.6 Analysis of authorised person per second. (Developed by Author.)

14.7.2 Privacy

During the insurance application process, users often want to keep their information hidden. In addition, they may want to keep account details and activities as private as possible. This means that using a method based on blockchain is the best option because it keeps all user data safe and lets people access it even when there are harmful hacks or sudden system crashes.

14.7.3 Data Tampering

All network nodes receive signed copies of transactions saved in the blockchain. This makes it very hard to change data because every node has an exact copy of the transactions. In addition, blockchain technology protects the privacy of data, creates records that can't be changed, and stops users from sharing their data across many social platforms (Figure 14.7).

14.7.4 Access Control

Ethereum lets you authenticate data and control who can see it, so you don't need a third party. Insurance companies can set up smart contracts with pre-defined entry rules that might only let hospitals deal with the contract. There's also a chance that the deal will limit the information that doctors and the public can see. This includes only letting hospitals that are approved by the insurance company that takes part in the insurance operations (Figure 14.8).

14.7.5 DDoS Attacks

Distributed Denial of Service (DDoS) attacks are a popular way for bad hackers to get into websites. The fact that hackers are flooding fixed systems with fake data to

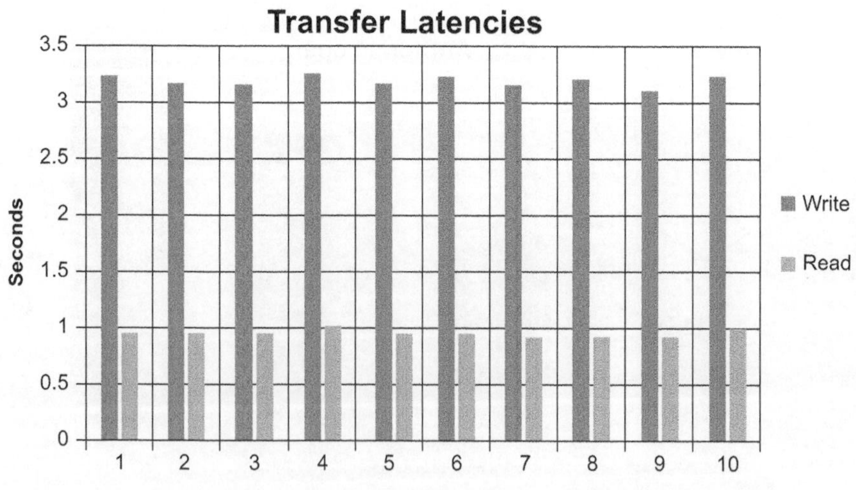

FIGURE 14.7 Analysis of transaction per second. (Developed by Author.)

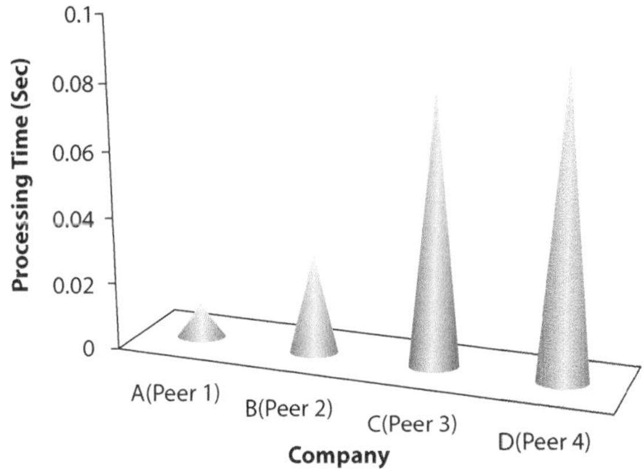

FIGURE 14.8 Analysis of company login with peer-to-peer. (Developed by Author.)

attack them is a big problem. For now, the blockchain's distributed structure lets it set aside resources to handle DDoS strikes, essentially stopping such an attack. This makes it less likely that people will not be able to receive insurance services. As a result, it promises that deals on the blockchain will go through without any problems, even if there are a limited number of them.

14.7.6 Conclusion

Health insurance claims framework to solve privacy breaches in blockchain-based systems. Current blockchain health insurance systems provide all nodes complete access to insurance, ownership, and transfer data. The health insurer risks having their private information revealed when they enter it into the smart contract for identity verification during the claim. Blockchain technology offers several benefits, including data tampering, access control, and DDoS attacks. Transactions saved in blockchain are signed and transmitted to all network nodes, making it difficult to modify data. This ensures data security, generates immutable records, and prevents user data from being shared across social sites.

REFERENCES

Abdul-Kader, Sameera A., and John C. Woods. "Survey on chatbot design techniques in speech conversation systems." *International Journal of Advanced Computer Science and Applications* 6.7 (2015): 72–80.

Aleksieva, Veneta, Hristo Valchanov, and Anton Huliyan. "Implementation of smart contracts based on hyperledger fabric blockchain for the purpose of insurance services." *2020 International Conference on Biomedical Innovations and Applications (BIA), 24–27 September 2020, Varna, Bulgaria*. IEEE, 2020.

Asquarepartners. "Collaborative insurance: Takeoff impending?" 2019. https://www.asquarepartners.com/collaborative-insurance-takeoff-impending/ (accessed 1 April 2021)..

Bertini, T., K. Butkute, and F. Canessa. "Smart Flight Insurance—InsurETH." 2015. http://mkvd.s3.amazonaws.com/apps/InsurEth.pdf (accessed 1 April 2021)..

Brill, Eric. "Transformation-based error-driven learning and natural language processing: A case study in part-of-speech tagging." *Computational Linguistics* 21.4 (1995): 543–565.

Buterin, Vitalik. "A next-generation smart contract and decentralized application platform." White Paper 3.37 (2014): 2–1.

Chowdhury, Mohammad Jabed Morshed, et al. "A comparative analysis of distributed ledger technology platforms." *IEEE Access* 7 (2019): 167930–167943.

Ethereum Team. Ethereum API—ProvableAPI 0.5 Smart Contract. 2019. https://github.com/provable-things/ethereum-.

Ferdous, Md Sadek, Farida Chowdhury, and Madini O. Alassafi. "In search of self-sovereign identity leveraging blockchain technology." *IEEE Access* 7 (2019): 103059–103079.

Gatteschi, Valentina, et al. "Blockchain and smart contracts for insurance: Is the technology mature enough?" *Future Internet* 10.2 (2018): 20.

Insure Chain—Blockchain Insurance Management. 2017. https://www.reply.com/en/content/insurechain (accessed 1 April 2021).

Jiang, Shan, Jiannong Cao, Hanqing Wu, and Yanni Yang. Fairness-based packing of industrial IoT data in permissioned blockchains. *IEEE Transactions on Industrial Informatics* 17 (2020): 1–11.

Jiang Shan, Cao Jiannong, Wu Hanqing, Yang Yanni, Ma Mingyu, and He Jianfei. Blochie: A blockchain-based platform for healthcare information exchange. *Proceedings of the 2018 IEEE International Conference on Smart Computing (Smartcomp)*, Taormina, Italy, 18–20 June 2018. IEEE: New York, 2018, pp. 49–56.

Joshua, D. "Peer to peer insurance on an Ethereum blockchain." 2018. http://www.dynamis-app.com/whitepaper.pdf (accessed 1 April 2021)..

Khan Shafaq Naheed, Loukil Faiza, Ghedira-Guegan Chirine, Benkhelifa Elhadj, and Bani-Hani Anoud. Blockchain smart contracts: Applications, challenges, and future trends. *Peer-to-Peer Networking and Applications* 14 (2021): 2901–2925.

Kunde, T., S. Herfurth, and J. Meyer-Plath. "Friendsurance: The P2P insurance concept." 2017. https://www.friendsurance.com/ (accessed 1 April 2021)..

Lamberti, Fabrizio, et al. "Blockchains can work for car insurance: Using smart contracts and sensors to provide on-demand coverage." *IEEE Consumer Electronics Magazine* 7.4 (2018): 72–81.

Lepoint, Tancrede, Gabriela Ciocarlie, and Karim Eldefrawy. "Blockcis—A blockchain-based cyber insurance system." *2018 IEEE International Conference on Cloud Engineering (IC2E)*, Orlando, FL, USA, April 17–20, 2018. IEEE, 2018.

McGrath, R. "How talluo improve customer service with chatbots." 2018, May 3. https://chatbotsmagazine.com/ill-never-buy-from-them-again- using-chatbots-to-avoid-bad-customer-service-e6a967360244 (accessed 1 February 2020)..

Moon, Junho, and Dongsoo Kim. "Design and implementation of distributed ledger based health data management system." *International Journal of Innovative Computing, Information and Control* 16.3 (2020): 1117–1124.

Nakamoto, Satoshi. Bitcoin: A peer-to-peer electronic cash system". 2008 https://bitcoin.org/bitcoin.pdf..

Okuda, Takuma, and Sanae Shoda. "AI-based chatbot service for financial industry." *Fujitsu Scientific and Technical Journal* 54.2 (2018): 4–8.

Pang, Bo, and Lillian Lee. "Opinion mining and sentiment analysis." *Foundations and Trends® in Information Retrieval* 2.1–2 (2008): 1–135.

Singh, Jaskanwar, and Siddhaling Urolagin. "Use of artificial intelligence for health insurance claims automation." In Patnaik Srikanta, Xin-She Yang, and Ishwar K. Sethi (Eds.) *Advances in Machine Learning and Computational Intelligence: Proceedings of ICMLCI 2019*. Springer: Singapore, 2021, pp. 381–392.

Suciu, George, et al. "Comparative analysis of distributed ledger technologies." *2018 Global Wireless Summit (GWS)*, Chiang Rai, Thailand, 25–28 November 2018. IEEE, 2018.

Vo, Hoang Tam, et al. "Blockchain-based data management and analytics for micro-insurance applications." *Proceedings of the 2017 ACM on Conference on Information and Knowledge Management*, Singapore, 6–10 November 2017. ACM, 2017.

Wu, Hanqing, et al. Data management in supply chain using blockchain: Challenges and a case study. *Proceedings of the 28th International Conference on Computer Communication and Networks (ICCCN)*, Valencia, Spain, 29 July–1 August 2019. IEEE: New York, 2019, pp. 1–8.

Zaboj, D. "Key chatbot statistics you should follow in 2020." 2020. https://medium.com/@yugasasoftware/key-chatbot-statistics-you-need-to-follow-in-2020-7c2dfeb53579.

Section D

Conclusion

15 Law and AI-Powered Actuarial Revolution

Navigating the Future of Insurance Risk Assessment

Neha Parveen

15.1 INTRODUCTION

15.1.1 Concept and Role of Artificial Intelligence in Actuarial Sciences

The use of artificial intelligence (AI) algorithms has now become frequent and is used in almost every field of life to know the utmost possible accuracy regarding collection of data. Hence, actuarial science is also not been immune from transformation either. In the contemporary times, AI is revolutionizing every façade of computation related to actuarial science that is connected to our day-to-day survival. Actuaries may find that their working environment modifications as a result of the rapid advances in machine learning (ML) and AI (Richman, 2018).

The insurance industry's roots trace back to the activities of maritime traders who funded voyages in search of new territories across the seas. According to Deloitte Insights, these ventures were partially supported by the Lloyd's subscription market, which has been active for over three centuries and remains a significant force in the worldwide insurance sector.

Today, actuarial science is instrumental in analysing the significant risks faced by the insurance and financial sectors, focusing primarily on life, health, and pension insurance products. Similar methodologies are favoured across various sectors, such as banking, agriculture, transportation, consulting, and the aerospace industry. As nearly every prosperous company relies on a team managing commercial insurance, actuarial scientists play a pivotal role in mitigating a diverse array of financial risks and payment annuities. Amidst burgeoning unrest in insurance markets, some scholars like Schreiber (2017) have foreseen the potential obsolescence of actuaries in the insurance sector due to rapid advancements in deep learning.

Conversely, others like Wuthrich and Buser (2023) argue that actuarial science will adapt and evolve to incorporate new deep learning methodologies, supported by burgeoning uses of AI across various domains, including telematics analysis, mortality modelling, claims reserving, life insurance valuation, and non-life pricing.

DOI: 10.1201/9781003472551-19

15.2 MANIPULATION OF BIG DATA THROUGH AI IN ACTUARIES AND MANAGING RISK MANAGEMENT

The potential to revolutionize actuarial science has emerged in 1990s with the advent of Analytics of Big Data, particularly in conjunction with ML and AI. Simultaneously, the insurance industry is evolving to meet the needs of a more informed, demanding consumer base amidst increased competition. Shapiro and Jain (2003) note that the insurance sector has long been utilized data collection and processing for various purposes, including underwriting strategies, fraud detection, risk assessment, claim management, and pricing models. According to Bearing Point Report (2020), entities benefiting from these innovations include data benefactors, data-sellers, automotive firms, aggregators and telecommunications companies, and their progress moulds the insurance market on the reliance of their services. These innovative approaches enhance customization capabilities, raising pricing complexities and socio-economic considerations, potentially leading to heightened regulation of big data and AI algorithms (Deloitte Insights Report, 2019). They must also monitor the ramifications of decisions and upgrades within existing insurance offerings (Berthele, 2018). While only 10%–15% of available data is currently structured, predominantly used in insurance analytics, this landscape is rapidly evolving (OECD Report, 2020).

According to a report by SNS Telecom & IT (2018), investments in big data are projected to reach $3.6 billion by 2021, indicating a growing reliance on data-driven approaches within the insurance sector. According to PWC's HR Technology report (2020), less than 10% of respondents thought they were currently utilizing all of the potential that was available, and more than half of respondents said it is difficult to find the right workforce expertise to take advantage of big data. Scholars like Topol (2015) and along with Meyers and Van Hoyweghen (2018) claimed that advances in big data analytics and capabilities are leading to an increase in schemes for the potential of personalized insurance products and benefits.

Alshamsi (2014) promoted to use random forest algorithms to help insurers predict customer decisions and create more alluring insurance offers. Wang and Xu (2018) used a Light-GBM algorithm to analyse data from over 60,000 auto insurance policies in order to pinpoint the key elements that influence consumers' decisions to stick with a specific insurer.

Xu and Wang (2018) introduce a novel deep learning methodology employing text mining techniques, particularly Latent Dirichlet Allocation (LDA), for the purpose of detecting fraudulent activities within the insurance sector. Subudhi and Panigrahi (2018) explore methods for fraud detection within the auto insurance domain, employing three prominent classifiers: Support Vector Machine (SVM), Decision Tree (DT), and Multi-Layered Perceptron (MLP). Furthermore, mortality modelling stands as a pivotal component within actuarial science, crucial for managing risks associated with longevity and for determining actuarial pricing of mortality-linked financial instruments and lifespan-related products (Silverman, 2011). Traditionally, regression-based methodologies, often coupled with extrapolative techniques, have been utilized to assess mortality concerns (Booth and Tickle, 2008). Additionally, various strategies such as ML, predictive analytics, and deep learning techniques are frequently employed in the realm of actuarial sciences. Deprez et al. (2017) employ regression trees to compute conditional odds pertaining to mortality within actuarial contexts, demonstrating how individual features can enhance mortality modelling. Similarly, Kopinsky (2015) utilizes tree models to forecast mortality rates and compile data relating to both mortality and maternity recovery.

It should be noted that a study conducted by Mill and Jones (2016) shows how vulnerable insurance companies and power providers are to the potential damage that can result from outages that follow disruption of the national grid. In his research, Biener et al. (2015) examined statistical characteristics to determine the extent to which cyber risk can be covered by insurance. According to his findings, there are several factors that will make it difficult to develop a sustainable cyber insurance market, including a dearth of data, severe information asymmetries, and the substantial interdependence of losses.

Similar conclusions were drawn by Eling and Schnell (2016) who discovered that there are the high risk of change and the even higher risk of accretion of risks when there is lack of data, which poses the challenges to analytically insuring against cyber risk. Some researchers have discovered that big data has the ability to produce the required data, despite the conclusions of the cited authors. It has been proposed that data can be categorized by combining supervised learning techniques to produce information that is security-aware; therefore, any information that could harm clients or insurance providers is kept private (Hassani et al., 2020).

15.3 EVOLVING ROLE OF AI IN RISK ASSESSMENT WITHIN INSURANCE-RISE OF INSURTECH

Predictive modelling is used by the insurance sector in India, which is a major user of actuarial services impacted by AI. Determining the regulatory framework for the application of technology, including AI, in the insurance industry has been a task for the Insurance Regulatory and Development Authority of India (IRDAI). To guarantee the ethical and responsible application of AI in actuarial procedures, regulatory frameworks were created.

Furthermore, by utilizing data analytics and AI, insurers may be able to make better investment decisions.This aids in satisfying legal requirements and optimizing investment portfolios. In an in-person interview, Ali (2019) underlined that the primary obstacle to improving the application of AI in business is that the development of AI capabilities does not always result in a rise in financial gains. There are no requirements to acquire these skills. It is imperative that consulting and insurance firms actively seek out and compensate AI expertise in order to provide actuaries with the proper incentives to proceed in this direction (Yunos et al., 2016).

Traditional loss reserving techniques are typically predicated on statistical models that are adjusted using elementary arithmetic operations. Li et al. (2018) and Sheshasaayee and Thomas (2018) proposed a number of identification techniques, such as expert systems, DTs, SVMs, artificial neural networks (ANNs), naive bayes, linear regression, random forests, and logistic regression, among others, that can be used to reduce the risk of insurance fraud.

According to Deloitte, InsurTech startups have amassed $16.5 billion in funding over the last decade, with investments in the first three quarters of 2021 surpassing the combined totals of 2019 and 2020 (Deloitte Insights Report, 2021). Driven by market pressures, insurance companies are increasingly embracing technology, which offers manifold advantages. These include more accurate measurement of insurance risk using big data analytics, improved investment strategies through AI and advanced algorithms, and heightened defences against operational risks like fraud and money laundering (Deloitte Insights Report, 2021). Notably, various entities, including non-financial businesses, are entering the insurance arena, providing ancillary services alongside innovative insurance offerings (Deloitte Insights Report, 2021). However, technology also offers solutions to these challenges; for instance, blockchain technology aids in fraud detection, identity protection, and compliance with regulatory frameworks (Nath, 2016). Moreover, lax regulation surrounding data security raises concerns about cybersecurity and data privacy. The insurance industry has been particularly susceptible to data breaches, with potential global ramifications. Reports suggest that coordinated cyberattacks could lead to substantial insurance claims, underscoring the urgency of robust cybersecurity measures (Bengaluru Reuters Report, 2019).

15.4 HOW IS AI USED IN ACTUARIAL SCIENCES AND INSURANCES IN RISK MANAGEMENT?

In actuarial sciences and insurance for risk management, AI is becoming more and more important. Large-scale datasets are analysed by AI algorithms to find trends and patterns, which helps with predictive modelling. Actuaries evaluate the probability of future occurrences, including insurance claims, death rates, and economic trends, using AI-driven predictive models. This facilitates the identification of possible hazards and the enhancement of risk mitigation tactics. ML algorithms are used by AI systems to spot patterns and anomalies that point to fraudulent activity. AI is used in insurance to identify and stop claim fraud. Actuaries can reduce the financial risks related to fraudulent claims by examining past data and spotting odd trends.

15.5 CYBERCRIMES, AI, AND INSURANCE

Cybercrimes may include conventional crimes like theft, fraud, forgery, defamation, and mischief that fall under the purview of the Indian Penal Code, 1860. Advanced offenses like tampering, hacking, publishing pornographic material, gaining unauthorized access to systems, violating privacy and confidentiality, and disseminating phony digital signature certificates are all covered under the Information Technology Act. Other offenses that carry legal consequences include sending threatening or defamatory emails, forging electronic documents, engaging in cybercrime, spoofing emails, web-jacking, and abusing emails. If someone is losing money as a result of these offenses, they can benefit from cyber insurance.

A tool for transferring cyber risk is cyber insurance. Exposure to damage or loss as a result of information system breaches or assaults is a frequent definition of cyber risk. The policyholders will be shielded from cybercrimes by this coverage. Liabilities to first parties and third parties resulting directly from a breach in cybersecurity are covered by cyber insurance. It pays for costs associated with cyberattacks, data breaches, human mistake, interruptions to business, and claims made through electronic media. Costs associated with emergency response, event planning, notification, company loss, and recovery are all covered. Customized plans are provided by insurance carriers in accordance with corporate and industry requirements.

15.5.1 Rise in Cybercrimes

As per the Telecom Regulatory Authority of India (TRAI) report 2023, the January–March 2023 report on Telecom Services Performance Indicators revealed that the total number of Internet subscribers in India surged to 881.25 million, up from 865.90 million in December 2022, marking a quarterly growth rate of 1.77%. In 2019, India ranked as the world's second-largest internet market, trailing only China. However, despite this growth, the literacy rate in India stood at 77.7% in 2023. Moreover, only 38% of Indian households were reported to be computer literate during the same period.

Digital literacy is comparatively greater in urban regions (61%), compared to rural ones (only 25%). In rural India, the profession profile that shows the largest number of digitally literate families is that of households reporting regular wages/salaries from non-agricultural occupations, at around 53%. On the other hand, with only 13%, casual labourers in the agricultural industry have the lowest degree of digital literacy. At 21% of households, Scheduled Tribes have the lowest degree of digital literacy overall. Digital literacy rates in urban India are 30% for casual workers and 73% for permanent wage/salaried workers (Dattopant Thengadi National Board for Workers Education & Development Report, 2023). People are more easily tricked by digital frauds due to a lack of digital literacy and awareness, which is increasing the number of digital offenses.

In regions with high digitalization and low literacy rates, cyberattacks are prevalent. Spoofing, an identity theft method, involves an individual trying to impersonate an authorized user. Cybercriminals employ various techniques such as SIM swapping, malware, and phishing. Phishing, for instance, aims to steal sensitive user data like bank account details. Spyware, categorized as malware, infiltrates or damages a user's computer, often without their knowledge, collecting personal data and sending it to external parties like data companies or advertisers. Even, according to Sophos data of 2023, almost 40% of board members in India have no acquaintance about cybersecurity threats and risks. As there is low literacy rate according to various reports, cybercrimes are increasing as there is no acquaintance about cybersecurity threats and risks. Hence, it is impacting the risk management in the insurance sector as well. As per data given in Table 15.1 on data crimes in comparison to 2021, in 2022, 65,983 were reported in 2022 of which cyber fraud were of 64.8% with high rate according to NCRB report of 2022 as given in Table 15.2. Whereas data given in Table 15.3 is showing the crimes in 2023 with detailed bifurcation of crime rate as per NCRP report, 2023.

TABLE 15.1
Data on Cybercrimes

Years	Case Reported
2022	65,983
2021	52,974

TABLE 15.2
Data on Crimes of Registered Cases in 2022

Crime	Crime Rate (%)
Cyber fraud	64.8
Extortion	5.5
Sexual exploitation	5.2

TABLE 15.3
Cybercrime Complaints in NCRP (per Lakh Population) in 2023

Crime	Crime Rate (%)
Customer care, refund-based and KYC expiry frauds	35
Sextortion	24
Online booking fraud	22
AePS frauds and biometric cloning	11
Android malware	8

According to the Computer Emergency Response Team of India (CERT-IN), the nation experienced 1.39 million cybersecurity incidents in 2022. This surge in cyberattacks and crimes against businesses and organizations has led to an increased demand for cyber insurance. Currently valued at \$50–60 million, the cyber insurance market is anticipated to witness remarkable growth, with a projected compound annual growth rate (CAGR) of 27%–30% over the next three to five years. Globally, the cyber insurance market surpassed \$12 billion in 2022 and is forecasted to exceed \$63 billion by 2029, with a compound annual growth rate of over 26%.

15.6 INTERSECTION OF LAW WITH AI IN ACTUARY SCIENCE

The convergence of law and AI in actuary science is strongly advised in the context of deepfake and cyberattacks to improve rights protection, enforce regulations, and ensure that rules and regulations are properly implemented to support the insurance industry's smooth operation. Actuaries are experts in evaluating and controlling financial risks, and they are now using AI technology to improve their analytical and decision-making skills. But the use of AI in actuarial science brings up important ethical and legal issues that need to be carefully considered.

15.7 EXAMINING LEGAL FRAMEWORKS, REGULATIONS, AND ETHICAL GUIDELINES THAT GOVERN THE IMPLEMENTATION OF AI IN ACTUARIAL PROCESSES

In India, the demesne of actuarial sciences operates within a regulatory framework aimed at ensuring transparency, fairness, and the protection of stakeholders' interests. Currently, there is a notable absence of specific legislation governing AI in India, as highlighted by IT Minister Ashwini Vaishnav, owing to the myriad moral and ethical concerns surrounding AI development. Nonetheless, the primary legislation governing digital and electronic commerce governance in India remains The Information Technology Act, 2000 (IT Act). It is to be noted that this act directly does not address AI, but various actions are covered under various sections of this act. Section 43 of this act provides compensation where there is negligence in handling subtle personal data, which leads to breaches of data privacy when AI is involved in managing the data of users. Section 73A of the act deals with electronic governance of cybersecurity, data protection, and digital signatures, creating a legal structure for using electronic signatures and electronic records in AI-controlled actuarial processes.

In the benchmark case of Justice K.S. Puttaswamy (Retd.) v. Union of India (2017), the Apex Court of India confirmed that right to privacy is the fundamental right under Constitution of India, which underscores the guarantee of preserving personal data from AI systems. Recently, substantial Personal Data Protection Act, 2023 is enacted to establish all-inclusive legal framework for the protection of personal data demarcating the responsibilities and commitments for institutions handling the data. This act integrates the principles of accountability, persistence, consistence, restraints, and data localization and also dictates for the establishment of jurisdictional authority called as Data Protection Authority to overlook and supervise the proper enforcement of the provisions, regulations, and guidelines of the Act, which includes tailored decision-making and profiling, imposing the requirement of written consent in processing personal data consuming AI algorithms dealing with interests and rights of individuals.

With the infiltration of AI-generated contents, deliberations have textured regarding copyright proprietorship and liability in case of infringement under the Indian Copyright Act, 1957. This act provisioned for safeguarding exclusive rights of creator and prevents unauthorized use or reproduction without authority. In the case of Gramophone Company of India Ltd. V. Super Cassettes Industries Ltd. (2011), the High Court of Delhi pronounced that AI-generated music is devoid of human creativity and thus is barred for protection of copyright.

Beside these, National e-Governance Plan is articulated to empower society through providing online government services incorporating AI as a vital constituent to enhance accessibility and efficiency of services of e-governance. To this end, many government agencies have integrated AI processes to enhance public services and decision-making process.

Additionally, National Education Policy is introduced by Indian Government to include coding workshops for sixth-grade students to make India as hub of e-innovations. The AI Research Analytics and Knowledge Assimilation Platform (AIRAWAT) is formulated by Indian Planning Commission called as Niti Ayog mandating for AI-equipped processes.

These are helpful in the insurance sector and are governed by Insurance Act, 1938, which provide regulations for actuarial assessment, solvency margins, and reporting obligations that are vital for operation of insurance business.

Actuaries play a significant role in assuring amenability with the regulatory requirements. The regulatory authority to overlook the insurance industry in India is Insurance Regulatory and Development Authority of India as per IRDAI Act, 1999. Insurance Companies are directed to adhere to regulations and standards fixed by IRDAI, which includes financial reporting, product design, and underwriting with the responsibility of actuaries for their compliance and application.

According to IRDAI, the panel actuaries have to work in accordance with various regulations, viz., IRDAI (Appointed Actuary) Regulations, 2017; IRDAI (Investment) Regulations, 2016 and IRDAI (Insurance Services by Banks) Regulations, 2002, etc., for protecting the interest of policyholders. For valuations, the IRDAI (Appointed Actuary) Regulations, 2017 were enacted to set the wide-ranging canons for the appointment and obligations of actuaries in insurance firms, which are vital for valuation, reserve establishment and guaranteeing pecuniary solidity. IRDAI (Investment) Regulations, 2016 set the guidelines for the operational investments for actuaries. IRDAI (Insurance Services by Banks) Regulations, 2002, fixed the guidelines for banks to provide insurance services.

Moreover, Companies Act, 2013 deals with establishment, registration, management, and dissolution of corporation, which require actuarial services in financial reserve assessment, reporting, and liability assessment. The Income Tax Act, 1961 provisioned for regulating pension schemes and insurance products with tax allusions for actuarial services for providing valuations.

Indian actuaries are often adhering to international norms to indorse quality and integrity of their work, viz., the International Standards of Actuarial Practice (ISAP), which are issued by International Actuarial Association (IAA) to provide guidelines on various actuarial practices. To protect the interest of stakeholders, Indian actuaries stay abreast of professional regulatory, legal, and ethical standards by following international and domestic norms.

IRDAI also issued policy guidelines in 2023 aiming to ensure proper compliance with all pertinent laws, regulations, standard guidelines, and codes including civil and criminal laws to meet regulatory, statutory, and contractual obligations which emphasized on compliance with security wants and information security laws. Statutes and contractual commitments to operate ethically and in consonance with the law of land, with active monitoring of compliance and prompt remedial actions in the case of breaches of standards. A clear strategy for ensuring compliance with relevant legal, statutory, regulatory, and contractual obligations is to be established and regularly updated.

Protocols must be established to ensure compliance with intellectual property rights and the usage of proprietary software products, with statutory rules made mandatory and formal risk analysis conducted to select controls addressing regulatory requirements and legal responsibilities. The legal department is tasked with providing guidance on legal requirements and ensuring compliance, promptly implementing necessary controls, and conducting regular compliance assessments. Regulatory circulars issued by bodies such as the Insurance Regulatory and Development Authority of India (IRDAI) mandate changes to security requirements and operational procedures, necessitating integration into insurance company operations to comply with IRDAI standards. Compliance with the Information Technology (IT) Act of 2000, its amendments, and relevant Acts is crucial, particularly regarding email communications, internet banking, and communication networks. Processes must be designed to align with revisions to the IT Act, 2000, or the introduction of supporting cyber laws or privacy legislation, with a deep understanding of the requirements of the IT Act, 2000 being essential for securing the organizational data environment and preventing fraud. Compliance with relevant laws, statutes, recommendations, and amendments to the Aadhaar Act is also imperative.

In support of these laws, rules, and regulations, guidelines are implemented to facilitate enforcement. The Information Technology (The Indian Computer Emergency Response Team (CERT-In)) Rules, 2013 empower the Computer Emergency Response Team to gather, analyse, and share cybersecurity incident data and enact emergency response measures. Guidelines issued by CERT-In in 2022 complement existing cybersecurity incident reporting obligations under the 2013 rules. Industry-specific regulations issued by entities such as the Reserve Bank of India and the Securities Exchange Board of India require regulated entities to maintain cybersecurity standards; compliance with the Indian Penal Code 1860 and the Companies (Management and Administration) Rules 2014 is mandatory for businesses to secure electronic records and systems against unauthorized access and tampering.

15.7.1 Institutional Framework

Considering that cybersecurity is a multifaceted issue, India has a sophisticated institutional architecture that spans many ministries, departments, and agencies, all of which play important roles in the field. For example, policy concerning IT, electronics, and the internet, including cyber legislation, is handled by the Ministry for Electronics and Information Technology (MeitY). As a nodal body for managing and coordinating cyber incident response operations, it established the CERT-In.

15.7.2 Security Measures

Under the IT Act, organizations handling sensitive personal data are obligated to adhere to state security requirements. These are delineated in the SPDI regulations, which stipulate that companies must implement operational, technological, managerial, and physical security controls. Moreover, in alignment with the ISO/

IEC 27001 global standards for information security management, these regulations necessitate that body corporates undergo audit assessments conducted by an impartial, government-approved auditor at least annually, or more frequently should they significantly expand their computing resources and procedures. Nodal authorities and sectoral regulators also enforce security measures.

15.7.3 Cyber Incident Reporting

In line with the regulations set forth in 2013, organizations are obligated to promptly notify CERT-In of cybersecurity incidents as they arise. These incidents encompass a range of potential threats including denial of service attacks, phishing and ransomware incidents, website defacement, and targeted network or website scanning.

15.8 REGULATORY CHALLENGES

Onerous regulatory constraints may cause a lengthy, steep, and capital-intensive burnout for these start-ups, and an unfavourable regulatory climate can be a major impediment to appropriate implementation and data access through InsurTech. According to Insurance Act, 1938 (Section 2C to 5), companies wishing to enter the insurance policy market through the sale, issuance, origination, or underwriting of insurance policies must first register and, upon registration, get the necessary licenses under the Insurance Act. These licenses must be renewed yearly. After each calendar year ends, create a balance sheet, a profit and loss account, and a revenue account in the required forms for each kind of insurance business according to Insurance Act, 1938 (Sections 10, 11, 12).

15.9 AMBIGUITIES IN LEGAL SYSTEM OF AI IN INDIA

The Indian landscape for AI encounters several hurdles. Currently, India lacks specific legislation tailored explicitly to address AI. While existing laws such as the Personal Data Protection Act of 2023 and the Information Technology Act of 2000 touch upon aspects related to AI, they fall short of comprehensively tackling the intricate complexities and challenges posed by AI technologies. A significant barrier obstructing AI research and adoption in India lies in the absence of clear and enforceable ethical guidelines. This deficiency in robust standards may result in inconsistent behaviours and potential misuse of AI systems.

15.10 CYBER INSURANCE IN INDIAN BANKING SECTOR

In accordance with provision of I4C, the "National Cyber Crime Reporting Portal" has been developed to allow the public to report occurrences related to all forms of cybercrimes, with a concentration on cybercrimes against women and children. The law enforcement agencies in question in each state or territory handle cybercrime occurrences that are reported on this platform, turn them into formal complaints, and take appropriate action in accordance with the law. In order to prevent financial criminals from embezzling money, the "Citizen Financial Cyber Fraud Reporting and Management

System," under I4C, has been introduced. In response to more than 4.7 lakh complaints, the Citizen Financial Cyber Fraud Reporting and Management System has saved over Rs. 1,200 crore with the help of a free Helpline with the number "1930."

15.11 IMPORTANCE OF CYBER INSURANCE IN INDIAN BANKING SECTOR

In today's advancing technological landscape, cybersecurity holds immense significance, particularly in the banking sector where maintaining customer trust and credibility forms the cornerstone. With the increasing shift towards cashless transactions and the widespread use of virtual currencies such as debit and credit cards, ensuring robust cybersecurity measures becomes imperative to safeguard stakeholder data and uphold privacy standards. Instances of data breaches not only undermine the trust of customers in banks but also pose a critical challenge for banking institutions.

According to DSCI India cyber threat report (2023), Data Security Council of India (DSCI) in collaboration with SEQRITE released the data on cybercrimes as given in Table 15.4.

In the face of an expanding threat landscape driven by the rapid increase in digitization, effective management of cyber risks becomes paramount. In this context, cyber insurance emerges as a pivotal strategy for both managing and mitigating risks, providing an additional incentive for the adoption of preventive measures encompassing products, services, and best practices. Tailored cyber insurance products serve to alleviate exposure to risk by covering expenses incurred in the aftermath of a cyberattack or breach.

TABLE 15.4
Data by DSCI India Cyber Threat Report 2023

Total detections	Over 400 million detections across approximately 8.5 million
Detection rate	Averaging 761 detections per minute
Behaviour-based detections	49 million detections constituting 12.5% of the total detections
Ransomware and malware incidents	Malware incident ratio: One incident/cyberattack per 38,000 detections
	Crypto-jacking: Over 5.28 million detections in a year
Dominant threats	Trojans (41%) and Infectors (33%)
Geographical hotspots (states)	Telangana (15%) and Tamil Nadu (14%) top the list in terms of malware detections
City-wise analysis	Surat (15%) and Bengaluru (14%)
Distribution of detections	Over 50% of detections are associated with removable media and network drives
Malicious links	Approximately 25% of attacks result from clicking on malicious links in emails and websites
Mobile threat landscape through Android devices	An average of three attacks per month per Android device were observed for the year 2023

15.12 BENEFITS FROM CYBER INSURANCE

The primary benefits of cyber insurance lie in its ability to provide coverage to organizations or individuals in the event of a cyberattack, mitigating financial losses and facilitating recovery. For businesses, cyber insurance can cover loss of revenue or additional expenses incurred during cyber incidents, offering protection against ransomware attacks to which hackers demand payment for data retrieval. Moreover, in cases of lost or corrupted digital assets, cyber insurance policies can assist with recovery and restoration costs. Additionally, in the event of a data breach, financial institutions or corporations are required to notify affected customers and address privacy infringement claims, with cyber insurance covering associated legal fees.

15.12.1 Data on Cyber Breach Cover

In a recent study carried out by cybersecurity firm Sophos (2023), findings unveiled that India ranks sixth among 14 nations concerning the proportion of businesses equipped with sufficient coverage for cyber breaches. This report includes 3,000 respondents for survey from the countries, which includes 300 respondents from India. The report probed into complicated dynamics among cybersecurity, cyber insurance, and ransomware. This report divulged that South Africa is at top with 98% organizations holding cyber insurance benefits, followed by Singapore with 97%, and Australia and the United States with 94%.

15.12.2 Data Recovery Cases

Foundations that are well-found with cyber insurance determines the suppleness in convalescing data post-ransomware occurrences when compared to those foundations that have not taken any protective measures of cyber insurance. Only 84% of foundations deficient in such insurance were successful in recovering their data.

The stringent cyber protocols mandated for eligibility in acquiring such policies strategically position organizations for effective data restoration, underscoring the imperative for secure backups and the adoption of a comprehensive incident response strategy. Additionally, the research indicates that victims of ransomware possessing standalone cyber insurance policies are nearly four times more inclined to opt for ransom payment to regain access to encrypted data than those lacking cyber coverage.

Across various industry verticals, the education sector, encompassing both higher and lower education, showcased the highest overall level of cyber insurance coverage at 96%. This was followed by the financial services sector, primarily favouring standalone cyber policies (59%), and the retail sector (56%). Notably, the IT, telecom, and technology sectors displayed a lower coverage rate of 35% (Kurmanath 2023).

15.13 LEGAL CONSIDERATIONS ARE PIVOTAL IN ENSURING ETHICAL, TRANSPARENT, AND COMPLIANT PRACTICES IN RISK ASSESSMENT-PROMOTING RESPONSIBLE AI IN INSURANCE

Legal considerations are indeed crucial in ensuring ethical, transparent, and compliant practices in risk assessment within the field of actuarial sciences in India. Adhering to applicable laws and regulations helps protect the interests of stakeholders, ensures fair practices, and maintains the integrity of the actuarial profession. With the adoption of AI in actuarial processes, questions regarding legal liability may arise in cases of errors, biases, or malfunctions in AI systems. Legal liability frameworks in India, including contract law, consumer protection laws, and tort liability principles, may apply to determine liability for damages resulting from AI-related errors or misconduct.

15.14 DISCUSSION

As a result of hiking, the rate of cyberattacks and cybercrimes, the utmost contemplation is protecting the customer data and to ensure privacy with the propagation of AI-empowered technologies, which mandates the actuarial sciences to update with technological advancement combating the striking rate of cybercrimes, hence contributing the insurance sector in minimizing the risk assessment. For this drive, there is need of collaborations of actuaries with data scientists, technology professionals, and legal connoisseurs to robust risk assessment frameworks. Such kind of interdisciplinary collaboration may foster novelty, augment risk assessment and management proficiencies, and warrant all-inclusive slants to address in curbing and monitoring legal challenges.

For better risk assessment for cybersecurity, actuaries have to observe data protection laws, viz., Personal Data Protection Act, 2023, to protect subtle information, hence preserving the trust of consumers. For this purpose, actuaries should also have to give priority to ethical contemplations in the development and dispositioning of AI algorithms. This includes considerations like biasness in data and algorithms, sponsoring non-discrimination and fair-mindedness and encouraging transparency in supervisory policymaking processes.

15.14.1 Conclusions

Conclusively, the juncture of AI-driven actuaries with the intersection of law provides a transformative and revolutionary landscape for minimizing the impending insurance risk assessment. The advanced technology experts, insurance, and actuaries' experts along with legal doyens have to circumnavigate a regulatory milieu to guarantee fair, legal, ethical, and yielding practices to reduce cyber risks. For this purpose, regulations and strategies are laid down by regulatory bodies, viz., Insurance Regulatory and Development Authority of India (IRDAI); hence, there is a need for proper enforcement and compliance by the Risk Management Authorities in assessing risk management policies in insurance practices.

REFERENCES

Alshamsi, Asma S. "Predicting car insurance policies using random forest." In *2014 10th International Conference on Innovations in Information Technology (IIT), Al Ain, UAE, 9–11 November 2014*, pp. 128–132. IEEE, 2014.

BearingPoint Institute. "The smart insurer: Embedding big data in corporate strategy." 2020, accessed on December 17, 2024, https://www.bearingpoint.com/en-us/our-success/thought-leadership/the-smart-insurer-embedding-big-data-in-corporate-strategy/.

Bengaluru Reuters Report. "Potential global cyber-attack could cause $115b-$261b worth of damage." The Straits Times, 29 January 2019, accessed on 15 February, 2024. https://www.straitstimes.com/world/potential-global-cyber-attack-could-cause-115b-261b-worth-of-damage-says-report.

Berthele, Emmanuel. "Using big data in insurance." *Big Data for Insurance Companies* 1 (2018): 131–161.

Biener, Christian, Eling Martin, and Wirfs Jan. "Insurability of cyber risk: An empirical analysis". *The Geneva Papers on Risk and Insurance - Issues and Practice* 40 (2015): 131–158.

Booth, H. and Tickle, L. "Mortality modelling and forecasting: A review of methods." *Annals of Actuarial Science* 3, nos. 1–2 (2008): 3–43

Data Security Council of India (DSCI). "Cyber Threat Report." 2023.

Dattopant Thengadi National Board for Workers Education & Development Report, Ministry of Labour & Employment, Govt. of India, 2023.

Deloitte Insights Report. "Sector spotlight: Insurance." *Global Risk Management,* 2019. Accessed on 17 December 2020. https://www2.deloitte.com/content/dam/insights/us/articles/4222_Global-risk-management-survey/DI_g lobal-risk-management-survey.pdf.

Deprez, Philippe, Pavel V. Shevchenko, and Mario V. Wüthrich. "Machine learning techniques for mortality modeling." *European Actuarial Journal* 7 (2017): 337–352.

Eling, Martin, and Werner Schnell. "What do we know about cyber risk and cyber risk insurance?" *The Journal of Risk Finance* 17, no. 5 (2016): 474–491.

Hassani, Hossein, Stephan Unger, and Christina Beneki. "Big data and actuarial science." *Big Data and Cognitive Computing* 4, no. 4 (2020): 40.

Kurmanath, K.V. "Cybersecurity. Indian entities embrace cyber insurance as attacks surge." The Hindu Bussinessline, 9 May 2023, accessed on 15 February 2024. https://www.thehindubusinessline.com/info-tech/indian-entities-embrace-cyber-insurance-as-attacks-surge/article66830069.ece.

Li, Yaqi, Chun Yan, Wei Liu, and Maozhen Li. "A principle component analysis-based random forest with the potential nearest neighbor method for automobile insurance fraud identification." *Applied Soft Computing* 70 (2018): 1000–1009.

Meyers, Gert, and Ine Van Hoyweghen. "Enacting actuarial fairness in insurance: From fair discrimination to behaviour-based fairness." *Science as Culture* 27, no. 4 (2018): 413–438.

Mills, Evan, and Richard B. Jones. "An insurance perspective on US electric grid disruption costs." *The Geneva Papers on Risk and Insurance-Issues and Practice* 41 (2016): 555–586.

Nath, I. "Fight insurance fraud: Data sharing with blockchain technology." *IBM Tech* 16 (2016).

OECD. "The *Impact of Big Data and Artificial Intelligence (AI) in the Insurance Sector*." OECD: Paris, 2020, accessed on 17 December 2020. https://www.oecd.org/finance/Impact-Big-Data-AI-in-the-Insurance-Sector.htm.

PWC's HR Technology Survey. "Professional service providers on tech related datas." 2020, accessed 17 December 2020. https://www.pwc.com/us/en/library/workforce-of-the-future/hr-tech-survey.html.

Richman, Ronald. "AI in actuarial science." Available at SSRN 3218082 (2018).

Schreiber, D. "The Future of insurance." Digital Insurance Agenda *DIA Munich*, 2017, accessed on 10 January 2024. https://www.youtube.com/watch?time_continue=1&v=LDOhFHJqKqI.

Shapiro, Arnold F., and Lakhmi C. Jain, (Eds.). *Intelligent and Other Computational Techniques in Insurance: Theory and Applications*. Vol. 6. World Scientific: River Edge, 2003.

Sheshasaayee, Ananthi, and Surya Susan Thomas. "A purview of the impact of supervised learning methodologies on health insurance fraud detection." In Bhateja Vikrant, Bao Le Nguyen, Nhu Gia Nguyen, Suresh Chandra Satapathy, and Dac-Nhuong Le (Eds.) *Information Systems Design and Intelligent Applications: Proceedings of Fourth International Conference India 2017*, pp. 978–984. Springer: Singapore, 2018.

Silverman, David. "*Interpreting Qualitative Data: A Guide to the Principles of Qualitative Research*." Sage Publication: London, 2011.

SNS Telecom & IT. "Big data in the insurance industry: 2018–2030—Opportunities, challenges, strategies & forecasts." 2018, accessed on 17 December 2020. https://www.snstelecom.com/bigdatainsurance.

Sophos Report. "The Critical Role of Frontline Cyber Defenses in Cyber Insurance Adoption." 2023.

Subudhi, Sharmila, and Suvasini Panigrahi. "Effect of class imbalanceness in detecting automobile insurance fraud." In *2018 2nd International Conference on Data Science and Business Analytics (ICDSBA), 21–23 September 2018, ChangSha, Hunan, China*, pp. 528–531. IEEE, 2018.

Topol, Eric. *The Patient Will See You Now: The Future of Medicine is in Your Hands*. Basic Books: New York, 2015.

Wang, Yibo, and Wei Xu. "Leveraging deep learning with LDA-based text analytics to detect automobile insurance fraud." *Decision Support Systems* 105 (2018): 87–95.

Wuthrich, Mario V., and Christoph Buser. "Data analytics for non-life insurance pricing." Swiss Finance Institute Research Paper No. 16–68, 2023.

Yunos, Zuriahati Mohd, Aida Ali, Siti Mariyam Shamsyuddin, and Noriszura Ismail. "Predictive modelling for motor insurance claims using artificial neural networks." *International Journal of Advances in Soft Computing and its Applications* 8 (2016): 126.

16 Charting the Future

Artificial Intelligence's Role in Revolutionizing Actuarial Work in the Insurance Sector

Mufaro Dzingirai and Rukudzo Dzapasi

16.1 INTRODUCTION

In a digitalized and globalized economy, the potential benefits of the adoption of artificial intelligence technologies across sectors are witnessed in modern societies and economies. Although sectors such as manufacturing, healthcare, software development, agriculture, and banking have been hailed for high uptake of artificial intelligence technologies and massive investment in artificial intelligence platforms, it is troublesome to observe that the insurance sector is largely neglected in the artificial intelligence movement and discourse.

In the insurance sector, it has been witnessed that artificial intelligence is revolutionizing the ways in which business is being conducted in the 5th Industrial Revolution. With the radical transformation of technology in the contemporary business world, insurance companies are adopting artificial intelligence in both developed and developing countries (Gürsev 2023; Khalisa 2024; Mangla et al. 2022; Prince & Taylor 2023). Artificial intelligence is playing a significant role in transforming the global insurance sector by revolutionizing various aspects of the industry, such as customer experience, underwriting, claims processing, fraud detection, and risk assessment. Although insurance companies in developed countries are at an advanced stage when it comes to the implementation of artificial intelligence, insurance companies in developing countries are also trying to accelerate the adoption of artificial intelligence. It is widely accepted that many organizations in developing countries are slowly adopting digital transformation mainly because they have weak financial health.

It is imperative to mention that the sustainability of various insurance firms depends on the extent to which the organizations adopt advanced technology (Malifete et al. 2022; Shamsuddin et al. 2023). As such, it is the duty of a proactive manager to provide resources with the aim of improving efficiency and effectiveness. Given that we are now in a global economy, it makes sense to harness the benefits of artificial intelligence so as to outsmart the competitors. Investment in artificial intelligence can lead to the generation of real-time data that can assist in risk management. By

DOI: 10.1201/9781003472551-20

ensuring effective risk management, the organization can enjoy market leadership, which can go a long way in ensuring competitive advantage.

Going forward, actuarial work in the insurance sector is becoming more data-based, which justifies the need for generative artificial intelligence. Given the importance of artificial intelligence in actuarial work, proactive insurers are implementing artificial intelligence technologies like natural language processing, machine learning, deep learning, and robotics processing automation as well as video and audio analysis with the aim to deliver exceptional products and services. It is worth noting that digital transformation in the form of artificial intelligence has improved speed, accuracy, and efficiency across branches of insurance companies (Gürsev 2023; Prince & Taylor 2023; Shamsuddin et al. 2023). Therefore, the need for relevant information technology infrastructure and mechanisms cannot be underestimated journeying toward data integration. Interestingly, artificial intelligence helps insurance companies to gather and analyze granular, timely, and accurate actuarial data.

It is a fact that artificial intelligence has been hailed for playing an instrumental role in accelerating digital transformation across sectors. With the need for actuarial excellence, a data culture strategy can support data-driven strategic decisions. Of late, it is slowly gaining momentum in the insurance sector (Mangla et al. 2022). Notably, the adoption of artificial intelligence in the insurance sectors of developing countries is still in the early stages. Although generative artificial intelligence is being incorporated into the insurance sector, its potential is not yet fully realized (Holland 2022). Consequently, this chapter aims to critically examine the role of artificial intelligence in revolutionizing actuarial work in the insurance sector.

16.2 ARTIFICIAL INTELLIGENCE AND INSURANCE SECTOR: A GLOBAL PERSPECTIVE

The exponential increase of artificial intelligence adoption worldwide has been associated with several merits for the insurance sector. The Oxford English dictionary defines artificial intelligence as "the theory and development of computer systems able to perform tasks normally requiring human intelligence, such as visual perception, speech recognition, decision-making, and translation between languages". With this in mind, global insurers allocate a significant portion of their limited financial resources toward the adoption of artificial intelligence technologies. For instance, a big insurer in Hong Kong invested HK$20 million in artificial intelligence technology in an attempt to shorten claims processing time (KPMG 2023). Artificial Intelligence-powered chatbots and virtual assistants are being used to provide personalized customer service, answer queries, and assist with policy inquiries, resulting in enhanced customer experience. These virtual agents can handle multiple requests simultaneously, leading to faster response times and improved customer satisfaction. This supports the notion that generative artificial intelligence is now a topical issue in corporate boardrooms with the aim of augmenting corporate strategies.

There is no doubt that artificial intelligence improves actuarial work in terms of artificial intelligence-enabled marketing, optimization of technological capabilities and competencies, improving customer experiences by using chatbots, automation of routine tasks, fraud deterrence, claims modelling, and robust risk management models.

In this regard, artificial intelligence algorithms play a significant role in analyzing voluminous data in supporting precise pricing models when it comes to the insurance sector (KPMG 2023). Therefore, it would be very easy for insurers to offer customized products and services, assess customer profiles, and then reduce risks. More interestingly, by leveraging artificial intelligence, data analysts can extract meaningful and valuable insights from voluminous unstructured and structured data collected from clients. Accordingly, artificial intelligence-enabled marketing strategies can be effectively implemented by insurers in this digitalized business world. According to Lior (2021, p. 467), "the artificial intelligence ("AI") industry is predicted to grow exponentially over the next decade, up to a 14.5% contribution share to Gross Domestic Product in North America by 2030". This shows how significant is artificial intelligence when it comes to socio-economic transformation.

In terms of OECD context, the adoption of the Recommendation on Artificial Intelligence was adopted in May 2019 and the Ethics Guidelines for Trustworthy Artificial Intelligence was also adopted in April 2019 (OECD 2020). The OECD's Insurance and Private Pensions Committee participated in discussing technology related to the insurance industry. It emerged that artificial intelligence was regarded as a powerful tool for automating the claims process, whereby OCR technology assists insurers in extracting relevant and accurate data from documents which can reduce errors associated with manual data entry. In addition, artificial intelligence helps insurers when applying predictive data analytics when it comes to the assessment of risk and the development of risk-elimination strategies. Admittedly, artificial intelligence algorithms can be used to predict potential risks and assist data analysts in formulating preventive measures. Consequently, artificial intelligence is a game changer in the insurance sector. It requires a comprehensive understanding of how new artificial intelligence projects in the insurance sector can deliver long-term benefits to insurers and their clients (Holland 2022).

16.3 DRIVERS OF THE ADOPTION OF ARTIFICIAL INTELLIGENCE IN THE INSURANCE SECTOR

With the widespread impact of advanced technologies in the corporate world, it is worth capturing the key drivers of the adoption of artificial intelligence in the insurance sector. Firstly, the availability of large data sources is considered to be one of the drivers of artificial intelligence adoption in actuarial work. This implies that large databases play an instrumental role in applying artificial intelligence in areas such as risk management and claims processing in the insurance sector (Leech et al. 2024). Secondly, the exponential rise in machine learning is also another chief drive of artificial intelligence adoption in the insurance sector. It is in this context that machine learning deals with training algorithms to learn from bid data, which is widely regarded as a subset of artificial intelligence (Baruah & Singh 2023; Poufinas et al. 2023). It is interesting to note that researchers can teach and train machines to make predictions and recognize patterns. Machine learning also encompasses the utilization of a plethora of applications that recognize speech and images. To this end, deep learning and neural networks can recognize problematic patterns in relation to sounds, text, and pictures.

Thirdly, perceived usefulness is another key driver of artificial intelligence adoption in the insurance industry. It is within this context that the insurers perceive artificial intelligence as a powerful tool for detecting and monitoring fraud. More interestingly, artificial intelligence is widely considered to be a strategic approach to risk reduction and mitigation in actuarial work. The application of a robust risk and network model helps to improve efficiency and effectiveness in the current digitalized world (Bao et al. 2022; Gupta et al. 2021; Nabrawi & Alanazi 2023; Owolabi et al. 2023). Fourthly, massive investment in research and development has been hailed as one of the key drivers of artificial intelligence in actuarial work. It is interesting to note that both government and private players are investing in research that is related to the application of artificial intelligence to different sectors of the economy although developing countries are lagging behind in terms of supporting research and development when it comes to artificial intelligence (Leal-Filho et al. 2023; Marino et al. 2023). This is the reason why most of the insurers are at the infancy stage of artificial intelligence adoption. The investment in research and development has led to the creation of robotics, computer vision, and natural language processing.

Fifthly, the demand for customized products and services necessitated the adoption of artificial intelligence in actuarial work. The prediction models supported by artificial intelligence allow insurers to deliver personalized insurance products and services (Khalisa 2024; Singh et al. 2022; St-Onge et al. 2022). Artificial intelligence technologies allow actuarial scientists to learn from big data about customer profiles. Sixthly, the rise in cloud computing also acts as the fertile ground that supports artificial intelligence adoption in the insurance market. It is interesting to observe that the emergence of cloud computing permitted voluminous data to be easily processed and stored in a manner that is scalable and cost-effective. Consequently, insurers and actuarial scientists can easily deploy artificial intelligence systems. Seventhly, Society 5.0 is another key factor that influences the adoption of artificial intelligence in actuarial science. Society 5.0 is a new society dominated by technological innovation, whereby humans address wicked problems by offering valuable technological solutions. With this in mind, it is not surprising that Society 5.0 has been associated with a massive explosion of big data. As such, voluminous data has permitted the application of machine and deep learning so as to augment artificial intelligence systems.

Eighthly, the support of innovative culture has demanded insurers to embrace artificial intelligence. It has been observed that the support of an innovative culture in the organization can lead to sustainable growth of the company (Malifete et al. 2022; Loh & Soo 2023). Therefore, insurance companies dominated by innovative culture can find it easy to embrace artificial intelligence. The sustainability of the company in a turbulent and dynamic business environment hinges on the adoption of advanced technology like artificial intelligence technologies and systems. Lastly, competitive pressure is another factor that can influence artificial intelligence adoption in the insurance sector. With this in mind, it is worth mentioning that the insurance market is associated with cut-throat competition (Pathak & Bansal 2024; Tanwar & Bhardwai 2022). As such, managers of insurance are forced to adopt artificial intelligence so as to reduce costs, improve efficiency, and access real-time data that assists managers in making informed strategic decisions.

16.4 CHALLENGES FACED IN FOSTERING ARTIFICIAL INTELLIGENCE IN ACTUARIAL WORK IN THE INSURANCE SECTOR

Despite the fact that artificial intelligence is relevant to the insurance sector, there are many challenges that can be faced by insurers when adopting artificial intelligence. To enjoy the benefits of artificial intelligence, the managers of insurance companies must address the hindrances of artificial intelligence adoption. Limited availability of quality data for artificial intelligence models is one of the challenges that can be encountered when adopting artificial intelligence. While actuarial work has been hailed for dealing with issues of in-depth financial records analysis, policyholder profile analysis, and extrapolation of historical data, it is a great challenge to assemble accurate data in many developing countries owing to a lack of expertise. Consequently, there is a challenge in training models of artificial intelligence using unreliable data.

According to Lauterbach (2019), insurance companies are mainly faced with a challenge related to difficulties in interpreting artificial intelligence algorithms mainly because of a lack of model transparency. With such difficulties, insurers are advocating for artificial intelligence training in order to have a broader and deeper understanding of artificial intelligence systems. Thus, the insurance sector needs to develop methods to make artificial intelligence algorithms more transparent and interpretable with the main purpose of ensuring trust and accountability.

In addition, ethical considerations and potential biases are also considered to be posing a significant challenge when it comes to artificial intelligence adoption. It is a fact that actuarial work deals with large data, which requires adherence to anti-discriminatory and respect for the privacy of the clients (Chikhaoui et al. 2022; Prince & Taylor 2023; Wilkinson et al. 2024). Worryingly, the historical data that is required for modeling can also be biased. In this regard, if unreliable data is used to train artificial intelligence models, there will be a great challenge of perpetuating existing biases especially when the insurers are making strategic decisions. With this in mind, it is imperative to augment compliance with laws and ethical considerations, which can be challenges to insurers.

16.5 METHODOLOGY

This study adopted a comprehensive literature review methodology to establish the role of artificial intelligence in revolutionizing actuarial work within the insurance sector. It was deemed an appropriate methodology given that the extant literature related to artificial intelligence in actuarial work is scattered and fragmented. This research methodology allowed the researchers to gather data from secondary sources. These sources include Web of Science, Google Scholar, organizational sources, and the Scopus database. Collected data was analyzed according to emerged patterns which is in tandem with thematic analysis. The results and discussion are reported as follows.

16.6 ROLE OF ARTIFICIAL INTELLIGENCE IN ACTUARIAL WORK IN INSURANCE SECTOR

It emerged that artificial intelligence plays an instrumental role in supporting actuarial work in the current digitalized economy. With the successful implementation of artificial intelligence in the insurance sector, companies are more interested in boosting productivity. This can be achieved by effectively and efficiently synthesizing big data extracted from customer profiles using machine learning. Insurance companies that leverage artificial intelligence have the potential to automate tasks that are done repetitively including data processing, data entry and verification as well as underwriting process. In this context, Gupta et al. (2021) argued that insurance companies that have a high affinity for artificial intelligence can outsmart their rivalry as they can streamline workflows and enhance decision-making processes in a manner that fosters advanced risk assessment.

Insurance companies that command market leadership are those that focus on personalized services. As such, artificial intelligence provides a benefit in enhancing customer experience. This can be done in the form of mixed reality and augmented reality. As a matter of fact, the application of artificial intelligence could allow insurance firms to engage customers personally by embracing robots and virtual assistants. It is a fact that personalized customer service is one of the positive business outcomes that can be derived from the efficient utilization of artificial intelligence. Customers can have various queries 24/7, which implies that it is imperative to employ artificial intelligence in dealing with such queries with the aid of online chatbots.

It is common knowledge that robust risk assessment is at the epicenter of business success in the insurance industry. Undoubtedly, advanced technologies like artificial intelligence can be powerful tools to deal with the negative effects of poor risk assessment in the insurance sector. In the same vein, fraud is one of the forms of risk that can be encountered by insurers, which demands the utilization of machine learning and neural networks. These kinds of technology can assist in real-time risk assessment, prediction of fraudulent claim activities, and accurate risk computation (Brown 2018). It is imperative to observe that artificial intelligence provides many benefits when insurance companies are dealing with claims management. In claims management, artificial intelligence plays a catalyst role in providing closer cross-examination of suspicious accounts. This suggests that red-flagging is very crucial in claims management, which demands the use of neural networks and deep learning.

In light of the above, cost-containment approaches embedded in artificial intelligence can add value to insurance especially when managing customer claims (Kewal & Saxena 2023; Khalisa 2024; Sinha et al. 2021). The claims related to on-demand insurance, usage-based insurance, and micro-insurance can be easily automated with the application of artificial intelligence. The main motive for automating claims management processes is to collect real-time data from various data sources like sensors and biometric machines utilizing trained artificial intelligence models. This can go a long way in assisting insurers to expedite their claims processes and introduce unique and innovative products and services. With the utilization of artificial intelligence models, insurance firms can unlock the potential values of real-time data and deliver excellent insurance products and services efficiently.

Artificial intelligence can quicken the process of new product development. It is evident that new insurance products and services are supported by the digitalization of the insurance process. Within the context of micro-insurance, on-demand insurance, and usage-based insurance, the need for portfolio innovation is at the center of excellent service delivery in the insurance sector (Khalisa 2024; Kumari et al. 2024; McDonald et al. 2024). Therefore, it is not surprising to mention that artificial intelligence helps insurance companies to accelerate their internal processes that support the development of new product portfolios. The artificial intelligence models can derive valuable insights that can be effectively utilized in the new product or service development process, and such an approach helps in streamlining the business operations.

Artificial intelligence can also help in developing robust risk prediction models in insurance work. This implies that advanced technologies can assist actuarial scientists in computing risk levels associated with different products and services. To be specific, machine learning plays a fundamental role in determining policy pricing systems in actuarial work (Khalisa 2024; Sadowski 2023; Xin & Huang 2023). This suggests that price optimization demands the application of artificial intelligence technologies. The refinement of pricing models in the insurance sector can be promoted by the use of data from telematics. These kinds of models can be applied to synthesize large amounts of data taking into account different variables and can be built upon to create user-friendly tools for non-technical staff, such as underwriters. More interestingly, predictive and prescriptive analytics models can be useful in gaining an in-depth understanding of improving operational resilience, risk computation, predictive customer behavior, and enhancing customer interaction in the insurance sector. To this end, the power of artificial intelligence within the context of underwriting and pricing perspectives cannot be underestimated.

More interestingly, artificial intelligence adoption can offer real-time and accurate data, which is of great importance to strategic managers of insurance firms. It is widely accepted that evidence-based management in the insurance sector demands the instant provision of structured data. Therefore, prudent managers of insurance companies are embracing artificial intelligence at an alarming rate, especially in developed countries. The availability of policy data, market trends, and claims history forces managers to look for advanced models of analyzing big data in the insurance market. Interestingly, artificial intelligence tools including machine learning algorithms allow insurers to extract and draw valuable insights from collected structured and unstructured data. This not only enables them to make informed decisions based on data but also helps in improving their operational processes, which is undoubtedly a game-changer in the industry.

Going forward, artificial intelligence adoption provides a benefit in terms of improving the underwriting process in the insurance sector. It is very difficult to keep up with advanced technology without embracing advanced artificial intelligence technologies that can assist in the underwriting processes (Khalisa 2024; Wilkinson et al. 2024). Application of artificial intelligence models has transformed the insurance's process of underwriting by utilizing predictive analytics. The quotes on demand and customization of policies can be done with the aid of artificial intelligence. Manual underwriting is no longer admirable when it comes to property, life, and casual insurance. Artificial intelligence technologies make the insurance underwriting process so fast and cost-effective. It is necessary at this juncture to note that artificial intelligence plays an instrumental role in ensuring robust monitoring and evaluation. With the adoption of artificial intelligence, it is much easier to monitor and evaluate the progress of the actuarial work. Artificial intelligence helps insurers to secure real-time structured and unstructured data associated with indicators of progress in terms of claims management and underwriting.

16.7 RECOMMENDATIONS

Given the instrumental role of artificial intelligence in promoting efficiency in the insurance sector, the following are the proposed recommendations:

Development of regulatory framework: It is recommended that the regulators of different economies can come up with regulatory frameworks related to artificial intelligence in the insurance sector. This could ensure that the rights and privacy of clients are respected when applying artificial intelligence models.

Tax relief on artificial intelligence technologies: Governments are recommended to apply tax relief on the importation of artificial intelligence technologies. This can assist insurers in reducing the procurement costs of artificial intelligence tools and technologies. This is more applicable to most of the developing countries that rely on the importation of advanced technologies.

Artificial intelligence knowledge hubs: The institutions of higher learning especially in African countries should establish artificial intelligence hubs. These hubs can be the center for training and development when it comes to the development and application of artificial intelligence technologies and tools.

Public–private partnerships: In this digitalized economy, it is recommended that the public and private players should work together in intensifying artificial intelligence adoption in insurance. This could assist in the sharing of knowledge and expertise.

Grants from non-governmental organizations: Non-governmental organizations are hereby recommended to offer grants to insurance companies associated with limited financial resources. These grants can be channeled toward harnessing the benefits of artificial intelligence.

Artificial intelligence awareness campaigns: It is recommended that the regulators in the insurance sector should design and implement a plethora of artificial intelligence awareness campaigns so as to sensitize the need for artificial technology in the current digital corporate world.

16.8 CONCLUSION

This chapter has critically examined the role of artificial intelligence in revolutionizing actuarial work in the insurance sector. Despite the fact that some sectors of the economy such as manufacturing, healthcare, software development, agriculture, and banking have been hailed for high uptake of artificial intelligence technologies and massive investment in artificial intelligence platforms, the insurance sector is largely neglected in this artificial intelligence movement and discourse. In the current 5th industrial revolution, the actuarial work can be made easier through the adoption of advanced digital technologies that support the transformation of the insurance sector especially with the aid of artificial intelligence technologies. As such, it was observed that artificial intelligence technologies are of utmost importance when it comes to the insurance sector in the sense that they boost productivity, augment customer experience through personalized services, foster automation of claims management, reduce fraud, support the development of customer predictive models, offer real-time and accurate data, improve underwriting process, quicken new product development, and ensure robust monitoring and evaluation. The study concludes that artificial intelligence is a powerful strategy toward superior competitive advantage in the insurance sector. Therefore, it is recommended that the management of insurance companies should effectively and efficiently embrace artificial intelligence as a game-changer in transforming the performance of insurance companies.

REFERENCES

Bao, Yang, Gilles Hilary, and Bin Ke. "Artificial intelligence and fraud detection." In Babich, Volodymyr, John R. Birge, and Gilles Hilary (Eds.) *Innovative Technology at the Interface of Finance and Operations: Volume I*, pp. 223–247. Cham: Springer, 2022.

Baruah, Prasanta, and Pankaj Pratap Singh. "Risk prediction in life insurance industry using machine learning techniques – A review." In *International Conference on Advances in IoT and Security with AI, 24–25 March, New Delhi*, pp. 323–332. Singapore: Springer Nature Singapore, 2023.

Brown, A. "Artificial intelligence in the insurance industry: Rise of the Insurtechs". *Journal of Cyber Policy* 3, no. 2 (2018): 165–187.

Chikhaoui, Emna, Alanoud Alajmi, and Souad Larabi-Marie-Sainte. "Artificial intelligence applications in healthcare sector: Ethical and legal challenges." *Emerging Science Journal* 6, no. 4 (2022): 717–738.

Gupta, Rohan Yashraj, Satya Sai Mudigonda, and Pallav Kumar Baruah. "A comparative study of using various machine learning and deep learning-based fraud detection models for universal health coverage schemes." *International Journal of Engineering Trends and Technology* 69, no. 3 (2021): 96–102.

Gürsev, Samet. "Digital transformation with artificial intelligence in the insurance industry." In *International Symposium on Intelligent Manufacturing and Service Systems, 26–28 May 2023, Istanbul, Turkey*, pp. 326–335. Singapore: Springer Nature Singapore, 2023.

Holland, Christopher. Artificial intelligence (AI) and digital transformation in the insurance market: A case study analysis of BGL group. (2022). https://scholarspace.manoa.hawaii.edu/server/api/core/bitstreams/dc20bb63-6143-4f40-9137-9ce1298d078c/content.

Kewal, Tamanna, and Charu Saxena. "Transition from traditional insurance sector to InsurTech: Systematic analysis and future research directions." In *International Conference on Data Analytics & Management*, pp. 473–487, London Metropolitan University, London, UK. Singapore: Springer Nature Singapore, 2023.

Khalisa, Arvidhia. "The digitalization in insurance broker industry: How artificial intelligence affect this industry." *Ilomata International Journal of Management* 5, no. 1 (2024): 261–279.

KPMG. Artificial Intelligence: How insurance can manage the risks of AI and stay ahead of regulatory development. (2023). https://assets.kpmg.com/content/dam/kpmg/cn/pdf/en/2023/11/artificial-intelligence-in-the-insurance-industry.pdf.

Kumari, Bharti, Jaspreet Kaur, and Sanjeev Swami. "Adoption of artificial intelligence in financial services: A policy framework." *Journal of Science and Technology Policy Management* 15, no. 2 (2024): 396–417.

Lauterbach, Anastassia. "Artificial intelligence and policy: Quo vadis?" *Digital Policy, Regulation and Governance* 21, no. 3 (2019): 238–263.

Leal Filho, Walter, Peter Yang, João Henrique Paulino Pires Eustachio, Anabela Marisa Azul, Joshua C. Gellers, Agata Gielczyk, Maria Alzira Pimenta Dinis, and Valerija Kozlova. "Deploying digitalisation and artificial intelligence in sustainable development research." *Environment, Development and Sustainability* 25, no. 6 (2023): 4957–4988.

Leech, Gavin, Simson Garfinkel, Misha Yagudin, Alexander Briand, and Aleksandr Zhuravlev. "Ten hard problems in artificial intelligence we must get right." arXiv preprint arXiv:2402.04464 (2024).

Lior, Anat. "Insuring AI: The role of insurance in artificial intelligence regulation." *Harvard Journal of Law & Technology* 35 (2021): 467.

Loh, Magdalene, and Terence Soo. "Opportunities and use cases of AI in the insurance industry." In Remolina, Nydia, and Aurelio Gurrea Martínez (Eds.) *Artificial Intelligence in Finance*, pp. 244–270. Cheltenham: Edward Elgar Publishing, 2023.

Malifete, Linda, Samuel Adekunle, and Clinton Aigbavboa. "Exploring digitisation as a solution to the long-term insurance sector efficiency quagmire." In *International Conference on Computing in Civil and Building Engineering, 26–28 October, Cape Town, South Africa*, pp. 357–374. Cham: Springer Nature Switzerland, 2022.

Mangla, Dolly, Renu Aggarwal, Mohit Maurya, Sweta Dixit, and Mridul Dharwal. "Application of artificial intelligence in insurance sector: A bibliometric view." In *International Conference on Advances and Applications of Artificial Intelligence and Machine Learning, 16–17 September 2022, Noida, India*, pp. 543–555. Singapore: Springer Nature Singapore, 2022.

Marino, Domenico, Jaime Gil Lafuente, and Domenico Tebala. "Innovations and development of artificial intelligence in Europe: Some empirical evidences." *European Journal of Management and Business Economics* 32, no. 5 (2023): 620–636.

McDonald, Angus, Kirsty Paynter, and Ernie Van der Vyver. "Embedded insurance." In Tarr, A. A., Julie-Anne Tarr, Maurice Thompson, and Dino Wilkinson (Eds.) *The Global Insurance Market and Change*, pp. 66–94. Abingdon: Informa Law from Routledge, 2024.

Nabrawi, Eman, and Abdullah Alanazi. "Fraud detection in healthcare insurance claims using machine learning." *Risks* 11, no. 9 (2023): 160.

OECD, Gennaio. The impact of big data and artificial intelligence (AI) in the insurance sector. (2020). https://web-archive.oecd.org/temp/2020-01-31/543595-impact-big-data-ai-in-the-insurance-sector.htm.

Owolabi, Toluwalope, Shahra, Essa Q., and Basurra, Shadi. "Auto-insurance fraud detection using machine learning classification models". In *International Congress on Information and Communication Technology, 19–22 February, London, United Kingdom*, pp. 503–513. Singapore: Springer Nature Singapore, 2023.

Pathak, Aman, and Veena Bansal. "Factors influencing the readiness for artificial intelligence adoption in indian insurance organizations." In *International Working Conference on Transfer and Diffusion of IT, 18–19 December 2020, Tiruchirappalli, India*, pp. 43–55. Cham: Springer, 2024.

Poufinas, Thomas, Periklis Gogas, Theophilos Papadimitriou, and Emmanouil Zaganidis. "Machine learning in forecasting motor insurance claims." *Risks* 11, no. 9 (2023): 164.

Prince, Anya ER, and Seamus Taylor. "Artificial intelligence: Attempts at developing an ethical approach for its use in insurance." In Burling, Julian M., and Kevin Lazarus (Eds.) *Research Handbook on International Insurance Law and Regulation*, pp. 647–673. Cheltenham: Edward Elgar Publishing, 2023.

Sadowski, Jathan. "Total life insurance: Logics of anticipatory control and actuarial governance in insurance technology." *Social Studies of Science* 54, no. 2 (2024): 231–256.

Shamsuddin, Siti Nurasyikin, Noriszura Ismail, and R. Nur-Firyal. "Life insurance prediction and its sustainability using machine learning approach." *Sustainability* 15, no. 13 (2023): 10737.

Singh, Gurinder, Manish Sharma, Shweta Nanda, and Sunil Kadyan. "Disruptive technologies and digitalization in insurance: Improving the value chain of insurance." In *2022 3rd International Conference on Computation, Automation and Knowledge Management (ICCAKM), 15–17 November 2022, Dubai, UAE*, pp. 1–5. IEEE, 2022.

Sinha, K. P., Sookhak, M., and Wu, S. "Agentless insurance model based on modern artificial intelligence." *In 2021 IEEE 22nd International Conference on Information Reuse and Integration for Data Science (IRI), 10–12 August 2021, Las Vegas, NV, USA*, pp. 49–56. IEEE, 2021.

St-Onge, Sylvie, Michel Magnan, and Catherine Vincent. "The digital revolution in financial services: New business models and talent challenges." In Nguyen, Duc Khuong (Ed.) *Handbook of Banking and Finance in Emerging Markets*, pp. 464–478. Cheltenham: Edward Elgar Publishing, 2022.

Tanwar, Samridhi, and Surbhi Bhardwaj. "Recent trends and inflows of foreign direct investment in India: With a specific reference to the insurance sector." In Sood, Kiran, Balamurugan Balusamy, Simon Grima, and Pierpaolo Marano (Eds.) *Big Data Analytics in the Insurance Market*, pp. 185–206. Bingley: Emerald Publishing Limited, 2022.

Wilkinson, Dino, Alec Christie, Anthony A. Tarr, and Julie-Anne Tarr. "Big data, artificial intelligence and insurance." In Tarr, A. A., Julie-Anne Tarr, Maurice Thompson, and Dino Wilkinson (Eds.) *The Global Insurance Market and Change*, pp. 22–46. Abingdon: Informa Law from Routledge, 2024.

Xin, Xi, and Fei Huang. "Antidiscrimination insurance pricing: Regulations, fairness criteria, and models." *North American Actuarial Journal* 28, no. 2 (2023): 1–35.

Index